Paratexts

Introductions to Science Fiction and Fantasy

James Gunn

THE SCARECROW PRESS, INC.
Lanham • Toronto • Plymouth, UK
2013

Published by Scarecrow Press, Inc.
A wholly owned subsidiary of The Rowman & Littlefield Publishing Group, Inc.
4501 Forbes Boulevard, Suite 200, Lanham, Maryland 20706
www.rowman.com

10 Thornbury Road, Plymouth PL6 7PP, United Kingdom

Copyright © 2013 by Scarecrow Press, Inc.

All rights reserved. No part of this book may be reproduced in any form or by any electronic or mechanical means, including information storage and retrieval systems, without written permission from the publisher, except by a reviewer who may quote passages in a review.

British Library Cataloguing in Publication Information Available

Library of Congress Cataloging-in-Publication Data

Gunn, James E., 1923–
[Essays. Selections]
Paratexts : introductions to science fiction and fantasy / James Gunn.
 p. cm.
A collection of introductions written by James Gunn for leather-bound collectors' editions called Masterpieces of science fiction and Masterpieces of Fantasy (published by Easton Press), and with the addition of original prefaces to several of his own works.
Includes bibliographical references and index.
ISBN 978-0-8108-9122-7 (cloth : alk. paper) — ISBN 978-0-8108-9123-4 (ebook) 1. Science fiction, American—History and criticism. 2. Science fiction, English—History and criticism. 3. Fantasy fiction, American—History and criticism. 4. Fantasy fiction, English—History and criticism. 5. Science fiction—Authorship. 6. Fantasy fiction—Authorship. I. Title. II. Title: Introductions to science fiction and fantasy.
PS3513.U797A6 2013
823'.087609—dc23
 2012050139

♾️ The paper used in this publication meets the minimum requirements of American National Standard for Information Sciences Permanence of Paper for Printed Library Materials, ANSI/NISO Z39.48-1992.

Printed in the United States of America

To Eric Stones,
whose vision and open mindedness got it all started

Contents

Preface	vii
Acknowledgments	ix
Prefaces to Books by James Gunn	1
Star Bridge	1
Station in Space	3
Breaking Point	5
The Immortals	7
The Joy Makers	10
The Magicians	13
Some Dreams Are Nightmares	15
The Burning	22
The Listeners	23
Human Voices	25
Gift from the Stars	27
The Dreamers	29
Kampus	30
Masterpieces of Science Fiction	31
Masterpieces and Me	31
The Foundation Trilogy Isaac Asimov	32
Stranger in a Strange Land Robert A. Heinlein	36
The World of Null-A A. E. van Vogt	40
A Canticle for Leibowitz Walter M. Miller Jr.	42
1984 George Orwell	45
A Clockwork Orange Anthony Burgess	51
Fury Henry Kuttner	54
Out of the Silent Planet C. S. Lewis	58

The Moon Pool A. Merritt	60
What Mad Universe Fredric Brown	64
Blood Music Greg Bear	68
Speaker for the Dead Orson Scott Card	71
Islands in the Net Bruce Sterling	73
The Postman David Brin	76
When Gravity Fails George Alec Effinger	79
Do Androids Dream of Electric Sheep? Philip K. Dick	82
The Hitchhiker's Guide to the Galaxy Douglas Adams	83
Childhood's End Arthur C. Clarke	86
Doomsday Book Connie Willis	87
Brute Orbits George Zebrowski	89
City Clifford D. Simak	90
Flatland Edwin A. Abbott	92
Flowers for Algernon Daniel Keyes	93
The Island of Dr. Moreau H. G. Wells	94
The Sword of the Lictor Gene Wolfe	95
Jem Frederik Pohl	97
The Lost World Arthur Conan Doyle	98
The Dead Zone Stephen King	99
Masterpieces of Fantasy	103
The Other Side of the Mirror	103
Nine Princes in Amber Roger Zelazny	104
Magician Raymond E. Feist	107
The Malacia Tapestry Brian W. Aldiss	110
Mythago Wood Robert Holdstock	113
The Unpleasant Profession of Jonathan Hoag Robert A. Heinlein	116
The Belgariad: Pawn of Prophecy David Eddings	120
The Chronicles of Thomas Covenant the Unbeliever: Lord Foul's Bane Stephen R. Donaldson	123
The Mists of Avalon Marion Zimmer Bradley	126
Three Hearts and Three Lions Poul Anderson	129
The Complete Compleat Enchanter L. Sprague de Camp and Fletcher Pratt	132
Darker Than You Think Jack Williamson	136
Black Easter and *The Day After Judgment* James Blish	139
Gather, Darkness! Fritz Leiber	142
Gormenghast Mervyn Peake	145
The Last Unicorn Peter Beagle	149
Little, Big John Crowley	152
The Lord of the Rings J. R. R. Tolkien	155
Lord Valentine's Castle Robert Silverberg	158

Signed First Editions of Science Fiction 163
   Falling Free Lois McMaster Bujold 163
   Ancient Shores Jack McDevitt 166
   Blue Mars Kim Stanley Robinson 169
   Cloud's Rider C. J. Cherryh 173
   Cosm Gregory Benford 176
   Destiny's Road Larry Niven 179
   Dragonseye Anne McCaffrey 182
   Dreamfall Joan D. Vinge 185
   Evolution's Shore Ian McDonald 188
   A Fisherman of the Inland Sea Ursula K. Le Guin 192
   Illegal Alien Robert J. Sawyer 196
   Lifehouse Spider Robinson 199
   The Memory Cathedral Jack Dann 202
   Moonrise Ben Bova 207

Index 211

About the Author 229

Preface

I've always been fond of introductions and prefaces. Maybe it's because I am fascinated by the process of creation or by insights into the reading experience. I spent many years as a teacher trying to understand what goes on when creation and reading happen and passing what I understand about them along to students. While I recognize the magic, I know that it can't be depended on; my approach has always been to demystify it—to make it a part of everyday life and ordinary experience.

I've written a lot of introductions myself. Some of them came through requests from authors or editors, and I looked upon them as an opportunity to give something back to the colleagues and the genre that have given me so much—in Robert Heinlein's words, to pay it forward—but also to explore my own experience with a lifetime of reading science fiction and fantasy and to share that with others. Most of the introductions, though, came about through my chance relationship with Easton Press recounted in my essay "Masterpieces and Me."

When my own stories and novels began to be reprinted, I seized the opportunity to add prefaces to them, to explain the act of creation, how they came to be written and how they were received in the marketplace of ideas and commerce. It helped me to remember the labors and the rewards involved, in my personal and creative lives. I hope it helped the people who read them, who were, like me, fascinated by the process.

I begin with those and continue with a selection of the introductions I wrote for the Easton Press Masterpieces of Science Fiction, then a selection of the extended collector's notes I wrote for Masterpieces of Fantasy, and end with a selection of the introductions I wrote for the Signed First Editions of Science Fiction.

Acknowledgments

The prefaces in this book were published originally in the novels and collections by James Gunn. The introductions and collector's notes were published in three series of collector's editions by Easton Press: Masterpieces of Science Fiction, Masterpieces of Fantasy, and Signed First Editions of Science Fiction, and are reprinted by permission of Easton Press.

My thanks to Bert Chamberlin, who retrieved a good number of the texts; to Ron Larson, who facilitated the project; to David Williams, who analyzed the Easton Press series; and to Pam LeRow, who turned everything into usable files.

Prefaces to Books by James Gunn

STAR BRIDGE

Some creations take on a life of their own. That's the way it was with *Star Bridge*.

Gerald Jonas reviewed a reprint edition of *Star Bridge* in 1977, twenty-two years after the first publication as a Gnome Press hardcover followed by an Ace Books paperback. Jonas wrote:

> The book is not a recognized "classic" of that period. . . . It stirred no controversy, won no awards, added nothing to the reputation of its authors. Not only had I never read it before, I had not even heard of it. I mention these facts only to help the reader understand my astonishment at discovering that this obscure collaboration between Williamson and Gunn reads more like a collaboration between Heinlein and Asimov. The concept is pure, classic science fiction. A vast empire spans the galaxy, controlled from the planet Eron which alone holds the secret to faster-than-light travel . . .

Neither Jack Williamson nor I had any idea we were up to anything like that. It was an accident it happened at all. I was working as an editor for Western Printing and Lithographing Company (which selected, edited, and printed Dell's paperback books) in Racine, Wisconsin, and talked the editor-in-chief into sending me to Chicago to attend my very first Science Fiction World Convention in late August of 1952. I'd been writing SF stories for four years and having them published for three, but it was my first encounter with other writers and editors and agents. I met some of my heroes, including John Campbell, Tony Boucher, Bob Bloch, Clifford Simak, and many others, including Fred Pohl (my agent at that time), who told me he'd sold four

1

stories that I didn't know about. On the strength of that I went back and told my boss that I was resigning to go back to full-time writing.

But the biggest event was standing in line at registration and turning to find behind me a face I recognized from the backs of some of my favorite novels. "You're Jack Williamson," I said, and he admitted that he was. It was the beginning of a long friendship that ended only with his death at the age of ninety-eight. We met again in early 1953 when Jack and his wife, Blanche, visited Kansas City, where her sister lived, and at that time Jack mentioned that he'd had a writer's block for the past decade and asked if I would be interested in working on a novel he'd started and couldn't continue. I was writing my first novel, *This Fortress World*, but I would finish that soon and I agreed to look at his manuscript.

Jack sent me the first fifty pages (the opening chapter as I rewrote it) and 150 pages of notes about the background and the characters. I developed an outline that Jack approved and then wrote the novel (and rewrote it once) in three months, and Jack approved that. Our mutual agent (Fred, again) sold it to Marty Greenberg of Gnome Press, a small specialty press that was publishing more science fiction than anyone. Gnome published *Star Bridge* and *This Fortress World* in 1955. He paid us a $500 advance for each book, but since I shared the royalties for *Star Bridge* with Jack, that amounted to a total of $750 for six months' writing. Even in the early 1950s, when my wife and I were living in my parents' home rent free (they had moved in with my physician brother a couple of miles away, and I was using a basement room as an office) and my brother was providing free health care, that wasn't a living wage. I decided to give up space epics and collaborations and focus on near-future issues and to break up future novels into novelettes or novellas publishable individually in magazines. That's when I derived my later motto: "Sell it twice." Most of my later novels were written that way.

Marty Greenberg was a good publisher but not so good at paying his authors. Jack and I never got any share of the paperback royalties, and it was only some years later, when Gnome Press went out of business and *Star Bridge* and *This Fortress World* and my other novels began to be reprinted in the United States and overseas, that we got some financial return. Actually, the three years I spent as a freelance writer selling almost everything I wrote but never earning more than $3,000 a year provided the basis for a literary career and financial return as reprints continued. *Star Bridge* has been in print, somewhere in the world, almost continuously.

But I had no idea that *Star Bridge* had any claims to classic status until writer Ed Bryant showed up in Missoula, Montana, where the Science Fiction Research Association met in 1976. Ed had just attended a convention in Washington and he told an audience that a novel named *Star Bridge* had turned him into a science-fiction writer, and he added, turning to Jack and me in audience, "I'm not sure I thank you."

A month later I was having breakfast in New York City with John Brunner and Samuel R. Delany, and I mentioned the incident. Delany said, "The same thing happened to me." And we put Delany's comment on the cover of the Berkeley reprint that Jonas reviewed.

Since then Bryant wrote, in an introduction to volume 4 of *The Collected Stories of Jack Williamson*: "I think I was about twelve, probably in the sixth grade, when the TAB Book Club delivered a paperback of *Star Bridge* by Jack Williamson and James E. Gunn. To this day, I refuse to understand why this novel is not accorded the same classic status as *The Stars My Destination* or *The Moon Is a Harsh Mistress*."

I don't know that I can really take any credit for it. Oh, I wrote it. I know that because it has my name on the cover, along with Jack's. But that was more than fifty years ago, and I read it now as if they were someone else's words. No doubt Jack's vision had something to do with it. He was always young in spirit and his imagination soared.

A number of years ago I was having lunch with David Hartwell in New York City, when he was editor of Timescape Books, and he said that he wanted to reprint *Star Bridge*. "I seem to reprint it whenever I move to another publisher," he said. "It has the ideal combination of Jack's experience and your youthful energy."

"You've got it wrong," I said. "It was my experience and Jack's youthful energy!"

STATION IN SPACE

In 1954 I had written my first two science-fiction novels, *This Fortress World* and *Star Bridge* (in collaboration with Jack Williamson). I was writing full time, living in a house rent-free and working in a basement room I had converted into an office in the house my parents shared with my brother. My wife and son and I even had free medical care from my brother, and still it was difficult to buy groceries and pay our few other bills.

I spent eight hours a day in my basement office, turning out ten pages a day and rewriting it once. That meant I could write a short story in a week, a novelette in two weeks, a short novel in four weeks, and a novel in three months. I wrote *This Fortress World* and *Star Bridge* that way, and both got published by Gnome Press in 1955, but I got a total of $500 ($450 when my agent took his percentage) for *This Fortress World* and half that (Jack got half) for *Star Bridge*. Both novels were reprinted later and translated into a number of foreign languages and provide a good return for my efforts, but I didn't know about those prospects then, and at the time $750 for six months' work seemed like a poor strategy for a struggling writer.

I made two decisions: I would place my stories in the near future, and I would write my novels in the form of short stories and novelettes that I could get published first in magazines and later collect as books. When I became a teacher of fiction writing, I passed it along to my students as "Gunn's Law" (*Sell it twice!*).

One of the ideas I was turning over in my head was the near future of space flight: how would the public's inertia ever be overcome? Willy Ley and Wernher von Braun had started the process by collaborating on an issue of *Collier's* dedicated to the construction of a space station, complete with evocative paintings by astronomical artist Chesley Bonestell. It was later reproduced in book form as *The Conquest of Space*. I sat down to write a story that might be published in the slick magazines (the ultimate aspiration of every pulp writer). I called it "The Cave of Night," and when it was done I asked my agent to send it to *Collier's* and, if *Collier's* rejected it, to the *Saturday Evening Post*. He sent it to *Collier's*, and when *Collier's* rejected it, he shipped it over to Horace Gold at *Galaxy*, who paid me three-and-a-half cents a word and published it in the February 1955 issue.

A couple of good things happened. "The Cave of Night" was dramatized on NBC's *X Minus One* radio program. I got $50 for that. A year or so later *Galaxy* told my agent it wanted to develop a television program that would broadcast dramatizations from the pages of *Galaxy*, as *X Minus One* had done on radio. *Galaxy* wanted "The Cave of Night" for its pilot program and bought the TV rights for $350. Not long afterward, apparently, that project fell through and the rights were sold to Desilu, which broadcast a version in 1959 on *Desilu Playhouse* under the title of "Man in Orbit" (with Lee Marvin and E. G. Marshall). That was too late to save my full-time writing career (by then I was working in the chancellor's office at the University of Kansas), but it was good to have something on television, even though somewhere along the line the point of the story had been changed (that would become a familiar feeling).

Back in 1954, however, I had gone on to write "Hoax." Horace Gold didn't like it ("Are you going to keep on writing stories about hoaxes?" he wrote), but James Quinn did and published it in *If* in December of 1955. I wrote "The Big Wheel" in 1955, and it got published in *Fantastic Universe* in September 1956. By that time I was editing the alumni publications for the University of Kansas Alumni Association, under an agreement that I could take off one week a month and a month every summer to write. I also enrolled in a writers' workshop course from mainstream author and editor Carolyn Gordon, who taught me (among other things) about Flaubert's invention of creating a sense of reality by describing places with appeals to at least three senses. I wrote "Powder Keg" in that class. I suspect that Ms. Gordon was a bit puzzled by it, but she didn't flinch. *If* published it in April of 1958.

Before that came out I had written in the summer of 1956 the short novel *Space Is a Lonely Place*, and Bob Mills, who later would become my agent, published it in his innovative magazine *Venture* in May 1957. By that time Bantam Books had decided to start a science-fiction line, and my then agent, Harry Altshuler, submitted *Station in Space*. Bantam didn't reply for several months (Harry would write that submitting a book to Bantam was like dropping it down a well, but eventually they always seemed to come through with an acceptance); then they sent us a contract for the unheard-of advance of $2,500.

So it seemed that my strategy had worked. The book was published in 1958. Meanwhile, however, something else had happened. A man-made satellite had been placed in orbit on October 4, 1957. It was called Sputnik, and the Russians had done it. The United States didn't launch one until 1958, and it was the third. *Station in Space* was out of date before it was published! I discovered that stories could be placed too close to the present.

Science-fiction writers get reputations as prophets. They aren't really in that business. Their intention is to write plausible scenarios about possible futures. Sometimes, by chance, one of them coincides with reality. I wasn't too good in my foreshadowing of the future of spaceflight. But what about the first American in orbit, John Glenn, on February 20, 1962? What do you call it when the town of Perth, Australia, turned its lights on and off as Glenn's flight passed overhead? Well, maybe somebody had read *Station in Space* or seen the television adaptation. Or maybe . . .

So *Station in Space* can be read today as historical science fiction like Jules Verne's *From the Earth to the Moon*. Or as alternate reality. Or as the way it should have been . . .

BREAKING POINT

"Breaking Point" began life as a three-act play. I wrote it in the final year of my master's program at the University of Kansas when I still nursed the illusion that I might become a playwright. I wrote it as a writers' workshop project with Professor Carroll Edwards, not a drama teacher like my erstwhile instructor Allen Crafton but an English teacher and authority on modern drama (he and his wife created the scholarly journal by that name). Partly I wanted the credit, partly I wanted to demonstrate that science-fiction drama was possible, and partly I wanted to write something I could turn into fiction and publish.

In my senior year of college, after returning from service in World War II, I wrote a play in playwriting class, *Thy Kingdom Come*, about the second coming of Christ, his running for president, and his being crucified again when people realize that they can't live up to his message. Crafton added it to the theater season for the spring of 1947, and on the strength of that I spent the summer writing another play for him, and then enrolled in the speech and drama program at Northwestern, famous for its theater department—but not for its playwriting, and I left after two quarters to pursue the notion of writing a series of radio plays about Kansas City history. When that encountered no enthusiasm, I began writing science-fiction stories and sold my first, "Paradox," to Sam Merwin Jr., editor of *Thrilling Wonder Stories*. I was a writer.

Being a writer didn't mean being able to support myself as a writer, however, and I returned to the University of Kansas in 1949 to pursue a master's degree in English. I continued to write and publish stories, eventually publishing nine of my first ten (the only one that didn't get accepted was "Sane Asylum"—*The Unpublished Gunn, Part One*, 1992)—all under the name of "Edwin James." The eleventh, "The Misogynist," was the first published under my own name and my first story in Horace Gold's *Galaxy* (November 1952).

It was not my first contact with Gold, however. That came when I converted the "Breaking Point" play into a lengthy novella and on October 17, 1950 (I used to keep records of such things) submitted it to *Galaxy* (I had already submitted it to *Astounding* on September 7, 1950, and got a written rejection on October 12, 1950). A couple of weeks later, I got a telephone call from someone who said, "This is Horace Gold, and I'd like to buy your story 'Breaking Point.'"

Wow! "Sure," I said.

"But it's too long," Gold went on.

"I'd be glad to cut it down," I said. It had been a play, after all, with lots of dialogue.

"I don't trust you to do it," he said bluntly.

Bluntness, I learned later, was the Gold standard.

"I'd like Ted Sturgeon to do it."

Ted, I learned, was working as a part-time assistant to Gold.

"He'd get one cent a word of your three cents a word payment."

I was getting only two cents a word from John Campbell at *Astounding* and less than that from the other magazines I was selling stories to. Besides I had been reading and admiring Sturgeon's sensitively written stories for more than a decade. "Sure," I said.

And I waited for "Breaking Point"—maybe my career breaking point—to be published in *Galaxy*. And waited. And waited.

Finally I couldn't wait any longer and wrote to Sturgeon. "Golly," he wrote back in his typical disarming way, "I'm sorry, Jim. I didn't get around to it for months, and when I did Horace said he didn't want it cut—he wanted it revised. He rejected it." I suspect that times had changed: when Horace wanted the story *Galaxy* had been in existence less than a year; he already must have been working with Fred Pohl, Isaac Asimov, Clifford Simak, Fritz

Leiber, Damon Knight, James Blish, Robert Sheckley, and Alfred Bester. A couple of years later he would convince me that I should rewrite a story for him, "Open Warfare," that he had already bought and paid for—because I was "writing so much better."

In 1952 I was editing Dell paperbacks for Western Printing and Lithographing of Racine, Wisconsin, and persuaded the editor-in-chief to send me to Chicago to attend the World Science Fiction Convention—to contact writers, I told him. That was true. It was my first contact with writers, and I met Jack Williamson, Clifford Simak, Richard Matheson, Robert Bloch, Frederik Pohl, and many others, as well as editors John Campbell, Tony Boucher, Ray Palmer, and Horace Gold's surrogate, Evelyn Gold. Fred Pohl was my agent then and told me he had sold four stories for me. I thought that was a sign, quit my job, and went back to full-time writing—this time sticking with it for almost three years before returning to Lawrence and a series of positions that saw me end my career as a professor of English as well as a writer.

In preparation for my second fling at full-time writing, I went to New York to visit editors and talked to John Campbell, Horace Gold, Harry Harrison, and Lester del Rey and met Ted Sturgeon. Horace offered me a job. John Campbell offered me an idea that turned into "Wherever You May Be" ("The Reluctant Witch"), which Horace published in the May 1953 *Galaxy*. And Lester told me he was going to publish "Breaking Point" in his new *Space Science Fiction* magazine, and he did, in the March 1953 issue. *Space* paid $400 (two-and-a-half cents a word) for the sixteen-thousand-word novella, and I gave Ted a third. He tried to decline, but I insisted.

I included it as the lead story (and the title story) in my 1972 Walker Books and Daw Books collection, *Breaking Point*. Piers Anthony once told me that reading the novella convinced him it was possible to write and publish stories like this. I'm sure he meant it as a compliment. I'm pretty sure.

THE IMMORTALS

Story ideas come at unexpected times and develop in unexpected ways and sometimes have lives of their own.

The idea for *The Immortals* came to me during my second stint as a full-time writer. The first was a twelve-month period back in 1948–1949 after I had given up the idea of becoming a playwright and then of becoming a radio writer. I sold a bunch of stories (the first ten under the pseudonym of Edwin James) but not enough to live on and decided to return to the University of Kansas to get a master's degree in English. Two years later I took a job as an editor for Western Printing and Lithographing Company of Racine, Wisconsin. It published paperback books and Disney comics for Dell and Little

Golden Books for Simon and Schuster. I was supposed to create a science-fiction line. But when I attended my first World Science Fiction Convention (and my first convention of any kind) in Chicago in 1952 and learned from my agent, Frederik Pohl, that he had sold four stories for me, I decided to return to full-time writing.

Halfway through that period of about two and a half years, I came up with the idea for *The Immortals*. Science fiction's appeal is its sense of wonder, its series of "what ifs." One day I began wondering about how humanity might actually achieve immortality. Those ideas are starting points; they develop into stories through research. Some creatures, I found, never die from natural causes. Another source suggested that people age because our circulatory system is inefficient; it doesn't provide food for the cells when they need it or remove the by-products of oxidation. What would happen if someone were born with a better circulatory system? And what if that improvement were capable of being transmitted to someone else through a blood transfusion? And what if the rejuvenating power might reside in a blood protein like the gamma globulins that provide passive immunity against infection when they are injected into other people (such as pregnant women, so that they don't catch German measles)? Then the rejuvenation itself might be only temporary, lasting only about thirty to forty-five days, like the passive immunity conferred by gamma globulins. Those were the "what ifs" that set off a process of story creation.

I sat down and wrote "New Blood," which my agent sent to John Campbell, editor of *Astounding Science Fiction*. It was published in the November 1955 issue. By then I had finished the second story in the series, "Donor." Campbell wasn't interested in more stories about immortal blood, so I sold it to *Startling Stories*; it was scheduled for publication in the winter issue of 1955—but the fall issue was the last (*Startling Stories* wasn't the only magazine I helped kill). I resold it to *Fantastic Stories of the Imagination*, where it appeared in the November 1960 issue.

By the time "New Blood" was published, I had moved my family from Kansas City back to Lawrence, Kansas, and had been asked to teach a couple of sections of English composition. Before the semester was over, I was invited to become managing editor of the university's alumni magazine. I made a deal to work only three weeks a month and get a month off in the summer for writing. During the first summer I wrote "Medic," which Bob Mills published in the July 1957 issue of *Venture Science Fiction* as "Not So Great an Enemy." The second summer I wrote "The Immortals," which Fred Pohl published in *Star Science Fiction No. 4* in 1958.

By that time Bantam Books had launched its science-fiction line. I had sold them *Station in Space* and *The Joy Makers*. The third book Dick Roberts accepted was *The Immortals*. It was published in 1962.

On the other side of the continent, Robert Specht, an aspiring screenwriter, was working in the Los Angeles office of Bantam Books. Each month a stack of paperback books arrived from the East Coast; one month Specht picked *The Immortals* to take home with him and, he later told me, decided immediately that he wanted to make it into a movie.

Four years later he was story editor for Everett Chambers on the *Peyton Place* television series, and he persuaded Chambers to go in with him to obtain the film and television rights to *The Immortals*. They contacted my agent, who by then was Harry Altshuler (Fred Pohl had gone out of the agenting business). We agreed upon a two-year option with modest payments every six months. I got three checks, but the fourth never came. I wrote Bob Specht who said that Chambers had dropped out, that he had tried the novel on every producer, director, and major actor in Hollywood without success, but that some new possibilities had opened up. We agreed upon a new contract that—to everyone's surprise—actually developed into a film.

ABC had decided that it would make its own television films rather than renting them from Hollywood and use them on what it called the *ABC-TV Movie of the Week*. Suddenly TV scripts were in demand, and Bob Specht sold Paramount on *The Immortals*. It was filmed in the spring of 1969 as "The Immortal," featuring Christopher George, Barry Sullivan, Ralph Bellamy, Carol Lynley, and Jessica Walter and directed by Joseph Sargent, and broadcast the following September. It was scheduled to be the first film in the new ABC series but at the last moment was edged out by "Seven in Darkness" with Milton Berle. Maybe the schedulers were saving the best for second.

Apparently the film rated well ("It ranked fourth in the eighty-city Nielsens," Bob told me later), although, to be sure, the film had changed the focus from the social change created by the reality of immortality for a few to a chase story in which Christopher George was pursued by rich and powerful aging people lusting for his blood. ABC decided to commission an hour-long series, also called *The Immortal*, for the following year. Only Christopher George was carried over from the film (Bob Specht didn't even get considered for story editor), and ABC decided to play the series for adventure instead of science fiction. But I won't go into that.

During the interim Bob Specht called and said that ABC wanted a novelization of the screenplay to promote the series. I was offered one-third of the royalties and said, "Go ahead." At the last minute I was phoned by Bantam to say that it couldn't find a writer to do the novelization, so I wrote it myself. It may have been the only time that the author of a novel wrote the novelization of the script (our director of special collections called it "cruel and unusual punishment"). My consolation is that it was easy money: I wrote it in six days so that it could be published before the series started in September 1970.

Flash forward about twenty-five years. Some interesting things happened in the interim: Bantam Books reprinted the novel in 1968 and Pocket Books in 1979, and it got translated into Italian, Japanese, German, Portuguese, and French and reprinted in Great Britain. But in the mid-1990s I got a telephone call from a woman who said she was calling from Disney Pictures and was looking for the person who owned the feature-film rights to *The Immortals*. "You've found him," I said. Back in 1968, Paramount, when it took over the contract from Bob Specht, had elected to buy only the television rights, not the more costly feature-film rights.

That began a series of Hollywood experiences (which Vonda N. McIntyre has characterized as "hysterical enthusiasm followed by total silence"). Touchstone Pictures, a Disney subsidiary, was interested in making a feature film. ("We see it as a major motion picture with a major star and a major director such as Sidney Pollack or James Cameron," the Touchstone president told me, when I visited him with my agent, Dorris Halsey.) But whoever at Disney was enthusiastic about the project got fired and Disney did not renew the option. Before the Disney option had expired, however, another producer was already pursuing the rights (tipped off, we heard, by a screenwriter who had been asked by Touchstone to offer a "take" on the film), and he took over the feature-film rights on the same terms. But then he, too, did not renew the option. A third and then a fourth producer took options and were unsuccessful. Now the novel is once more under option, to Warner Brothers.

During all this film hope and hype, I resold the reprint rights to Pocket Books and, at the editor's request, updated some of the material and added a new twenty-thousand-word section in the middle. The Touchstone president had commented (perceptively, I thought) that it was really the doctor's story, so I filled in a middle section about Dr. Russell Pearce's search for the *elixir vitae*.

People have not yet discovered immortality, though a recent article in *The New York Times* speculated that by 2200 people may be living for six hundred years. But until then our only immortality lies in progeny and books.

THE JOY MAKERS

The origins of many novels are obscure, but I have a clear memory of how *The Joy Makers* came into existence. I was in the middle of my second period of full-time freelance writing. The first period had been an accident. After two semesters of graduate study in the theater department at Northwestern University, I had given up the idea of becoming a playwright but, inspired by a course on radio writing, I had returned to Kansas City with the idea of writing a series of radio plays about Kansas City history. That was 1968 and no radio station was interested. So I decided to write a science-fiction story (I had read and loved science fiction since 1933), and on the third try, Sam Merwin Jr., editor of *Thrilling Wonder Stories*, bought "Paradox." In the following year I wrote eight more stories but sold only three more of them until the magazine boom that began in 1951 took all but one ("Sane Asylum," for the curious). But by the summer of 1949 (even before my first accepted story got published), I had returned to the University of Kansas to get a master's degree in English. It took me a couple of years (my bachelor's degree had been in journalism), but I continued to write during graduate school and during my subsequent employment as an editor for Western Printing and Lithographing of Racine, Wisconsin (it edited and printed the Dell line of paperbacks, as well as Little Golden Books, Disney comic books, and its own Whitman line). In 1953, as a result of attending the 1952 World Science Fiction Convention in Chicago (my first convention of any kind) and discovering that my agent, Fred Pohl, had sold four of my stories, I returned to Kansas City and full-time writing, intending to make a career of it.

Back in 1950 we bought a set of the *Encyclopedia Britannica*. It cost $300, I think, and that was a lot of money in those days, particularly for a struggling writer and graduate student, even if I did get help from the GI Bill. But we rationalized it as an investment in solid information that any writer ought to have, and it would be a resource, as well, when our toddler son started school. But it was only rationalization: there they sat, complete with bookcase, containing the wisdom of the ages. Book lovers unite! You have nothing to lose but your indebtedness!

But books have a way of repaying the love that longs to possess them. From the pages of the *Encyclopedia* I got the idea and did the research for *The Immortals* and other stories and novels, I am sure. Particularly *The Joy Makers*. I can point to the exact inspiration. I was doing research for something I wanted to write about (that part I don't remember) when I came upon an article on "Feeling." Don't look for it in any edition but the one published in 1950 (by 1954, at least, the article on "Feeling, the Psychology of" was substantially different). The article discussed not the way we "feel" but how and what we "feel," mostly our feelings of happiness and other emotional states. In a fascinating and relatively untechnical way, the article described techniques for achieving happiness (you will find most, and maybe all, of them exemplified in the novel) and avoiding pain and disappointment. Insightfully it commented that there are two ways to be happy: you can get what you want, or you can want what you get. The first strategy demands that you reshape the world outside to your own desires (or think that you do); the second requires that you develop the internal discipline to feel properly (which includes happiness) no matter what happens. You will find those two strategies fighting it out in *The Joy Makers*. But what finally turned my fascination into a novel was the final sentence: "But the true science of applied hedonics is not yet born."

This was a period when I had adopted my own strategy for financial success as a freelance writer. I had published two novels and earned only $675 for six months' work, so I had decided to write my novels in the form of novelettes or short novels that I could publish first in the magazines and later as novels. That later become codified as Gunn's Law: Sell it twice. I had become well enough known that Samuel Mines, the current editor of *Thrilling Wonder Stories* and *Startling Stories* (which had bought and published my first two stories), asked me if I would write a lead short novel for his magazine. It was a pretty certain sale, so I gave up the idea of marketing to better-paying markets and turned my "happiness" idea into a short novel called "The Hedonist." Mines published it in the winter 1955 issue of *Thrilling Wonder Stories* as "Name Your Pleasure." I decided I needed a lead-in story for the novel I had in mind and wrote "Hedonics, Inc." *Fantastic Universe* published that one (Mines must have turned it down) in its February 1955 issue (even before "Name Your Pleasure" appeared). And then I finished it up with "The Angry Man," which Mines published in the final issue of *Startling Stories* as "The Naked Sky."

A couple of years later Bantam Books became interested in starting a science-fiction line under editor Dick Roberts. Bantam accepted *Station in Space*, and then I submitted *The Joy Makers*. Through my agent, Harry Altshuler, Roberts asked for some alternate titles, and I submitted a dozen and a half of them. A few months later I made a trip to New York and visited the Bantam offices to meet Roberts for the first time. I asked him what he had decided to call the novel. "*The Joy Makers*," he said. "Do you like it?"

Those were the days when rates were low (my first Bantam Books sold for 35 cents a copy, and my royalty was one-and-a-quarter cents per copy—but they offered an advance of $2,500, and that was half a year's salary in those days) and sales were high (though not high enough to pay out the advance): *Station in Space* sold almost 100,000 copies and *The Joy Makers*, maybe 130,000, and another 50,000 in a reprint half a dozen years later. *The Immortals* sold as well. My final book with Roberts, a collection of stories called *Future Imperfect*, sold considerably fewer (as collections do). But then Roberts was hired by another publisher and my relationship with Bantam was over—until Fred Pohl became editor there, a couple of decades later.

But the books that Roberts edited live on, particularly *The Immortals*, which became a television movie in 1969 and an hour-long series the following year, has been under option half a dozen times in as many years as a possible feature film, and, at this writing, is under option again. *The Joy Makers*, as well, has attracted film interest that always gets cut off just before it gets translated into reality—but that, after all, is what happiness is all about. Being happy is not wanting anything anymore, and not wanting anything anymore is the same as death. . . . Besides, just the other day an agent called me saying what a great movie *The Joy Makers* might be . . .

THE MAGICIANS

Back in the early days of science fiction—just thirteen years after the founding of the first science-fiction magazine in 1926 and only a bit more than a year after John W. Campbell Jr. became editor of *Astounding Stories*, changed its name to *Astounding Science Fiction*, and inaugurated the Golden Age—Campbell created a companion fantasy magazine named *Unknown* (renamed *Unknown Worlds* in 1941). But it wasn't just any fantasy magazine. In its first issue Campbell wrote, "*Unknown* will be to fantasy what *Astounding* has made itself represent to science fiction. It will offer fantasy of a quality so far different from what has appeared in the past as to change your entire understanding of the term." What *Unknown* would publish was the fantastic concept treated realistically, magic as if it were a science, the supernatural considered as part of the natural world: what later became known as rationalized fantasy. It represented a clash of ideologies, an oxymoron, but in that internal conflict authors found the opportunity to create something new, often comic, sometimes insightful.

The magazine lasted only thirty-nine issues. It was discontinued in 1943 because of wartime paper shortages, but between 1939 and 1943 it published many classics of later fantasy, including Eric Frank Russell's "Sinister Barrier"; Robert A. Heinlein's "They" and "The Devil Makes the Laws"; Theodore Sturgeon's "It"; Fritz Leiber's *Conjure Wife* and "Two Sought Adventure," the first of his Fafhrd and the Gray Mouser stories; L. Ron Hubbard's "Fear" and "Typewriter in the Sky"; L. Sprague de Camp and Fletcher Pratt's Harold Shea novels, later gathered into *The Incompleat Enchanter*; and de Camp's *Lest Darkness Fall*, Jack Williamson's *Darker Than You Think*, and many others. Its passing was lamented by fantasy lovers.

I was too young to publish anything in *Unknown*, but Horace Gold wasn't. He contributed "The Trouble with Water" and collaborated with de Camp on "None but Lucifer," among others. So when Gold founded *Galaxy* in 1950, he soon thought of a companion fantasy magazine. It took him a little longer than Campbell—three years instead of a year and a half—but *Beyond* appeared in 1953. By that time I had published several stories in *Galaxy*, as well as a number in *Astounding* and other magazines. In fact, I was in the midst of my longest period of freelancing and turning out a short story a week or a novelette every two weeks, or a short novel every four weeks, and working on my first two novels at the rate of ten pages a day. A. J. Budrys, assistant editor of *Galaxy* in 1953, later told me that Gold wanted to use my short novel "Wherever You May Be" (aka "The Reluctant Witch") in *Beyond* but needed a lead story for *Galaxy* (it was published in May 1953). A couple of months later I finished a short novel I called "Beauty Is a Witch." Gold's first reaction (his first reaction to almost any story) was a rejection, and my agent, Harry Altshuler, sent it over to Fletcher Pratt, who was starting another fantasy magazine. Pratt wanted a change or two that I was prepared to make (even though he was going to pay only one cent a word, while *Beyond*, for which I had written the story, paid two), but before I could get started on the changes Gold asked for my short novel to be returned—he was desperate for a short novel to lead the May 1954 issue. Of such accidents are careers made—and broken.

I sold Gold only one more story for *Beyond*, "The Beautiful Brew," but *Beyond* lasted for only ten issues and was gone by January 1955. My short novel was published in May 1954. Gold changed the title to "Sine of the Magus." That was his habit (and one that did not endear him to his writers), changing titles and sometimes parts of the story as well. *The Encyclopedia of Fantasy* wrote that "*BFF* sought to bring the same sophistication to fantasy as *Galaxy* had to sf. It succeeded to a large extent, and is generally acknowledged as the natural successor to *Unknown*." The entry listed "Sine of the Magus" as one of the classics.

Six years later I persuaded Dell Books editor Gail Wendroff to publish "The Reluctant Witch," "The Beautiful Brew," and "Sine of the Magus" (renamed "The Magicians") in a collection I called *The Witching Hour*, and six years after that Scribner's editor Burroughs Mitchell let me expand "The Magicians" into a novel.

Between the publications of "Sine of the Magus" and *The Magicians*, fantasy had undergone a sea change. Tolkien's *The Lord of the Rings* had redefined the sales potential of fantasy, Howard's *Conan* novels had been rediscovered, Ursula Le Guin had launched her Earthsea juveniles and Peter Beagle had published *The Last Unicorn*, and, perhaps most importantly, Ira Levin's *Rosemary's Baby* and Peter Blatty's *The Exorcist* had become best sellers and, more significantly, successful motion pictures. What John Campbell in his introduction to *Unknown* had referred to as "anathema" had become a category even more successful than science fiction.

The Magicians reflects that. In fact, the observant reader may detect in its pages certain sly references to *Rosemary's Baby* and *The Exorcist*. But *The Magicians* is in the tradition of *Unknown*. I had always enjoyed the romantic fantasies of Thorne Smith, particularly *The Night Life of the Gods*, and I wanted *The Magicians* to be published in the same tradition, but editors preferred to promote the novel for shivers and suspense. I'd prefer more smiles and maybe an occasional chuckle.

SOME DREAMS ARE NIGHTMARES

> A novel is a prose narrative of some length that has something wrong with it.
> —Randall Jarrell

This book contains four stories: one short story, one novelette, and two short novels. They are related in some interesting ways, which I will get to a bit later, but one important thing they have in common is that they are distilled novels.

The ideal length for science fiction is the novelette.

This is not true of other genres such as the Western or the mystery, whose shorter versions are markedly less successful and almost invisible; they are known almost entirely for their novels.

Science fiction, on the other hand, can display hundreds of great short stories but few great novels. "It's doubtful," Anthony Boucher wrote in 1952, "if any specialized field can lay as much proportionate stress on the anthology as science fiction does today." More than twenty years later, the stress is even greater, with hardcover and paperback anthologies competing with magazines for original short fiction.

Now that the great slick fiction magazines are dead and gone, the last refuge of the popular American short story may be the science fiction magazine and anthology.

On the other hand, the science fiction novel is often—perhaps usually—a disappointment. Those which avoid the common fate of most science fiction novels are not the purest form of science fiction: that is, they are primarily adventure stories or fantasy stories or stories of mood or character whose goals and methods approach those of the mainstream . . .

This brings us to definition—at best a sticky place where one must thrash about to find a place to stand. Perhaps it is sufficient to observe, if we wish to be complete, that science fiction covers a broad variety of fictional forms that may have little or nothing to do with science, that the term "speculative fiction" is a bit more descriptive but has blanketed a great many stories that are related in only the broadest and least meaningful ways, and that the hard core of science fiction is a literature of ideas—unfortunately for accuracy, this also includes fiction that is not science fiction at all and fiction that is only related, such as the satire and the utopia.

The English critic Edmund Crispin has called science fiction "origin of species fiction," which views Man "as just one of a horde of different animals sharing the same planet. . . . Science fiction's real subject-matter is the present, seen against the perspectives of history. . . . It is about us, here, now—about us as we have been shaped by our genesis, our biology, our environment and our behavior."

What lies at the heart of every hard-core science-fiction story is an idea—perhaps an "if this goes on" kind of extrapolation from present tendencies into a future where those trends have come to fruition; perhaps a "what if" kind of speculation about a unique occurrence; perhaps an insight into the nature of man or the nature of his society or the nature of the universe and man's relation to it; or the conflict between man and his creation, between what he can dream and what he can do. In its essence, science fiction is a Platonic fiction dealing with ideals, even in characterization, of which the physical representations we see around us are only imperfect copies; or eschatological fiction dealing with last or final things.

The implications of all this are what create problems for the science-fiction novel. A hard-core science-fiction novel should take for its theme a major problem: pollution, overpopulation, racial survival, social survival, the exhaustion of resources, immortality, happiness, god, man's conflict with his environment, his surrender to it or symbiosis with it, war, progress, superpowers, superman ... To these problems or suggested problems there are no easy solutions and perhaps no solutions at all, but a novel, because of the promise of its scope and length, is under some compulsion to provide a solution. The mainstream avoids what science fiction traditionally finds obligatory—explanation—and in a mainstream novel the matter of resolution presents a smaller problem: a resolution must be provided only for a single character or group. Any attempt to resolve larger problems risks the ridiculous; if the larger problems were solvable they would have been solved already. Science-fiction writers either take their chances or avoid the danger by one of several expedients. The favorite for many authors is to ignore what they say the problem is and solve some other problem, or allow the problem to be solved by accident.

The best example of this kind of misdirection is Michael Crichton's *The Andromeda Strain*, a novel which begins with the threat of cataclysm: a deadly virus has been brought back from space which will wipe out all mankind unless something is done. The complication of the novel is the gathering together of a group of scientists in an excellently detailed underground laboratory that has been carefully prepared for such an eventuality. The scientists are unsuccessful in coping with the virus, but fortunately it mutates into a harmless form. In other words, everything the author told the reader about the virus and the situation turned out to be unimportant: the results would have been identical if no one had done anything or, in fact, if no one even had known about the plague. Only two endings would have played fair with the premise (and the reader): either the scientists discover effective countermeasures (which might have been unconvincing) or humanity is wiped out (which might have been too grim for popularity). Two novels that did not shrink from the consequences of their premises are Nevil Shute's *On the Beach* and John Christopher's *No Blade of Grass*.

Another science-fiction expedient is to tell the reader something that is incomplete or untrue. An example of this approach is Jack Williamson's *The Humanoids*, an otherwise admirable novel that tackled a major theme and an impossible problem. The origin of the novel is instructive: Williamson submitted to John W. Campbell, editor of *Astounding Science Fiction*, a beautifully conceived and delicately crafted novelette entitled "With Folded Hands . . . ," which was based upon the creation of the ultimate robot (that Platonic ideal) called a "humanoid." The Prime Directive of the humanoids is "to serve, obey, and keep man from harm." Since they are an ultimate form of the machine, the humanoids, however benevolently, can do everything better than humans, including their arts, and they keep humans from handling dangerous objects or engaging in dangerous activities. When humans become frustrated, the humanoids remove their unhappiness by means of lobotomies. In the end the humans can do nothing but sit with folded hands.

In the ellipsis that followed the title of the novelette, Campbell saw a sequel, a novel that he persuaded Williamson to write entitled " . . . And Searching Mind." It begins with the same premise as "With Folded Hands . . . " but concludes with humans discovering unique psychic abilities that they now can exploit to the greater glory of mankind. In effect, the author begins by saying that humanoids can do everything better than humans and ends with, "But I didn't mean *everything*!"

Other solutions of the inherent problem of the science-fiction novel are the conversion of the problem into a special case that can be solved or the elimination of a problem in novels that stress adventure, romance, mystery, intrigue, or mere description.

The structure of a science-fiction novel, therefore, is almost always the same: (1) a suspenseful situation, (2) rising through thrilling incidents to a shattering climax, and (3) an anticlimax in a resolution that cannot ultimately resolve. Even those novels that do not dare the impossible, that do not risk a major theme, suffer from the same inevitable pattern of excitement, suspense, and letdown. The science-fiction novel starts too high and builds even higher: when what is at stake is racial survival or the fate of galaxies, a society, a nation, a city, or even customs, traditions, or beliefs, the fate of any single individual or group is of relative insignificance.

The science-fiction novelette, on the other hand, can reduce its scale to the manageable. Length does not compel it to resolve its themes; the novelette—and its reader—is satisfied with the problem dramatized, not solved. The single case stands for many.

I distinguish between the science-fiction novelette and the short story because the short story is too short to encompass an entirely new world. Some science-fiction short stories succeed, and succeed magnificently, but those that do depart from the here and now only in small ways; usually the stories take place in our time and involve only a single intrusion of the strange. Only a few can provide greater separation without resort to special conventions that rely on an experience of the reader outside the scope of the particular story.

I include the short novel or novella within my ideal length, although the story that extends much beyond thirty thousand words begins to assume some of the same obligations—and problems—as the novel.

As a small proof of these controversial statements, let me suggest that the reader pick up a good anthology—I recommend the *Science Fiction Hall of Fame*, particularly the second volume (published, to make confusion total, in two volumes, A and B), which contains only novelettes and short novels. These stories say in fewer and more effective words what the novels cannot say in many. The best novelettes do not develop from smaller ideas than novels. Most are novel-sized ideas distilled into purer form. In the *Science Fiction Hall of Fame, Volume Two*, for instance, the reader will find such classic novelettes as Poul Anderson's "Call Me Joe," John W. Campbell's "Who Goes There?" Robert Heinlein's "Universe," C. M. Kornbluth's "The Marching Morons," Lawrence O'Donnell's "Vintage Season," Eric Frank Russell's " . . . And Then There Were None," Cordwainer Smith's "The Ballad of Lost C'Mell," H. G. Wells's "The Time Machine," Isaac Asimov's "The Martian Way," Theodore Cogswell's "The Spectre General," E. M. Forster's "The Machine Stops," Frederik Pohl's "The Midas Plague," James H. Schmitz's "The Witches of Karres," T. L. Sherred's "E for Effort," Clifford D. Simak's "The Big Front Yard," and Jack Vance's "The Moon Moth." Where in the entire literature of science fiction will one find novels to equal these?

In the same book, incidentally, the reader also will find Lester del Rey's "Nerves," Theodore Sturgeon's "Baby Is Three," Jack Williamson's "With Folded Hands . . . ," James Blish's "Earthman, Come Home," Algis Budrys's "Rogue Moon," and Wilmar Shiras's "In Hiding." All of these were developed, in one way or another, into novels—and all of the novels were less satisfying, in one way or another, than the novelettes or short novels from which they were developed.

Why, then, does anyone write science-fiction novels?

A variety of reasons can be offered, some of them economic, some, artistic. To dispose first of the economic, science fiction traditionally has paid for its stories by the word, and words in a novel come much easier than a comparable number of words in novelettes; and a novel published in book form has a chance of making a great deal more money. Second, the novel is the more glamorous publication: it exists alone, when it is published in a book, and leans on nothing else; it is a single monument to an author's intention and accomplishment. Third, aside from the intrinsic merits of the various lengths, readers prefer novels to shorter stories; most readers wish to immerse themselves in an imaginary world for several hours rather than be forced back to cold reality in half an hour or an hour. My two sons, for instance, were reading science-fiction novels long before they could be persuaded to read an anthology of the best short fiction, much less a magazine. As a consequence, serials almost always rank higher than short stories in magazine readership polls. Fourth, as a result of reasons two and three, the reputations and careers of writers are built more rapidly on novels than on shorter stories. The writers of shorter fiction have difficulty reaching the eminence that novelists have thrust upon them. In the fantasy field, for instance, John Collier and H. P. Lovecraft were writing marvelous short stories for years before they were recognized, and the same could be said, in science fiction, for Henry Kuttner and C. L. Moore, Theodore Sturgeon, Cordwainer Smith, and Harlan Ellison. Sturgeon, A. E. van Vogt, and Robert Heinlein were writing magnificent short stories and novelettes in 1940 and 1941, but van Vogt also wrote *Slan* and Heinlein wrote *If This Goes On . . .*, *Methuselah's Children*, and *Beyond This Horizon*.

I was aware of most or all of these arguments for the shorter lengths back in the early '50s, when I was writing full time. My convictions were reinforced by the fact that I had written two novels that had not been serialized in magazines and had done poorly as hardcovers. Part of the reason they had not done well could have been the times (no science-fiction novels were selling many copies, with the possible exception of juveniles), part, the financial predicament of the publisher; but whatever the reasons the conclusions were clear: if I hoped to be a successful freelance writer, I needed to be assured of magazine publication. (From this I derived Gunn's first law for freelance writers: nothing is worth writing if you can't use it at least twice.) When I got a novel-sized idea, I thought of how I could break it into smaller segments that I felt sure I could sell to the magazines and later bring together in book form if I was lucky.

A novelette can be developed into a novel in several ways. It can be expanded—I do not use the word "padded," though sometimes it might be appropriate. Usually a novelette is expanded by developing characters and incidents more fully and by inventing additional incidents. "Rogue Moon" was expanded into a novel in this way, as was Daniel Keyes's "Flowers for Algernon" (available in the *Science Fiction Hall of Fame*), which won a Hugo Award as a short story and a Nebula Award as a novel, and Lester del Rey's "Nerves." A novel can be extrapolated from a novelette, as in the case of *The Humanoids*, or extended with additional stories as was "Earthman, Come Home" (as well as Blish's "A Case of Conscience" and "Surface Tension") and Shiras's "In Hiding" and Sturgeon's "Baby Is Three."

I have the feeling (I could be wrong) that most of these novels were afterthoughts, the result of having written a superlative story and then recognizing its book-length potential. Not in my case: not only was I convinced that the best length for science fiction was the novelette and that the way to obtain the greatest immediate return (not, perhaps, the greatest final return) on my investment of time and thought was by writing the shorter form, but I felt that a novel-length idea treated in this way made possible artistic effects not available to the novel.

(I remember my first editor at Bantam, Dick Roberts, asking me if I thought *The Joy Makers* might be published as a novel, and I said, a bit amazed, "But it is a novel! The characters may change and it may extend over some two centuries, but the hero continues throughout the book—and the hero is an idea: the science of happiness.")

I would not be forced, I thought, to provide any specious solutions to any eternal problems. I could deal with an idea over a considerable span of time and over the lifetimes of several characters. I could dramatize, show the impact of the idea on individual lives, show how it works out for them, and allow the idea itself to complete its destiny, clarified but unresolved, after the book has ended.

I have written five novels in this fashion: *Station in Space*, *The Joy Makers*, *The Immortals*, *The Burning*, and *The Listeners*. They are novels of ideas in which the idea itself is hero: the conquest of space and the ordeals and sacrifices it will require, in *Station in Space*; the science of happiness, in *The Joy Makers*; the implications of immortality, in *The Immortals*; the interrelationship between laymen and the scientists who are beginning to control their lives and shape their futures, in *The Burning*; the difficulties of communication, particularly in the search for intelligent life on other worlds, in *The Listeners*.

The four stories in this book are the beginnings or the hearts of three novels. "The Cave of Night" was the story that began *Station in Space*. It was published in 1955, and events have dated its projections and proved me a poor prophet: the first satellite was not American but Russia's Sputnik in 1957, and the first manned spaceship was Russian, Vostok I, which carried Yuri A. Gagarin into orbit on April 12, 1961, and set a record for dating a book (*Station in Space* was published by Bantam Books in 1958) less than three years after publication. And yet perhaps my prophecy was not all that bad: the American launchings did take place on the east coast of Florida at Cape Canaveral (near Cocoa, Florida), rumors of Russian cosmonauts dying in orbit or possibly not going up at all floated around, and when John Glenn made his first orbital flight on February 20, 1962, the city of Perth, Australia, turned its lights on and off to signal its good wishes (my wife called me—I had gone to work after watching the capsule safely into orbit—and said, "Somebody's been reading 'The Cave of Night'").

"The Hedonist" is the central portion of *The Joy Makers*, the novella in which is most thoroughly brought out the nature of "hedonism"—the science of happiness—and its inherent conflicts. I got the idea from the *Encyclopedia Britannica*—people are always asking me where I get my ideas (usually, less tactfully, "Where do you get those crazy ideas?") and this is the example I often give because I can trace it accurately. I was doing research for another story, and I looked up the *Britannica* article about "Feeling." It was a fascinating piece which analyzed the various ways to be happy: modify, substitute, anticipate, daydream, and delude on one side, and devalue, project, and suppress on the other. One can be happy, that is, by getting what one wants—or by wanting what one gets. The article ended with the statement—like waving a red flag in front of a science-fiction writer—"But the true science of applied hedonics is not yet born." Ah, I began to imagine, what if there were a science of happiness so that we could seek happiness directly rather than through the various surrogates we think will make us happy, such as love, fame, success, money . . .

"New Blood" and "The Medic" are the first and third sections of *The Immortals*. In "New Blood" the reader will meet the Immortal man, a mutation whose blood and circulatory system is improved, whose cells do not age and die, who may live forever, and whose blood can rejuvenate older persons—only there's a catch. In "Medic" the reader will see the result of those facts, a world in which the search for longer life, for immortality, has become obsessive and has warped society into something nobody wanted.

I do not present these stories as proof for my argument that science fiction is at its best in the novelette (I have tried to do that with my other examples), but these stories have been successful. All of them were originally printed in magazines ("The Cave of Night" was included in a best-of-the-year collection) and provided key portions of books that together have sold more than half a million copies in this country and have sold more copies abroad in translation. Moreover, they have seemed unusually appealing to other media: "The Cave of Night" was dramatized over NBC's *X Minus One* radio series as "Man in Orbit" with Lee Marvin and E. G. Marshall on television's *Desilu Playhouse* in 1959; *The Immortals* was dramatized under the title of "The Immortal" as the second ABC-TV Movie of the Week in 1969 and became an hour-long series (alas, short-lived) the following season, with Christopher George; and *The Joy Makers* has attracted the attention of at least three different motion-picture producers.

These stories share a common concept: man has dreamed for centuries about space flight, about happiness, about immortality. "If only I could fly to the moon!" he has told himself. "If only I could find true happiness, if only I could live forever . . . then I would be like a god." These stories, however, go on to demonstrate that every dream come true brings unforeseen consequences. The power of man to dream and make his dreams come true is unlimited, but each step forward must be paid for, there is no such thing as a free lunch, and some dreams are nightmares.

THE BURNING

The nightmare began with the House Un-American Activities Committee and Senator Joseph McCarthy. We lived in Wisconsin for a year and a half where I had a job as a junior editor of paperback books but left in the fall of 1952 so I could return to full-time writing in Kansas City, but not before we had a chance to cast a vote against McCarthy. While we were in Wisconsin, my wife, Jane, went to a McCarthy campaign rally and reported that McCarthy had a personal magnetism that made her understand how people could be swayed by him. In 1953 we bought our first television set. In 1954, we were glued to it by the Army-McCarthy hearings. In 1955 I began thinking about an idea for a short novel that dealt with the American anti-intellectualism I saw as the reason for the success of HUAC's and Senator McCarthy's witch hunts. They were acceptable because people were eager to believe that writers, filmmakers, academics, and scientists would betray their country in the name of their soft-headed ideals. Emotions seemed heated enough to spill over into mob action.

I wanted to write about the way in which attitudes had changed toward the wise men of the community, the sachems, the witch doctors. Once they were considered gifted with special powers that they used on behalf of the tribe to placate or manipulate the supernatural forces and beings that controlled the world. They were special; they were revered. But in modern times, when everybody could educate themselves to wisdom and power over nature, people saw themselves as victims of scientific and technological change that were being created by scientists. They believed that scientists were pursuing knowledge without considering how it would be used and that ordinary humanity paid the price. The story I contemplated imagined a revolution from which eventually—in two sequels that might be combined with the first story into a novel—science would be restored to its original position as a respected member of the tribe with a special talent for making miracles.

In 1956 I exchanged some letters with John W. Campbell, the editor of *Astounding*. In his characteristic contrarian way, Campbell took the opposite position—that people had a right to be upset at the scientists, and my scientist, fleeing from their righteous anger, ought to realize this and return to give himself up. I was convinced—or, if not convinced, persuaded, since it was Campbell who would authorize payment, wrote "Witches Must Burn," and saw it published in *Astounding* in August 1956. But the sequels I had planned got hung up on my inability to get past the ending of that short novel to the beginning of the next. Twelve years later I finally realized why my hero had returned (it wasn't Campbell's reason), and I wrote "Trial by Fire." Frederik Pohl accepted it. "Witch Hunt" followed immediately, and the two short novels were published within a couple of months of each other—"Trial by

Fire" in the February 1969 issue of *If*, "Witch Hunt" in the April 1969 *Galaxy*.

That same year the World Science Fiction Convention was held in St. Louis. I took my two teenaged sons and a friend of my older son. There we met a charming young woman named Gail Wendroff who had just been named science-fiction editor at Dell Books. We invited her to join us at the Hugo Awards ceremony. She told me later that she had felt so out of place that she was about to return to New York. Perhaps it was no coincidence that a year later she published *The Witching Hour* and two years after that, *The Burning*.

THE LISTENERS

After a decade when there never had been a day when I wasn't working on some story or novel, I accepted a position as the first administrative assistant to the chancellor for university relations at the University of Kansas. Those were the turbulent 1960s, and between learning my job and trying to explain student unrest to the various university publics, I had no time for writing. *The Joy Makers*, *The Immortals*, and *Future Imperfect* were published between 1961 and 1964, but they had been written in the 1950s.

By the middle of the 1960s I was feeling serious withdrawal symptoms, and I resolved to take the month's paid vacation that I was due. I prepared for that month—August after the end of the summer session and before the beginning of the fall semester—for months ahead so that when the time came I wouldn't have to think or do research, I could sit down and write. Beginning in 1966, I wrote the second and third novellas that completed *The Burning* (and published them in *If* and *Galaxy*), the second chapter of what later became *Kampus*, and the novelette I called "The Listeners."

"The Listeners" was inspired by Walter Sullivan's *We Are Not Alone*. Sullivan was the long-time science editor of *The New York Times*. He had attended a seminal conference of scientists in Washington, D.C., along with many of the people who were being attracted to the idea of listening for messages from the stars—what now is called SETI, the search for extraterrestrial intelligence—including Frank Drake and Carl Sagan. His book described the fascination people have displayed over the centuries about the possibility of life on other worlds and various proposals for communicating with aliens. The availability of radio telescopes had led to recent discussions among such scientists as Giuseppe Cocconi and Philip Morrison about the possibility of picking up signals from space, and Cocconi had written a letter (reprinted in the first "Computer Run" section) to Sir Bernard Lovell proposing that some time on the Jodrell Bank radio telescope be devoted to a search for signals from space.

Sullivan's book was fascinating and included a good deal of material that later found its way into my novel, but what stimulated my writer's instinct was the concept of a project that might have to be pursued for a century without results. What kind of need would produce that kind of dedication, I pondered, and what kind of people would it enlist—and have to enlist if it were to continue? I wrote "The Listeners," which in the novel is called "Robert MacDonald." My then literary agent thought it was overwritten for its audience and had too many foreign-language quotations, and anyway, he wrote, I should make my hero a young man fighting against the tyranny of tired old men. Another agent didn't care for it enough to take me on as a client, but when *Galaxy* announced that it was going back to monthly publication (and, I realized, would need more material), I sent it to Fred Pohl and he wrote back saying that he'd be happy to publish it if I'd include translations of the foreign-language quotes. The following year Donald Wollheim included it in his *World' Best Science Fiction* anthology.

In the next few years (I was working on other projects as well), I wrote five more chapters and saw all but the final chapter published in *Fantasy and Science Fiction* and *Galaxy*. Meanwhile Charles Scribner's Sons had decided to develop a science-fiction line under editor Norbert Slepyan, and one of the novels he signed up was *The Listeners*. He asked me once if I was going to add anything to the six chapters and I said I was planning on broadening the perspective to include some of the materials that were being gathered by the computer to aid in its recognition (and translation) of alien communications, as well as the beginnings of artificial intelligence (observant readers may watch it happen).

The novel was published in hardcover in 1972 as "a novel" (not a science-fiction novel). The same year it became a selection of the Science Fiction Book Club. The following year it was published by Signet Books and a decade later it was reprinted by Del Rey Books. It has been translated into Italian, German, Polish, Japanese, and Chinese. Three decades have passed since the novel was published, and more than a fourth of the century-long project. SETI projects on both coasts are still hard at work, trying to pick up messages from the stars, and they continue—without positive results. If the novel has any claims to vision, its insight may be found in its evaluation of human desire and persistence in the face of continuing discouragement. But we are approaching the period when the novel begins, and maybe the signal we all have been awaiting—that we are not alone—will soon be received.

If it is, if our search is rewarded, maybe *The Listeners* will have played a part in it, and the book that started in 1966 in a hot August sleeping porch, in a college town in eastern Kansas, will have made a difference. After all, one of the SETI project directors told me recently that *The Listeners* had done more to turn people on to the search than any other book. My thanks go to Walter Sullivan's *We Are Not Alone*. I hope the title is right.

HUMAN VOICES

Raymond Chandler introduced a volume of his short stories with an insightful essay about what he called "the gentle art of murder," in which he remarked that "everything one learns about writing takes away from your need to write." That hasn't been my experience. People do get busier, however, as they get deeper into life, and they find less time to write stories. Time is the problem.

In my case, I got involved in directing university relations for the University of Kansas and teaching, writing novels, and writing about science fiction. So the short stories that I enjoyed so much—and feel are the ideal form of science fiction—became less frequent. Even some of the short stories were written as part of novels.

In this volume, then, I have gathered together the stories of my past quarter century. There aren't a lot of them, fewer than one every two years, but they represent the more mature vision of the years after fifty. The earlier stories had been influenced by the magazines I had grown up reading and the postwar anthologies that had recapitulated the experience for me. They were written when I felt that I was primarily a writer and actually had spent several years as a full-time writer, earning my living with what I was able to sell. But the stories in this volume were written by a man who took time away from other occupations to devote to fiction, who had the experiences of an editor, a teacher, a director of university relations, and a professor, as well as the earlier experiences of student, naval officer, and husband and father.

So the stories were much more difficult to categorize, and sometimes more difficult to find a publisher for. "The Old Folks," for instance, was written for my fiction-writing class, as an example for my students of what I wanted them to produce as weekly assignments—and to trick myself into writing again. I would like to have sold the story immediately and presented the publication to my students as a validation of everything I had told them. But the science-fiction magazines said the story wasn't science fiction, and the slick magazines—there still were some of them around—said they didn't publish science fiction. Then I met Harry Harrison at the World Science Fiction Convention of 1968, in Oakland, and he said he was publishing a new anthology of original stories. Categories didn't bother him, he said, and he published "The Old Folks" in *Nova Two*, and then it appeared in a best SF of the year collection. So there was a kind of validation after all, although it came after half-a-dozen years.

"The Voices" was written as the second part of my novel *The Listeners*. I had been working as the first administrative assistant to the chancellor for university relations, and the job was so demanding that I hadn't taken any vacation for the first half-dozen years, nor had I found any time for writing anything of my own. Finally, in 1967, I decided to take my month off in the summer and devote it to writing. I started my novel *Kampus* one year, wrote the second and third sections of *The Burning* in two other years, and wrote the novelette "The Listeners," which was published in *Galaxy* and later became the first chapter of the novel and was reprinted as part of my second short-story collection, *Breaking Point*. "The Voices," which also was published in *Galaxy*, became the second chapter.

I wrote "Fault" after I returned to full-time teaching in 1970 and after a long spell of writing such novels as *The Listeners* and such complicated historical surveys as *Alternate Worlds: The Illustrated History of Science Fiction*. The idea came from a geology professor who wanted me to write a scenario for him dealing with the psychological problem of earthquake prediction. I thought it would make a good story and so did Ben Boom, the new editor of *Analog*, who later told me that a government agency had requested copies. "Guilt" came along a couple of years later. For that I drew upon the expertise of a psychology professor who directed me to certain texts in the university's library.

"Child of the Sun" started as a proposal for a television series. CBS was looking for a series to compete with the then-popular "The Six-Million-Dollar Man," and at the suggestion of my agent, I "pitched" the idea to the West Coast office. The executives who listened seemed interested, but when it didn't get picked up, I decided to write it as a story. It was published in *Analog* and the following year in a collection of the world's best SF. That attracted the attention of a Hollywood producer who took a year's option on the TV and film rights. When that didn't work out, I decided that the people who make decisions about television series believed that there weren't enough such stories to justify a series. So I wrote five more of them and published them in *Analog* and then as a novel called *Crisis!*

"The North Wind" was a sidelight of my long-time work on a millennial novel called *Catastrophe!* (published in 2001 as *The Millennium Blues*). "Among the Beautiful Bright Children" was written for Harlan Ellison's long-postponed *The Last Dangerous Visions*. I later added two more substantial sections and some interchapter materials and published it as *The Dreamers*. "The Futurist" was almost another "The Old Folks." I tried it on a great many magazines in two different forms before Kim Mohan at *Amazing Stories* started working on it with me and, after some tinkering, published it—calling its publication one of his greatest pleasures as an editor.

"Man of Parts" emerged from my reading of a colleague's work on futurism. He quoted Adam Smith's anecdote in *The Theory of Moral Sentiments* that is repeated early in the story, and I began to consider what might happen if someone really was convinced that he could save people by cutting off a finger—and other pieces of himself. *The Magazine of Fantasy and Science Fiction* published that one.

Finally, "The Gingerbread Man," "The Day the Magic Came Back," and "The Lens of Time" were the products of my retirement from full-time teaching in 1993. I finished *The Millennium Blues* and decided that I'd like to write some more stories, maybe even enough to reach at least one hundred publications. "The Gingerbread Man," which was published in *Analog*, was a response to Isaac Asimov's "The Bicentennial Man," a marvelous story whose sentimental conclusion seemed to run counter to the basic rationalism displayed in Isaac's other fiction. Only a few readers recognized that the two stories were related, in spite of identical names of the protagonists and the date. "The Day the Magic Came Back," published in *Science Fiction Age*, I thought of as a response to the world's contemporary fascination with fantasy and fantastic phenomena. I had noted an increasing number of reflexive stories in SF, and I decided to write one: "The Lens of Time" was my tribute to Fitz-James O'Brien's marvelous 1858 story "The Diamond Lens." In doing my research for it I discovered that the story had made O'Brien's reputation, that he had been accused of plagiarizing the idea from a colleague who had died tragically young, and that he had defended himself by telling how he had used the expertise of an acquaintance, Dr. J. D. Whelpley. Whelpley, incidentally, also wrote SF, and his story, "The Atoms of Chladni," was published a year after "The Diamond Lens." Everything in "The Lens of Time," except the description of the meeting and the conversation, is true.

"The End-of-the-World Ball" is the final chapter of *The Millennium Blues*, although I wrote it first as a way of finding out about the characters who would wend their way through the millennial year 2000 before they ended up on December 31 at the End-of-the-World Ball. Then I went back and picked up the story on January 1, with my six characters viewpointing three chapters each as the year progressed inexorably toward the end of the second millennium. But meanwhile I answered a friend's request for a story, and George Zebrowski published it in his original anthology series, *Synergy*.

In 1999 I began a new series of novelettes, with "The Giftie," published in *Analog*. Carl Sagan sent me a copy of his novel *Contact* thanking me for the inspiration of *The Listeners*, but as I watched the film adapted from his novel, I thought: It wouldn't happen like that. So I decided to write about the way it would really happen. I hope to develop the series into a novel made up of six such episodes. I've done four of them. And I still have one more story to go before I reach one hundred.

GIFT FROM THE STARS

In 1972 Scribner's published a novel of mine called *The Listeners*. The Scribner's promotion director sent out galleys to a number of authors and scientists, and, among others, Carl Sagan was kind enough to read them and offer a quote: "One of the very best fictional portrayals of contact with extra-terrestrial intelligence ever written." It was used as an above-the-title blurb on every edition published after Sagan became even better known when he created his popular-astronomy television show *Cosmos* in 1980.

The following year Sagan signed a contract with Simon & Schuster to write a science-fiction novel called *Contact*. It was finally published in 1985.

When the film version of *Contact* finally was released in 1997 (delayed even more than the writing of the novel), my reaction was mixed: I enjoyed the film and yet I felt that it was romantic rather than realistic. The novel *Contact* had portrayed working scientists realistically and the film perhaps a bit less so, but the plans transmitted were fantastic and the method and purpose of the space journey, not only fantastic but a letdown (a common fault of SF novels). And the question of why aliens would send the plans was never adequately explored.

That isn't the way it would happen, I told myself, and I was "inspired" to write *Gift from the Stars*, a response not only to *Contact* but to every novel of humans encountering the unknown. I wrote it as a series of novelettes, just as I had written *The Listeners*, and published them over a period of half-a-dozen years in *Analog*, beginning with "The Giftie," which won the *Analog* readers' poll for best novelette of the year. I have kept that pattern in the book, even though I planned it from the beginning as a novel exploring "the way it would really be." It is a novel in six parts instead of a dozen or so chapters.

If aliens sent us plans for a spaceship, the novel suggests, they would arrive without fanfare and their arrival would be greeted not with surprise or joy or gratitude but with suspicion and resistance. A few space enthusiasts would want to implement them to reach the stars, but the great masses of humanity—and the bureaucrats who make decisions for them—would ignore the plans or want to suppress them. Most of all, why would aliens send us spaceship plans? Are their intentions beneficent or inimical? Damon Knight raised the question in a classic short-short story "To Serve Man," but *Gift from the Stars* pursues the question in detail and arrives at an answer, like the spaceship the humans construct and name, *Ad Astra "Per Aspera."* "To the stars through difficulty."

Gift from the Stars is a more lighthearted look at the issues of alien contact—the plans, for instance, are discovered as an appendix in a book on a UFO remainder table—and I enjoyed writing them and living with the characters: Adrian Mast, Frances Farmstead, Jessica Buehler, and the troubled genius Peter Cavendish. I liked Frances so much I couldn't bear to let her die from old age before the novel was over, so I invented a rejuvenation process. I hope you enjoy them as much.

THE DREAMERS

Sometime in the late 1950s I ran across accounts of what was then called "chemical memory." The way in which memory is transferred to the neurons in the brain for storage was mysterious at that time (and no one really knows today how the brain remembers). Robert Jordan and James McConnell, while still graduate students, began doing experiments with planarian worms at the University of Texas, studies that McConnell continued while a professor at the University of Michigan. His work and that of others was published in a publication whimsically titled *The Worm-Runners Digest*.

Other researchers picked up the research: Holgar Hyden, George Ungar, David Krech . . . All that, if the reader is interested, is summarized (in quotes from journal and magazine articles) in the middle channel of the Mnemonist's ruminations. The final statement in that brief history, in the Mnemonist's last section, speculates about the future potential of chemical memory. Such speculations are the spark to the rocket of the writer's imagination.

I included references to chemical memory in my novel *Kampus*, in which they became pills of instruction that students could pop instead of going to class—though there they became a metaphor for getting knowledge—or information—without having to work for it. But they also contained a central core of possibility: that learning itself could be encapsulated, so that one could learn to be a computer technician, say, or a surgeon by popping a pill. If that became possible, civilization would be transformed more radically than it was by the industrial revolution or by science.

The Dreamers assumes that the chemical memory revolution has already occurred. All the everyday problems of existence have been resolved. Now chemical memory is being applied to the arts, and people have the opportunity to indulge themselves in the ultimate escape fiction: the living of other people's lives through memories that have been encapsulated for them.

But there still will be a need for a few people who hold themselves apart from the common pool of pleasure, who must make decisions, create dreams, and supply the basic materials for the dreamers and their poppets.

Even in the 1950s and early 1960s, the concept of chemical memory was viewed skeptically by most biologists and physiologists, and today it has been discarded. An article in the January 2001 *Analog* by Kyle Kirkland, a postdoctoral scientist at the University of Pennsylvania, dismisses chemical memory and describes what scientists today think about the way memories are recorded in the brain. Synaptic physiology, he wrote, is one of the most important areas of neuroscience research. Just because you can't inject other people's memories, he goes on to say, doesn't mean that you can't *replicate* them. But chemical memory always was more potent in what it implied about the human condition than in what it might achieve in the real world. (Science fiction, editor John W. Campbell once wrote, exists in the gap between the laboratory and the marketplace.) Memory is what makes us individuals, and the creation of memories is what, when it structures our dreams, we call art.

KAMPUS

In the half-dozen years between 1964 and 1970, the college and university campuses of the country were torn by political upheavals inspired by civil rights demonstrations in the South and fueled by Vietnam War protests. Free-speech movements disrupted the University of California, Berkeley, and radical student groups exported their views and methods to other campuses. The rhetoric was heated, and sometimes the protests became violent: sit-ins turned into confrontations, buildings were burned, bombs exploded, and finally, at Kent State University, students were killed. With the end of the war in Vietnam, the radical student movements subsided.

At issue during this period were questions of justice, governance, and the obligation and right of universities to act as parents to their students, placing limits on their personal behavior. The nature and purposes of education were debated, as was who should be in charge of the process. Students insisted that they were consumers of education and had all the rights of consumers to pick and choose and evaluate, and even to hire and fire. Universities have not been the same since. Although most students have become more conservative in their political beliefs and more concerned about jobs after graduation than the politics of university governance, the authority of the universities, and particularly of their faculties, to determine curricula and establish standards has never been entirely regained, nor the high esteem in which universities were held or the financial support they enjoyed before the 1960s.

The student rebels were idealistic and drunk with power, filled with rage against the injustices of society and sanctimonious in their belief that they were the first generation to feel that way. The purity of their motives gave them license to strike out against any opposition and to throw off society's inhibitions against drugs and sex and sloth. It was the best of worlds; it was the worst of worlds.

I was in the midst of all this, as administrative assistant to the chancellor for university relations at the University of Kansas, one of the universities that developed as a kind of underground radical railroad from coast to coast. *Kampus* grew out of that experience. Its events occur in the world the student radicals might have created if they had won.

Masterpieces of Science Fiction

MASTERPIECES AND ME

In Kurt Vonnegut's *The Sirens of Titan*, Unk says, "I was the victim of a series of accidents, as are we all." That's been true of my life as well.

My association with Easton Press was no exception. In the middle of the 1980s I got a flyer from Easton Press announcing a new series of leather-bound collectors' editions to be called Masterpieces of Science Fiction. On an impulse, I wrote the publisher, David Ward, and suggested that Easton send a complimentary set to Special Collections in Spencer Research Library. I was surprised when Ward wrote back and said Easton would be happy to contribute the series to Special Collections. I also included a list of titles I recommended for inclusion in the series.

But that was not the end of it. A month or so later I got a letter from Eric Stones, the senior editor at Easton in charge of the series, thanking me for my suggestions and enclosing a couple of sample collector's notes for the first two books in the series, H. G. Wells's *The War of the Worlds* and Arthur C. Clarke's *2001: A Space Odyssey*. I wrote back that the notes had some inaccuracies. A few days later I got a telephone call from Eric asking if I would rewrite them. Before we had concluded our conversation, I had agreed to write all the collector's notes. Then he asked if the books should include introductions. I said that I thought introductions added class and might be useful, too, in explaining why the titles were "masterpieces." When Eric asked whom we would get to write the introductions, I volunteered to secure the services of some well-known writers. Eric thought that was a great idea.

For a dozen years, then, working with half-a-dozen different editors, I wrote collector's notes and solicited writers and scholars for introductions. When I couldn't find anyone to write an introduction and a deadline was looming, I or my late colleague, Stephen Goldman, would do it. That's how our names got on so many title pages. We also suggested some illustrations for some of the early editions, and I recommended some SF illustrators as well. Some of the Verne illustrations in one volume were watercolors, and I offered my opinion that SF illustrations needed hard edges.

Easton was paying $500 for an introduction, but Eric thought it would be great if writers would accept as payment a subscription to the series. That worked well for a time—and all but a few writers opted for the subscription—but as the series stretched past the original fifty planned volumes to seventy-five and beyond, billing all these free subscriptions to the series became a financial burden. At that point, payment for introductions was cut to fifty volumes and then to twenty-five. Finally, in 1995, the series was put on hold because older volumes had gone out of stock and the requests of new subscribers couldn't be fulfilled. A year or so later, however, Easton began to reprint half-a-dozen books a year, and then, in 1999, new titles began to be added again. This time the selections were made by Easton from recent award winners.

The Masterpieces of Science Fiction series and the subsequent Signed First Editions of Science Fiction series have been good for science fiction—besides adding to the income (and shelves) of authors, they have provided some great books to collectors, some of whom, like David Williams, Bert Chamberlin, and Ron Larson, have gone to considerable trouble and expense to get their editions signed. These well-crafted leather-bound editions with gilded edges and frontispieces by well-known SF artists have conferred some prestige on the field. When Easton mailed out its flyers, science fiction was listed alongside the complete works of Shakespeare, Faulkner, and Hemingway; the Harvard Classics; Library of the Presidents; Great Books of the 20th Century; Books That Changed the World; and the 100 Greatest Books Ever Written, not to mention the Complete Arabian Nights, *Winnie the Pooh, The Wizard of Oz*, and others. Easton always has done a fine job of publishing and a first-class job of mail-order solicitation and customer service.

The Masterpieces of Science Fiction series also has been good for Easton. At one time, one of the supervising editors told me, Masterpieces was Easton's fourth most popular series. He also told me that the other series had four consulting editors doing what I had been doing all by myself—but that's another story.

THE FOUNDATION TRILOGY
ISAAC ASIMOV

The first thing to understand about *The Foundation Trilogy* is that it is not a trilogy. There isn't a novel in the book. It is a series of nine stories: five of them novelettes, four of them novellas. The World Science Fiction Convention of 1966 voted them "the greatest all-time science-fiction series." If you read them with this in mind, you will read them not only as they were written but as they were intended to be read.

The second thing to understand is that the stories in the series were written one at a time, with no idea in the author's head (after the first one was published) what the next would deal with. This will not decrease your enjoyment of the book you are about to read, but it should control your expectations. Books put together in this way are not novels, even though they are published to resemble them. What you have here is a saga.

More important, it is a saga that not only is typical of the times in which these stories were first published, but it is central to much that came later. *The Foundation Trilogy* is a foundation book on which much that followed was built. Donald A. Wollheim, long-time SF editor and founder of the DAW line of paperback books, has called it "the point of departure for the full cosmogony of science-fiction future history."

What it presumes as a background, which many later SF writers adopted as a reasonable assumption for many of their stories about the future, is that humanity has expanded outward into the galaxy without encountering aliens and created a galactic empire that falls because of its size or corruption or communication problems or the inevitable cycles of history. In Asimov's future history, even the origin of humanity has been forgotten.

Asimov's galactic empire has grown into a vast collection of solar systems—some twenty-five million planets—united under the rulers of the administrative center, the planet of Trantor. The planet is a vast bureaucracy, so large and complex that Trantor has been entirely roofed over with metal. It is here the story starts, with the empire about to fall after twelve thousand years of peace—and one psychohistorian knows it, has been able to predict it, and has taken steps to shorten to only a millennium the thirty thousand years of barbarism and misery that will follow.

Hari Seldon has set up a Foundation of scientists and technologists, like a medieval monastery, on the remote planet Terminus at the edge of the galaxy, to preserve knowledge and skills in the midst of the chaos to come. And "at the opposite end of the galaxy," Seldon has set up a Second Foundation—but I will tell you no more about that, because it figures large in the plots of the second and third volumes.

And on the planet Terminus recordings of Seldon appear at critical points to comment on the situation. He is not simply a fortune teller; his mastery of the mathematical discipline of psychohistory has allowed him to predict the grand flow of human events, although not individual behavior. Psychohistory and the Foundations—these are the two Asimov inventions upon which one of the great achievements of science fiction was written, psychohistory to provide a recognizable pattern and the Foundations, Asimov's extension of his own rationality, to shape that pattern into situations more favorable to humanity.

The third thing to understand about *The Foundation Trilogy* is that the ability to predict the future does not make these stories an exercise in determinism—the philosophical idea that an omniscient deity or an omnipotent rule of cause and effect has laid down inexorable paths that humans must follow like puppets. Seldon is wise, but he is not always right, and he is right only when determined men and women in the *Trilogy* make him right.

What Asimov is writing about that is very important in our times is the way in which free will can exercise itself even in a world of science and high technology. A number of critics have accused *The Foundation Trilogy* of incorporating a kind of debased Marxism, which also has its philosophy of historical determinism. But Asimov has said that in his early discussions of the idea with editor John W. Campbell, in whose magazine, *Astounding Science Fiction*, all the stories originally were published, Campbell suggested "symbolic logic" as the justification for psychohistory. Symbolic logic, when perfected, Campbell said, would so clear up the mysteries of the human mind that human actions would be predictable. Asimov made *his* comparison to the kinetic theory of gases, "where the individual molecules in the gas remain as unpredictable as ever, but the average action is completely predictable."

Some other aspects of the book at hand that may add to the enjoyment of the reader: the young Asimov got the idea for the series in 1941. He was twenty-one, and he had been selling stories to Campbell (and other editors, although, for Asimov, Campbell was the only one that mattered) for two years. Asimov had made a practice of visiting the editor frequently, and upon this occasion, riding the subway toward Campbell's Street & Smith office and searching for an idea, he happened to look down at a collection of Gilbert and Sullivan plays opened to Iolanthe and saw a picture of the fairy queen kneeling in front of Private Willis of the Grenadier Guards. His mind wandered to soldiers, to a military society, to feudalism, to the breakup of the Roman Empire. When he reached Campbell's office, he told the editor that he was planning to write a story about the breakup of the galactic empire. "He talked and I talked and he talked and I talked and when I left I had the Foundation series in mind," Asimov recalled in an article for the *SFWA Bulletin* titled, "There's Nothing Like a Good Foundation."

What he had in mind, however, was not the entire book but the initial situation upon which episodes would be built like one floor of a skyscraper on another. The series, incidentally, started with chapter 2, which was called "Foundation." The first chapter in the book was written especially for the book version published in 1951 (ten years after the publication of "Foundation"), as a way of providing an introduction to the empire before it had fallen and background for the stories to follow. The outer stories appeared over eight years, while its author aged from twenty-one to twenty-eight; while the author was writing his robot stories and others, getting a Ph.D. in chemistry, getting married, and serving in the U.S. Army during World War II; as the author needed money and came up with ideas for further developments. The last installment of the last serial appeared in January 1950.

The Foundation Trilogy is an exercise in ingenuity. Much of its developments, as well as some of its characters, are taken from the fall of the Roman Empire. Asimov got some early criticism for this, but he responded that history is cyclical and that empires fall for similar reasons and produce similar responses. And the situation of the galactic empire is only vaguely similar, not identical, to that of the Roman Empire. The problems of shortening the long dark ages demand not only ingenuity but a philosophy of human behavior.

The reader will note that out of the solution to each problem grows the next problem to be solved. Not only does this tie the stories neatly together, but it also suggests the philosophy that nothing is permanent: history is dynamic, never static. There are no final answers. One generation's solution is the next generation's problem. Thus the series develops—the overriding goal, pushing back the dark (as Asimov has tried to do throughout his career with his more than 350 books on science, history, literature, and many other subjects); the individual action—the solution of the problem at hand creating a problem that itself must be solved and create the next problem.

Asimov is saying that life is a series of problems to be solved, but life itself, as an unending series of problems, one inside the other like Chinese puzzle boxes, can never be solved. Asimov would be pleased that this is so, just as the reader will be pleased with Asimov's simulation of the life-process in *The Foundation Trilogy*.

A further note: By 1978 *The Foundation Trilogy* had sold more than two million copies; since then, at least another million. In 1982, in response to the demands of those millions of readers, Asimov returned to his fictional creation of the 1940s and wrote a sequel, *Foundation's Edge*, which immediately appeared on *The New York Times* best-seller list. *The Foundation Trilogy* covered only about four hundred years of Hari Seldon's predicted one thousand years; *Foundation's Edge*, which is about half as long as the entire *Trilogy*, picks up about one hundred years later. And if readers wish to continue the saga, *Foundation and Earth* was published in 1986. Miraculously, these novels read as if hardly any time at all had passed since *Astounding* published the final installment of *Second Foundation* in 1950.

STRANGER IN A STRANGE LAND
ROBERT A. HEINLEIN

Robert A. Heinlein never won a Nebula Award, but he was the first writer to whom the Science Fiction Writers of America presented its Grand Master Award. No one who knows science fiction had any doubt about that; Heinlein was the Grand Master.

He had earned that title not by awards, although he earned a good many, but by accomplishments. Not only did his fiction realize the potential inherent in the science-fiction form, but he also experimented with new forms and, in the process, explored new worlds for science fiction to conquer.

When Heinlein launched his career as a writer in 1939, the only avenues for publication were the science-fiction magazines that had been created by Hugo Gernsback in 1926 with *Amazing Stories* and brought to a new state of readiness by John W. Campbell as editor of *Astounding Science Fiction*. With occasional exceptions, Heinlein became Campbell's most popular author almost with his first story, "Lifeline," and together with a few other authors who met Campbell's standards of good fiction told in science-important worlds established what has since become known as SF's Golden Age.

Born in Butler, Missouri, in 1907, Heinlein was graduated from the U.S. Naval Academy in 1929, twentieth in a class of 243. He served on active duty until 1934, when he was retired, permanently disabled, with tuberculosis. He tried several other avenues for his ambitions, including the study of astronomy, the practice of politics, silver mining, architecture, and real estate, without success. Then he noticed an announcement in *Thrilling Wonder Stories* of a contest for writing amateurs, but by the time "Lifeline" was finished, he discovered that Campbell would pay more for it.

For four years, before World War II intervened, Heinlein sold most of his stories to Campbell. In the process he discovered some "truly remarkable techniques," as Campbell put it later, "for presenting a great deal of background and associated material without intruding into the flow of the story." Then Heinlein joined the Naval Air Experimental Station of the U.S. Navy Yard in Philadelphia as a civilian engineer and persuaded L. Sprague de Camp and Isaac Asimov to join him there.

After the war Heinlein began systematically breaking down the walls that had enclosed the science-fiction "ghetto" and had kept it almost exclusively a magazine genre. Virtually no science-fiction books had been published between 1926 and 1946; one of the first authors the fan press, as well as the commercial publishers, turned to after World War II was Heinlein.

Another stronghold of resistance was the slick magazines, which had rigorously excluded SF. Beginning in 1947 Heinlein stories began appearing in the *Saturday Evening Post*, *Argosy*, *Town and Country*, *Blue Book*, *Boys'Life*, and the *American Legion Magazine*.

Although the principal audience for science fiction, beginning with Jules Verne, had been adolescent males, a significant juvenile literature did not exist until Heinlein began publishing his Scribner's series of novels for young readers, beginning with *Rocketship Galileo* in 1947 and *Space Cadet* in 1948, and then hitting his stride with *Red Planet* in 1949. After that his juveniles appeared every year, and often were serialized for adult readers in the SF magazines, until 1958, when Scribner's rejected *Starship Troopers* (as too militaristic for its intended audience); it was published the next year by Putnam, who also published his final juvenile, *Podkayne of Mars*, in 1963. A generation of SF readers has grown up with Heinlein's juveniles.

SF films enjoyed flurries of interest, most significantly in 1925 with *The Lost World* and in 1926 with *Metropolis*, but experienced the biggest boom in the 1930s with *Just Imagine, Frankenstein, The Island of Lost Souls, King Kong, The Invisible Man, Deluge, Transatlantic Tunnel,* and *Things to Come*. A long dry spell followed until Heinlein used parts of *Rocketship Galileo* in his screenplay (with collaborators) for the 1950 film *Destination Moon*, which film critic John Baxter credits as the beginning of the SF film boom of the 1950s.

Heinlein's final breakthrough for science fiction came in 1961 with the publication of *Stranger in a Strange Land*, the book at hand. His novels, like SF in general, had always sold well to a small and loyal audience. His juveniles, which reached a larger and less well-defined readership, were the exception to the publishing rule that one could never lose money publishing SF because SF readers were so hungry for books that they would buy several thousand copies of any SF novel and perhaps ten thousand or so of those by the better-known authors such as Heinlein. But, publishers said, that was the limit. It was a self-fulfilling prophecy: some regular publishers would print no more than five thousand copies of any title and never reprint.

Paperback books were different. A few, such as Bradbury's early pieced-together novels, Walter Miller Jr.'s *A Canticle for Leibowitz*, and Pat Frank's more mainstream treatments, managed to accumulate substantial totals by remaining in print year after year. *Stranger in a Strange Land* did not achieve best-seller success in hardcover, but it sold in massive numbers in paperback, where it became the first SF paperback best seller. It also won a Hugo Award.

Stranger in a Strange Land was not the first, nor the last, Heinlein novel to be honored by SF fans. Although many of Heinlein's stories and novels appeared before the World Science Convention began presenting its Science Fiction Achievement Awards (in 1953, picked up again as a regular feature in 1955), the fans voted Heinlein's *Double Star* the best novel of 1956, *Starship Troopers* the best novel of 1959, and *The Moon Is a Harsh Mistress* the best novel of 1966.

What distinguished *Stranger in a Strange Land*, besides its remarkable ascent into the best-seller stratosphere, and what may have contributed to its breakout into a general audience was its subject matter. Up to this point, Heinlein's fiction had been concerned mostly with plausible scenarios of near-future developments created with remarkable concern for detail, an infectious pride in humanity's competitive survival instincts, and an engaging optimism that competent individuals would solve most of the difficult problems that lay ahead for the species.

Stranger in a Strange Land deals with the creation of a religion based on firsthand knowledge of an afterlife. Heinlein's fiction is a search for the meaning of life and the best way to lead it in the absence of any certainty. Heinlein's characters end up with a set of rules for behavior that involve curiosity, education, honor, and obedience to legitimate authority. The first three are either innate in the best of humanity or learned through experience; the last always is subject to reevaluation as to what is "legitimate."

A Heinlein hero or heroine always begins with potential that must be realized through education, usually in the school of experience, often reinforced or codified by an older person who already has been through the process. The same pattern holds true in *Stranger in a Strange Land:* Valentine Michael Smith is a true innocent—as innocent as an angel, to which he is compared—who must be educated in the ways of humanity because he has been raised from birth among Martians. He learns from a skeptical, even cynical, father figure, a man somewhat like Heinlein himself, Jubal Harshaw.

But Smith is not a complete innocent. He, like the angels, has knowledge that ordinary humans lack. He knows, for instance, how to control his body, his thoughts, his emotions. He knows how to understand situations and other people; and not just to understand them but to understand them completely, holistically. He knows how to "grok" (a word that captivated a generation of readers). And he knows that when beings are "discorporated," they continue their existence on another plane. He's learned these things from the Martians.

Once Smith has learned enough about humans and human society, he sets about teaching people a better way of life; he shares with them what he has learned from the Martians. And, since the only institution free from public control is the church, Smith creates his own religion as a vehicle for the education of all humanity.

Perhaps that is as much as one ought to reveal in an introduction; the joy of a book like this, after all, is in the personal discovery, the "grokking" of the novel. But perhaps it should be pointed out that Heinlein is not advocating any religion—as a libertarian he was skeptical of any political or social institution that demanded conformity or obedience it had not earned—nor was he rationalizing the "discorporation" of bad people. In *Stranger in a Strange Land*, that depends upon a certainty, grokking, we have not mastered and a knowledge that discorporation is only a stage in a chain of existence.

Stranger in a Strange Land also is a satire of contemporary follies, including religion, that foreshadows, like its depiction of water beds, much of the return to fundamentalism we have seen in recent times.

And although its opening phrase, "Once upon a time," identifies the novel as a kind of contemporary fairy tale, and its ending as a kind of Christian fable, Jubal Harshaw, who shares at least a good many Heinlein characteristics (just as Valentine Michael Smith may share a good many Heinlein aspirations), remains skeptical until the end. And although he may finally be converted, the reader feels that he has not given up his innate skepticism and keen sense of his own individuality.

Stranger in a Strange Land became a cult book of the 1960s, and "grokking" and "water brother" and "thou art God" became part of the vocabulary of the generation that grew up then. More important, perhaps, the novel demonstrated that a vast, untapped audience, unsuspected by the publishing industry, was ready for science fiction. It prepared the way for the success, in paperback, of Frank Herbert's *Dune* (1965) and later the first hardcover bestseller, *Children of Dune* (1976), and then, in the 1980s, for the regular appearance of science fiction, by Asimov, by Arthur Clarke, by Heinlein himself, and by others, on the best-seller lists. It also led to the million-dollar advance. It may also have contributed to the success of *2001: A Space Odyssey*, *Star Wars* and its sequels, *E. T.*, and the SF film phenomenon, which has turned the list of many popular films into one almost entirely populated by SF and fantasy. Rather than *Star Wars* expanding the audience for written SF, Heinlein and other SF authors may have provided the audience for *Star Wars*.

Stranger in a Strange Land also represented a turning point in Heinlein's own work: it marked the end of the second major stage in Heinlein's development and the beginning of the third. The first stage was Heinlein's apprenticeship. Remarkably successful though they were, the first ten years of his career represented a period when Heinlein was learning his craft. For the next ten years, beginning with *Red Planet* and *The Puppet Masters*, and continuing through his other juveniles and among his adult novels *Double Star* and *The Door into Summer*, Heinlein was at his artistic peak. With *Stranger in a Strange Land* Heinlein turned, with the possible exception of *The Moon Is a Harsh Mistress*, to his third, and more discursive, style; it was to be in many ways his most successful, though not always the favorite of Heinlein connoisseurs.

Heinlein died on May 8, 1988, at the age of eighty. It would be difficult, if not impossible, to imagine science fiction without him; he was the most important SF writer since H. G. Wells. In recognition of that fact, I submitted two of the four volumes of my historical anthology *The Road to Science Fiction* as "From Wells to Heinlein" and "From Heinlein to Here." Like

Moses, he led science fiction into the promised land of art and commerce. *Stranger in a Strange Land* was one of the milestones along the way.

THE WORLD OF NULL-A
A. E. VAN VOGT

In 1945 the magazine *Astounding Science Fiction* announced the forthcoming publication of *The World of Null-A* with a great fanfare. No wonder. It was the ultimate science-fiction serial of SF's Golden Age, it had been written by one of the authors who had combined their talents with those of editor John W. Campbell to create that Golden Age, and it pushed the concepts of the human species and its undiscovered potentials as far as they would go.

It was not A. E. (for Alfred Elton) van Vogt's first success in the field. Born in 1912 in Winnipeg, Canada, the son of a lawyer, van Vogt grew up in a rural Saskatchewan community. He discovered fairy tales at the age of eight and was shamed out of reading them at the age of twelve. Without money for education (his father lost a good job at the start of the Depression), van Vogt did not attend college. He worked at a series of jobs and then started writing true confessions, love stories, trade-magazine articles, and radio plays.

When he broke into SF in 1939, he had already developed writing skills and theories. His first published story, "Black Destroyer," in the July 1939 *Astounding* (in the same issue as Isaac Asimov's first *Astounding* story, "Trends"; Robert Heinlein's first story "Lifeline" would be a month later; Theodore Sturgeon's "Ether Breather" a month after that), was immediately recognized as the work of a master. Its alien menace—a big, black, enigmatic catlike creature that consumes "id" and can teleport itself through space—was matched against the human crew of the visiting spaceship. It seemed like an unequal battle against the fearsome Coeurl, but the Earthmen had the use of a new science called "Nexialism."

Here was a writer who would produce one startling concept after another, who would match and sometimes surpass Heinlein in the polls for top story and favorite writer of the period. Over the next ten years (he would emigrate to Los Angeles in 1944), he produced for *Astounding* and its companion fantasy magazine *Unknown* almost fifty stories in lengths ranging upward to the one-hundred-thousand-word serial. In 1940 the serial *Slan*, built around the concept of superintelligent humans with tendrils in their hair that permit telepathy, and their persecution by the rest of humanity, created such excitement that fans began calling themselves Slans: here was the perfect symbol for their own status—the persecuted elite.

The principal characteristic of van Vogt's fiction was narrative excitement, unremitting tension, concepts pushed to their ultimate limits. To a

1947 book of essays titled *Of Worlds Beyond*, van Vogt contributed a chapter on "Complication in the Science Fiction Story" in which he described his practice of writing in eight-hundred-word scenes and then coming up with enough ideas to fill out each scene. He also developed a habit of putting every current thought into the story he happened to be working on; if it seemed to have no relevance, he could usually find an approach that would make it usable.

Some of the ideas that fascinated him that he incorporated into stories were Oswald Spengler's ideas of history that he used as background for "Black Destroyer" and *The Voyage of the Space Beagle* (1950), of which it became a part; the Bates eye exercises that provided the background for "The Chronicler" (1946); and General Semantics, Alfred Korzybski's theory of non-Aristotelian systems discussed in his 1933 book *Science and Sanity*, which formed the theoretical background for van Vogt's *The World of Null-A*. Van Vogt also became fascinated by L. Ron Hubbard's Dianetics, the psychological theories that preceded Scientology, and dropped out of writing SF for several years to become a Dianetics practitioner.

Null-A, or non-Aristotelianism, takes off from Korzybski's idea of the distinction between words and objects. The word is not the thing, Korzybski says; the map is not the territory. Failing to make these distinctions results in mental confusion that keeps people from achieving the mastery of mind over body and mind over matter that is its potential.

Van Vogt's quotations from Korzybski, which he uses as epigraphs for several chapters, and the discussions of non-Aristotelian thinking within the book popularized General Semantics in a way that Korzybski and his followers never did, and perhaps helped create a significant intellectual discipline that is still studied in colleges. S. I. Hayakawa, former president of San Francisco State College and former U.S. Senator, served as president of the International Society for General Semantics. But the novel is not simply a dramatization of a theory; the theory has created a fascinating new world, governed by a Games Machine to whose tests the leading intellects of Earth submit themselves for a month to demonstrate their right to join the Null-A thinkers on Venus. The losers get to be the top administrators on Earth.

Thrown into that situation is a man, Gilbert Gosseyn (pronounce it "go sane"), who discovers that his memories are not his own, who must find out who and what he is, who finds himself caught up in a vast conspiracy, and who is killed at the end of the first section of the novel—and that is only the beginning. Before the novel is over, we have a second body, a second brain, aliens, invasion by a galactic empire and the response of the Venusian Null-As, and most of all Gosseyn's discovery of himself and his fascinating new powers through the discipline of Null-A. James Blish, writing as a critic, called van Vogt's technique "the intensively recomplicated story," and readers may have difficulty following the ins and outs of it. But they will have no problem being carried along by it. They may wish to be carried on to its sequels, *The Pawns of Null-A* and *Null-A Three*.

Perhaps the best explanation for the appeal of van Vogt's stories and novels is to go back to his early fascination with fairy tales. His stories are the stuff of fairy tales, wish fulfillments every one of them. That does not make them fantasy, however, because our world is a product of wish fulfillments: that machines could be made to work for people and perhaps even think for them, that people could fly, that people could have ice in the summer and heat in the winter, that people could talk to each other from a distance, that people could have artificial light in the darkness, that pictures could be made to move, that sounds and pictures could be brought into our homes . . . Science is organized, systematized wish fulfillment, and van Vogt's stories are wish fulfillments treated as if they were sciences. In another context I have called them "fairy tales of science": the cloak of invisibility, seven-league boots, the cat with eyes as big as saucers, shape-changing, mind-reading—here they are treated as the products of science, or the discoveries of time and distance.

John W. Campbell once wrote: "Fiction is simply dreams written out, and science fiction consists of the hopes and dreams and fears (for some dreams are nightmares) of a technically based society." More than anyone else, van Vogt summed up the hopes and dreams and fears that are science fiction. His characters are larger than life, supermen facing situations that would deter the most intrepid ordinary characters, or super-realistic characters confronting super-menaces. Van Vogt's stories have all the authenticity and all the logic and all the abrupt shifts of dreams and nightmares, but his characters can cope with them.

And his readers can enjoy them.

A CANTICLE FOR LEIBOWITZ
WALTER M. MILLER JR.

A Canticle for Leibowitz is one of the classics of post-catastrophe science fiction. When it was first published at the height of ban-the-bomb fever in 1960, the novel found an audience among SF readers (who awarded it the Hugo) and in the public at large (who have kept it in print almost continuously ever since). As Willis E. McNelly pointed out in *Survey of Science Fiction Literature*, some mainstream reviewers dismissed the novel as "mere science fiction," while others thought it was so good that calling it "science fiction" was an insult.

Nevertheless, science fiction was what it was, written by a science-fiction writer as the capstone of his career, published as three novelettes in a science-fiction magazine and as an SF novel and within the post-catastrophe tradition. Post-catastrophe means that the novel dealt not with the catastrophe but with its aftermath. The catastrophe category itself is one of the oldest in human storytelling, going back at least to the biblical account of Noah, as well as the Moses-in-Egypt story and the Sodom-and-Gomorrah episode. In fact, virtually every culture has a catastrophe story in which angry or vengeful supernatural beings destroy all but a small remnant of humanity, who then must try to reestablish civilization and perhaps a more sane or more worshipful world.

In science fiction the tradition began with *The Last Man* (1826) by Mary Wollstonecraft Shelley (of *Frankenstein* fame). It was followed by Richard Jeffries' *After London* (1885), H. G. Wells's *The Time Machine* (1895) and "The Star" (1897), M. P. Shiel's *The Purple Cloud* (1901), George Allan England's *Darkness and Dawn* (1912), Jack London's *The Scarlet Plague* (1915), and many others, including Thomas Calvert McClary's *Rebirth* (1934), Alun Llewellyn's *The Strange Invaders* (1934), and John Collier's *Tom's A-Cold* (1933). The threat of nuclear holocaust not only gave the tradition new energy but shifted the focus from the supernatural or the natural to the man-made disaster. Subsequent examples that involved nuclear catastrophe run from Judith Merril's *Shadow on the Hearth* (1950), Wilson Tucker's *The Long Loud Silence* (1952), Pat Frank's *Alas, Babylon* (1959), and Nevil Shute's *On the Beach* (1959) down to Kate Wilhelm's *Where Late the Sweet Birds Sang* (1976) and Russell Hoban's *Riddley Walker* (1980), as well as such non-nuclear classics as George R. Stewart's *Earth Abides* (1949), John Wyndham's *The Day of the Triffids* (1951), John Christopher's *No Blade of Grass* (1956), and a group of J. G. Ballard's 1960 novels.

What distinguished Miller's novel from the others was the remoteness of the post-catastrophe period and its emphasis on believable characters involved in everyday activities, in a narrative that was carefully detailed and stylistically written. These qualities made it acceptable far beyond the audience for which it was originally published.

But it was clearly science fiction. The first part, called "A Canticle for Leibowitz" ("Fiat Homo"—let there be man!—in the novel), was published as a novelette in the April 1955 *Fantasy and Science Fiction*. The second part, called "And the Light Is Risen" ("Fiat Lux"—let there be light!—in the novel), was published in the August 1956 *F&SF*. The third part, called "The Last Canticle" ("Fiat Voluntas Tua"—let thy will be done!—in the novel) was published in the February 1957 *F&SF*. They were extensively rewritten for the novel. What took up eighteen pages in the original magazine publication of the first novelette turned into ninety-eight pages in the book version. The narrative grew richer and darker in the process.

More significant than its publishing history was its demonstration of the science-fiction ideal of "idea as hero." The first section begins six hundred years after the holocaust, the second six hundred years after that, and the third six hundred years after that. None of the characters, with the possible exception of the Wandering Jew, carries over from one section to another. What the author offers instead is the cyclical nature of history and the persistence of basic truths such as those contained in religion, and in the working out of the novel, the action flows not from character, although character is involved, but from the idea. The novel actually may have originated in the notion that just as the monasteries preserved and copied Greek and Roman writings without understanding, future religious orders might preserve scientific and technological information. The time spans themselves are instructive: six hundred years from the Dark Ages to the Renaissance; six hundred years more from the Renaissance to the Age of Science.

Miller's novel was one of the first SF texts to make religion a central issue without either satirizing it or treating it as parable or apologetics, and thus opened the way, perhaps, for such religiously oriented works as Robert A. Heinlein's *Stranger in the Strange Land* and Frank Herbert's *Dune*. It is not so much that it is Christian, and Catholic at that, but that the novel opposes the life of the world with the life of the spirit and makes believable what moves men of faith. As Robert Scholes and Erik Rabkin comment in *Science Fiction: History, Science, Vision*, "Miller is using his holocaust novel to show that nobility resides in the faith of men, not in the objects of their faith." In the process it deals with the religious impulse toward imagery and mythmaking, showing in its very first episode how a chance encounter gets turned into legend.

The title of the novel promises a celebration—a canticle is a little religious song of praise—and there are, to be sure, songs sung in praise of Isaac Leibowitz, an atomic scientist who founded the Albertian Order of Leibowitz in the American Southwest. Its mission was to conserve and preserve knowledge during the historic process known as "the simplification"—an anti-intellectual uprising that destroyed books and hunted down scientists, in a planetwide paroxysm of revulsion at the destruction of civilization by the scientifically created nuclear war.

The novel is filled with ironies such as the fact that, like the Christian religion, the Catholic Order of Leibowitz was founded by a Jew, as well as the repeated ironies of the most sacred relics being recognized by the reader as the most prosaic of items from contemporary times, like the discovery of the shopping list and blueprint that launch Brother Gerard's lifelong labors. But life itself is filled with ironies, and religion is no exception.

In the end the novel must justify itself, and the judgment of critics and public alike is that it deserves its position not only in science fiction but in the broader field of literature. As John Clute writes in *The Encyclopedia of Science Fiction*, "The novel is full of subtly presented detail about the nature of religious vocation and the way of life of an isolated community, deals ably with the questions of the nature of historical and scientific knowledge which it raises, and poses and intriguingly answers ethical questions about mankind's proper relation to God and the world."

Its author was born in New Smyrna, Florida, in 1922. He flew combat missions in World War II, converted to Catholicism in 1947, attended the University of Tennessee before the war, and was graduated from the University of Texas in 1949. He began publishing SF in 1951 and published some forty stories, many of them influential on the field, such as "Conditionally Human" (1952), "Crucifixus Etiam" (1953), and "The Darfsteller" (1955). *A Canticle for Leibowitz* was his only novel and his final publication in the field.

1984
GEORGE ORWELL

The world seems to await some years with special anticipation.

The end of the first millennium was one of those years. It was supposed to be the time of the Second Coming, and multitudes gathered on mountaintops to await the Day of Judgment. The end of the second millennium after the birth of Christ will be another, enhanced by the popularity of at least two books: Edward Bellamy's *Looking Backward, 2000–1887* and Arthur C. Clarke's *2001: A Space Odyssey*, and the Stanley Kubrick film that sprang from it.

Perhaps more anticipated than either was George Orwell's *Nineteen Eighty-Four*, which has been published and filmed as *1984*. It was written in the bleak Scottish Hebrides in 1948 as its author, whose real name was Eric Arthur Blair, was dying of tuberculosis. It became a tremendously popular novel: it sold more than eleven million copies in English before 1984 (how many more were sold that year?) and was translated into thirty foreign languages. It survived in the public imagination longer than most best sellers, assisted more than a little by its adoption by innumerable teachers as a standard high school text.

Why did it last? Why did the public adopt its title as a shorthand for tyranny, and even for any tendency *toward excessive governmental information-gathering or prying?*

One answer: like many science-fiction novels *1984* seemed to be involved in prediction. Let's look at the novel's record. Some predictions seem reasonably on target. In the area of technology, which has significantly shaped the world since 1949, when the novel was first published, *1984* includes: a nuclear stalemate; bombers superseded by rockets as weapons of destruction; the omnipresence of television; and a machine for turning the spoken word into the written word, which Orwell called a "speakwrite." The last hasn't quite been created, but technologists are working on it.

But three out of four isn't bad.

Orwell also describes contemporary military research with success that might depress critics of the military-industrial complex, although he places considerable emphasis on the importance of Floating Fortresses to control strategic spots on the sea lanes. Maybe Orwell got that notion from M. P. Shiel's 1901 *The Lord of the Sea*.

Many of the details of what seem like successful predictions, however, are just a bit askew. The nuclear stalemate in *1984* came after an atomic war Orwell dates about 1955. Television, which he calls "telescreens," is received on oblong metal plaques like dulled mirrors; they can't be turned off (by anyone except the elite) not only because they transmit propaganda but also because they monitor the activities of the citizens. And the rockets are loaded with conventional explosives like the V-2 rockets of World War II, which Britain had so recently experienced.

Orwell's geopolitical predictions aren't that accurate, either. In *1984* the Soviet Union has absorbed Europe and become "Eurasia," encompassing all the Northern European and Asiatic landmass from Portugal to the Bering Strait. The United States has absorbed Great Britain and together with South America, "Australasia," and the southern portion of Africa has become a second great world power called "Oceania." The third world power is "Eastasia," which is smaller; it is made up of China and the countries south of it, the Japanese islands, and large parts of Manchuria, Mongolia, and Tibet. All of this seemed reasonable in 1948 and even had some vague similarities when 1984 actually rolled around, but seems much less prescient today. But then few experts predicted the recent fragmentation of the Soviet Union.

Oceania, in alliance with Eurasia or Eastasia, is in a constant state of war with the other major power (it doesn't matter which, though it becomes a matter of necessary Party "doublethink" to be able to switch enemies and remember that the current one always has been the enemy). The three world powers confine their struggles to a quadrilateral area between Tangier, Brazzaville, Darwin, and Hong Kong, which contains about one-fifth of the earth's population. They fight over cheap labor, which can be used to make weapons and to wield them.

The wars in Southeast Asia and in Africa and even in the Middle East would seem to fall easily into this prediction, but not (geographically, at least) the war in Korea, and certainly not the guerrilla wars in Central America. Still, one should give Orwell credit for the insight that made World War II enemies into allies, and allies into enemies.

But the point of the wars seems to be a clear miss. Cheap labor is more a problem for the economies of the industrialized nations than an asset, and today's technological war equipment requires skilled workers and even skilled soldiers. Most of the conflicts in our world have concerned political control or ideology. Orwell did not foresee the rise of Israel or its wars for survival in the Middle East. His world of *1984* did not concern itself with the population problem or the energy shortage (and the rise of economic power of the oil-rich nations) or the resurgence of religious fundamentalism of several kinds. His world, indeed, is "bare, hungry, dilapidated" but it is kept in that condition by the three world powers and, in fact, the continuing war is a means of keeping people too poor to rebel.

Orwell's social and political predictions have not come true, either. Even with today's superior technology, governments seem no closer to total control of their populations than they were during World War II. The People's Republic of China was able to subdue dissenters, but the existence of dissent was in itself remarkable. And the forces of governmental control were unable to cope with the desire for democracy and self-expression in Eastern Europe and the Soviet Union. Only in the United States does government control, through the sophisticated use of the media, seem to have grown.

To be sure, *1984* should receive credit for sensitizing the world to the potential for tyrannies to seek and cling to power for its own sake. As O'Brien says in the novel, "One does not establish a dictatorship in order to safeguard a revolution; one makes a revolution in order to establish the dictatorship." The novel also led the world to inspect new technologies that allow increasing inroads on human freedom, and to be alert to mind-altering techniques that not only can make people believe that falsehood is truth but can make them want to believe it.

But prediction is not what *1984* is about. Science fiction is not about prediction but dramatization, not about the future but a variety of possible futures, not about the then and there but the here and now; and *1984* is more about 1948 than about 1984, and more about the human condition than about technology. What remains true about *1984* is what always has been true; Orwell put it in perspective.

One human trait has been the need to deify leaders. In *1984* that leader is Big Brother. His face is on posters plastered everywhere along with the warning, or for some the assurance: Big Brother Is Watching You. Orwell describes Big Brother's face as that "of a man of about forty-five, with a heavy black mustache and ruggedly handsome features." It is easy enough to identify Big Brother with Stalin, and Oceania's scapegoat, arch-traitor, and head of the legendary underground "Brotherhood," Emmanuel Goldstein, with Trotsky. It even is possible to point to the deification of later leaders such as Mao Tse-tung or the Ayatollah Khomeini. One should also note, however, that in *1984* "Big Brother will never die." In the real world Stalin and Mao died, and it was necessary for the surviving leaders to denounce or reshape the images of their predecessors in order to govern. The cult of the personality leads to catastrophic errors.

Another key element in *1984* is the rewriting of history. The job of the novel's hero, Winston Smith, in the Ministry of Truth is to rewrite yesterday's news to make it consistent with today's Party line. Orwell was a journalist, and his insight was that the past has no concrete existence: it is only what is written down and what people remember. "Who controls the past controls the future," Winston repeats during his torture; "who controls the present controls the past."

It is easy to find examples of this in today's world. There were plenty in what was formerly the Soviet Union, but they are not scarce elsewhere. Japanese textbooks, for instance, have downplayed its war with China. Americans say it can't happen in the United States, and yet what gets into history textbooks is under constant review and often turns out to be what is acceptable to review boards in Texas and California. What is "true" turns out to be what the fewest and least vocal people object to.

The fact that there is no historical reality is deeply disturbing to Winston Smith, but that the past can be reshaped is comforting to many political leaders and, if people would only admit it, to many others who want to see their convictions or their interpretations embodied in the official records. The *Congressional Record* is rewritten every day. People excuse themselves by the belief that their convictions *are* truth, and if the records do not agree, the records are wrong. But the Party in *1984* had the same excuse arrived at by the process of "double-think," which most people today are pretty good at as well.

The widespread use of the computer, which Orwell did not envision, soon will make revision of history much simpler. Soon nobody will keep files of newspapers (which even now are being widely replaced by microfilms). In *1984* they had to be reprinted each time Winston or his coworkers made a change, and encyclopedias had to have offending pages trimmed, as they were in the Soviet Union after Beria was purged in 1953. Soon all that will be necessary is to hit a few computer keys.

The computer also has been used to assemble information about citizens. Although Orwell does not suggest any such mechanism for keeping track of people, any mention of a national data bank or national identity cards has been greeted with shouts of "1984!" or accused of having "Orwellian" implications.

Surveillance is another significant aspect of *1984*. Its citizens are watched not only by their television sets but by their colleagues, their children, and members of the "thoughtpolice," who are believed to be everywhere though no one ever knows for certain until the moment of arrest. In this situation where nothing is illegal (there are no longer any laws) and even a rebellious thought or a careless expression is punishable by twenty-five years in a labor camp or death, citizens must be careful of " thoughtcrime " or " facecrime. "

Today, though technology has not perfected the two-way television screen, improvements in electronics and miniaturization have made devices available that Orwell never imagined. The point of these devices, however, is to film or overhear without suspicion; the point of the situation in *1984* was the constant awareness that citizens were always being watched and listened to. Logically, however, the idea of everyone's activities being monitored all the time seems far-fetched. For that to work, half the Party members (the Proles, who make up 85 percent of the population, don't count) would have to continually watch the other half, and then half the watchers would have to watch the other half of the watchers, and so on.

But the terror of betrayal is something that everyone can understand. Some U.S. citizens felt that terror during the McCarthy era, and citizens in Nazi Germany, particularly the Jews, and those in the Soviet Union lived with it as part of their daily lives.

A third aspect of *1984* that touches people's deepest fears about themselves is the willingness of the characters to torture each other. In the Ministry of Love, which is *1984*'s euphemism for the headquarters of the police power of the state, Winston Smith is subject to a seemingly endless series of tortures designed not simply to punish nor deter, but to convert. Winston must be made to surrender to his tormentors of his own free will; "we make the brain perfect before we blow it out," the brutal and intellectual O'Brien says. How Winston is brought not only to agree with what his tormentor says but also to love him is the heart of the novel.

To its shame, the world still resorts to torture: in such places as the former Soviet Union, Argentina, Iran, Iraq, first by one side, then by the other, in every place where people of the same country are in conflict with each other and passions run deeper than humanity, they torture each other. But the refinements that Orwell imagined have not been produced. Clubs, clamps, privation, starvation, applications of electrical shock to sensitive parts of the body, cages in which one can neither stand up nor lie down . . . these seem more than adequate for their beastly purposes.

Motives are different, too. Winston is tortured to cure him of the insanity of believing in a truth different from that of the Party. Once he is given a jolt of something that seems like electroshock in order to get him to see four fingers as three or five, whichever the Party requires. While it is true that Soviet dissidents reportedly were committed to mental institutions and dosed with drugs, perhaps even "treated" with electroshock, most torture in today's world seems still to be an act of vengeance or an act of terror.

The world also has perfected methods of behavior modification that Orwell never dreamed about: techniques of reward and punishment, drugs, electrodes into the brain . . . Some of these techniques have been used to teach children difficult to reach by other methods. Drugs make it possible for some mental patients to cope with their symptoms or make them accessible to other kinds of therapy. Research into the operation of the brain has helped scientists understand how the brain works and how to treat those damaged in various ways. Aversion therapy has been used to help people cope with addictions or bad habits. Tranquilizers, mood elevators, or depressants: doctors prescribe them every day to help patients deal with personal problems or handle the stresses of ordinary existence.

But all of these have the capability of being used to control behavior for purposes that are not so benign, and even some of the seemingly benign purposes are arguable (as Anthony Burgess demonstrated in *A Clockwork Orange*). Governments, including the United States, have conducted experiments to determine the effects of drugs or behavior modification techniques on soldiers and perhaps even on citizens. And yet the process of actually controlling thoughts seems just beyond the world's grasp: for the moment.

Finally, Orwell turned his attention to the ability of language to control people. Part of the confirming detail of his novel is his invention of "Newspeak." He devoted an appendix to it, describing it as the medium of expression for the world view and mental habits proper to the citizens of Oceania. Moreover, once perfected and made universal, Newspeak would make "a heretical thought . . . literally unthinkable." Newspeak is the verbal equivalent of "doublethink," the technique by which the Party member can hold two contradictory beliefs simultaneously.

In Newspeak, "War Is Peace," "Freedom Is Slavery," and "Ignorance Is Strength," which are the three mottos of the Party; anything thrown into the "memory hole" is instantly vaporized; the Ministry of Truth (Minitrue in Newspeak) is in charge of rewriting history; the Ministry of Peace (Minipax) concerns itself with war; the Ministry of Love (Miniluv) maintains law and order; and the Ministry of Plenty (Miniplenty) is responsible for universal deprivation.

All social groups, to be sure, try to describe their virtues in the most favorable terms and clothe their flaws, when they must be mentioned, in euphemisms. One of Hitler's favorite techniques was the "big lie." Other cultures are susceptible to the same temptations: the great decline in Chinese industrial production after the misguided effort to decentralize the industrial process by such measures as building thousands of backyard steel mills was called a "u-shaped development."

But the healthiest tendency in Western society is to label efforts to clothe events in deceptive or obscurantist language as "Newspeak." President Truman had his "police action" in Korea. U.S. leaders saw "light at the end of the tunnel" in Vietnam, not once but many times, and U.S. citizens heard that "we had to destroy the village to save it." All recent presidential terms have been rife with "Newspeak " but the Nixon, Reagan, and Bush years seemed to be unusually prolific. During that time, the United States learned that officials had to preserve "deniability" and that some statements were not lies but "no longer operative." The "Teflon" presidency meant that Truman's slogan that "the buck stops here" was no longer applicable, and public officials no longer assumed responsibility for their statements or their actions.

Every effort to persuade people of the advisability or desirability of some action is clothed in Orwellian language. Campaign rhetoric is a major creator of Newspeak, and complex problems get stated in simplistic slogans that later make solutions difficult. "A balanced budget," for instance, competes with "full employment." "Read my lips" becomes a noose around the presidency. The "Moral Majority" calls for a return to the values of church and home, and bumper stickers proclaim "The Moral Majority Is Neither." The "right-to-life" fights for victory over the "right-to-choice" movement: who can be against either life or choice?

The tendency to oversimplify is a human trait, and so is the effort to deceive. But so is the need to point out these characteristics and to pillory the worst examples of it. One of the horrors of *1984* is that Orwell described a world in which the ability to criticize has been eliminated, forever. The novel does many things, including the dramatization of a nightmare that still haunts humanity's dreams. It did not happen, but Orwell and his influential novel were two reasons why it did not happen. The deification of leaders, the rewriting of history, surveillance of citizens and the loss of individual liberties, torture and behavior modification, the perversion of language, and the ability of modern tyrannies to determine reality itself: these have not yet been realized.

One major reason they have not yet stolen from humanity everything that it finds precious in life is that *1984* existed.

A CLOCKWORK ORANGE
ANTHONY BURGESS

When Anthony Burgess spoke at the University of Kansas a half-dozen years ago, he said that he had learned just one thing about writing, and it was all he needed to know: he could write one thousand words a day. If he wrote one thousand words a day, in two to three months he had accumulated enough pages to make a novel. Actually, his production over thirty years has been estimated at two thousand words a day.

His productivity may have emerged from his own restless creativity (Brian W. Aldiss says "some deep wound or anger"), but it was nurtured by a diagnosis, sometime in 1959, that he had a brain tumor and only a year to live. He had already published, between 1956 and 1959, three novels about his Malayan experience but now he sat down to write a series of novels whose royalties would provide some support for his wife after his death. In what he called his "pseudo-terminal year" he produced something between four and six novels before doctors discovered that the tumor had disappeared.

Thirty-three years later, in 1993, he died in London of cancer, the author of a substantial number of novels, variously estimated between thirty and fifty-three (he wrote some novels under the pseudonym of Joseph Kell, some books for children, and some book-length poems). He was a worldwide literary figure who felt underappreciated by the literary establishment in his native England (and was an expatriate until his final illness), which may have been alienated by his productivity (which made creation look easy), his refusal to write in a consistent style or to return to any subject (which made a critical appraisal difficult), and his broad-ranging interests (he wrote plays and operas, as well as criticism and translations, and composed music).

He was an unlikely Renaissance man. Born John Anthony Burgess Wilson in Manchester, England, in 1917, during the worst of World War I, he lost his mother to the influenza epidemic of 1918 and was raised by his father and an Irish stepmother. He was educated at Catholic schools and earned a degree from Manchester University in 1940, just in time to join the British armed services as musical director of a special services unit. After the war, he taught in an adult education program for the armed services from 1946 to 1948 and then as a lecturer in phonetics at Birmingham University from 1948 to 1950. He was English master for Banbury Grammar School from 1950 to 1954 and Senior Lecturer in English at the Malayan Teachers Training College in Khata Baru from 1954 to 1957, where he got the background for his Malayan novels.

He was not strictly speaking a science-fiction author. In fact, his SF writing, if it can be called that, was an accidental by-product of what Aldiss called his "hatred of the past, real or assumed" and "his loathing for English nostalgia." Among his many novels were only four that a SF reader would recognize as having "the right stuff." They were *The Wanting Seed* (1962), which uses an overpopulated world "to replay the Manichean dilemma," as David N. Samuelson comments *in Twentieth-Century Science-Fiction Authors*; *1985* (1978), which is a narrative/critique of Orwell's *1984*; *The End of the World News* (1982), which revisits the colliding-planets end-of-the-world scenario and plays a filmed short life of Sigmund Freud against a filmed Broadway musical about Leon Trotsky aboard a spaceship escaping the destruction. And, of course, *A Clockwork Orange* (1962), which should have been written during Burgess's "pseudo-terminal year" but came just after.

The greater part of the reputation of *A Clockwork Orange* came from the 1971 film by Stanley Kubrick, which was criticized, is considerably more violent than the novel, and was banned in Britain — and, at last account, still is. From the film Burgess earned only a consultant's fee, but no doubt it helped the later reprints of the novel as well as the sales of his other books.

The novel belongs to the long-honored SF tradition of the dystopia such as Frederik Pohl and Cyril Kornbluth's *The Space Merchants* (1952/1953), John Brunner's *Stand on Zanzibar* (1968), Aldous Huxley's *Brave New World* (1932), or George Orwell's *1984* (1949). In the case of *A Clockwork*

Orange, society has deteriorated into a socialistic police state in which youth gangs are nevertheless free to murder and rape virtually at will. It is not, however, a traditional SF novel. It is not about outer space but inner space, that is, it concerns itself with the human soul rather than human adaptability; in fact it asks whether the state's efforts to change human nature are not as sinful as the violence they are intended to prevent.

The novel is about such theological questions as free will and good and evil, like James Blish's *A Case of Conscience* (1958) or Walter M. Miller Jr.'s *A Canticle for Leibowitz* (1960). Unlike science-fiction novels that deal with religious questions, *A Clockwork Orange* offers no clues to what brought about the condition of Great Britain, so that we can gain some insight into what decisions to make or to avoid; in Ursula K. Le Guin's formulation, it is not about there and then but about here and now. It is, so to speak, a mainstream novel in the form of a science-fiction novel. Nevertheless, in imagining his fantastic world in believable detail, particularly in the language the characters speak, Burgess offered his readers the credibility that all good SF provides.

The novel challenges the reader on several levels. The first is the language: true to his love for words and his linguistic background (he not only taught linguistics, later in his career he invented a language for the French film *Quest for Fire*), he paid tribute to the way in which language changes with time and circumstance by developing a slang for the street gangs of *A Clockwork Orange*. Burgess called it "nadsat," and it is explained by a character as "odd bits of rhyming slang. A bit of gipsy talk, too. But most of the roots are Slav. Propaganda. Subliminal penetration."

As prediction, even as extrapolation, the expansion of Soviet influence over culture as well as politics has proved to be inaccurate. But as a device to set rebellious youth apart from the rest of society (as teenage slang does today), the invented language functions artistically as well as science-fictionally. Moreover, stylistically it makes the reader work harder to understand Alex, whose life of violence and crime has only a single redeeming quality— his love of classical music, particularly Beethoven—and whose Ludovico aversion-therapy treatment, as well as his experiences on the street, make him, in the English phrase, "as queer as a clockwork orange." The slang is difficult to decipher at first (some versions of the novel provide a glossary developed by critic Stanley Edgar Hyman), but even without a glossary the meaning quickly comes clear.

Samuelson comments that "verbal violence both shields the reader from and exposes him to physical violence, while learning to understand Alex leads to condoning his behavior, and accepting the conditioning effects of society in general."

The second difficulty the novel presents is the characters, who seem irredeemably evil, though in Burgess's view, perhaps, no more evil than the society in which they were born and bred—indeed the question of the redemption of one human soul is what the novel is all about. Burgess said that "I had to write *Clockwork Orange* in a state of near-drunkenness in order to deal with material that upset me very much."

The final challenge is the ending. The British and American versions differed; the American version left off the final twenty-first chapter of the British version (Kubrick's film version chose the bleaker vision of humanity), but after 1986 has generally included the longer moral version that Burgess insisted was his vision.

Burgess told the *Paris Review* in 1973: "The ideal reader of my novels is a lapsed Catholic and failed musician, short-sighted, color-blind, auditorily biased, who has read the books that I have read." He was, of course, describing himself, in his customary self-deprecatory style. Readers will have to decide whether he was also, in meaningful part, describing them.

FURY
HENRY KUTTNER

Fury is a novel that readers remember. Although it was first published as a serial in *Astounding Stories* in 1947, it was not reprinted in book form until 1950, and it has often been out of print. Nevertheless, in the mid-1980s, William Burroughs told me that *Fury* was one of his favorite SF novels, and I asked him if he remembered the final two words. He quoted them.

Fury was a novel of its time, and yet ahead of its time, like most of the stories and short novels that Henry Kuttner wrote with his wife, C. L. Moore, for *Astounding* during the 1940s, and particularly between 1942 and 1945. It was of its time because it dealt with the threat of nuclear destruction and with a vision of Venus as a watery world in a period of ravening, Jurassic struggle for existence, and because of the pulp vigor that drove the narrative.

To understand why *Fury* was ahead of its time one must consider what was going on in science fiction when *Fury* was written. In 1942, the United States was readying itself for war after the Japanese attack upon Pearl Harbor a few weeks before. Industrial production was being turned toward munitions and weapons, men were being drafted, men and women were volunteering for military service, and those who weren't eligible for service were getting jobs related to the war effort.

John Campbell, the influential editor who took over Street & Smith's *Astounding Stories* in 1937, had gathered together a cadre of writers that had made a significant impact upon the nature of the science fiction being published. They would be looked back upon as creating a "Golden Age": Eric Frank Russell, L. Sprague de Camp, and Lester del Rey in 1937 and 1938; Isaac Asimov, Robert A. Heinlein, Theodore Sturgeon, and A. E. van Vogt in

1939. And others. But many of them had left for wartime service: de Camp, Heinlein, and later Asimov for the Naval Air Experimental Station in Philadelphia; Sturgeon for various kinds of service in the British West Indies; and van Vogt for the Canadian Department of National Defense.

Campbell needed replacements to keep his revolution going, and the Kuttners stepped forward. Between 1942 and 1947, they contributed forty-one stories (forty-eight by 1965) to *Astounding*, including three two-part serials and *Fury*, a three-parter. *Fury* was mostly Henry Kuttner's work (80 percent, Moore estimated later) and has been attributed to him. Most of their stories appeared under the names of "Lewis Padgett" and "Lawrence O'Donnell," pseudonyms used to avoid the appearance of two or more stories in an issue by the same author, to raise word rates, and to satisfy Campbell's desire to keep up the illusion of progress by introducing new writers. They would use another fifteen pen names for other publications.

Kuttner and Moore had been publishing stories in the pulp magazines since the mid-1930s. Moore, born in 1911 in Indianapolis, was forced by the Depression to leave Indiana University after a year and a half and take a secretarial job in a bank. She published a classic romantic fantasy, "Shambleau," in *Weird Tales* in November 1933, and continued with such epic characters as Northwest Smith and Jirel of Joiry. She also sold four stories to *Astounding* between 1934 and 1939.

Kuttner, born in 1914 in Los Angeles, worked for a Los Angeles literary agency after graduation from high school. In 1926 he had discovered *Amazing Stories*; in the mid-1930s he came into contact with the Lovecraft circle of correspondents and began contributing to *Weird Tales*, first a poem in February of 1936 and then a story, "The Graveyard Rats," in March. He became a regular contributor to that magazine and to such hybrids as *Strange Stories* and *Thrilling Mysteries*. He also sold a story to *Astounding* in 1938.

In 1938 Kuttner went to Indianapolis to meet Moore; in 1940 they were married. Afterward, Moore said, everything they wrote was a collaboration of one kind or another, but in varying degrees. In an introduction to a 1972 edition of *Fury*, she wrote:

> It worked like this. After we'd established through long discussion the basic ideas, the background and the characters, whichever of us felt like it sat down and started. When that one ran down, the other, being fresh to the story, could usually see what ought to come next, and took over. The action developed as we went along. We kept changing off like this until we finished. A story goes fast that way.
>
> Each of us edited the other's copy a little when we took over, often going back a line or two and rephrasing to make styles blend. We never disagreed seriously over the work. The worst clash of opinion I can remember ended with one of us saying, "Well, I don't agree, but since you feel more strongly

than I do, go ahead." (When the rent is due tomorrow, one tends toward quick, peaceful settlements.)

They became the most famous husband-and-wife collaborators in science-fiction history.

Writing for the pulps was never an easy life. *Astounding* paid one cent a word in 1942, raised to one and one-quarter cents in 1943 and to two cents in 1945, and the other magazines paid one-half to one cent a word at the most, and then only upon publication. Anthologies (with one exception), book publishers, foreign sales, or film rights provided no additional income until after the war. If the nearly forty stories the Kuttners sold to *Astounding* during the war years averaged ten thousand words, their total income from them would have been about $5,000, little more than $1,000 a year. They may have sold almost as many stories to the other markets, though for less money, but they would have found it difficult to live on their income from writing alone. Kuttner had a service income: disqualified by a heart murmur from active service, he entered the Army Medical Corps in 1942 and served at Fort Monmouth, New Jersey, until 1945. Of course, that makes the Kuttners' writing accomplishments during those years even more remarkable.

The Kuttners remained in the New York area until 1948, then moved to Laguna Beach. Henry Kuttner attended the University of Southern California with the aid of the G.I. Bill, earning a bachelor's degree in three and a half years. He had nearly completed a master's degree in English when he had a heart attack and died on February 4, 1958. C. L. Moore also attended Southern Cal, earning a bachelor's degree in 1956 and a master's degree in 1963. She later remarried. She died April 4, 1987.

After their return to California, the Kuttners produced much less science fiction. They had published two mystery novels in 1946 and would publish five more. They wrote nine romantic fantasy novels or short novels for *Startling Stories* and *Thrilling Wonder Stories* between 1947 and 1952, which have only recently been revalued and some reprinted. Kuttner taught a writing course at USC, and Moore continued it for four years after his death. She also wrote screenplays for Warner Brothers and scripts for such television shows as *Maverick* and *77 Sunset Strip*.

But the stories that the Kuttners wrote for John Campbell over those four wartime years, plus the two or three that followed, created a substantial body of short fiction that includes some of the finest yet written: "The Twonky," the Gallegher series, "Clash by Night," "Mimsy Were the Borogoves," "When the Bough Breaks," "The Children's Hour," "No Woman Born," the Baldies series, "What You Need," "Judgment Night," "The Fairy Chessmen," "Tomorrow and Tomorrow," "Private Eye," "Two-Handed Engine," "Vintage Season," and many more. "Mimsy Were the Borogoves" and "Vintage Season" were selected for inclusion in the Science Fiction Hall of Fame, and the other stories are often reprinted as well.

Fury, which began running as a serial in May 1947, was published under the name of Lawrence O'Donnell, which had been invented in 1943 for a story called "Clash by Night" because Henry Kuttner had stories in the same issue under his own name and under the pseudonym Lewis Padgett. "Clash by Night" also contains the background that would be used for *Fury* four years later: Earth has been destroyed (turned into another sun) by a nuclear accident. An ironic monument labels it "Man's Greatest Achievement." Humans had colonized Venus, however, even though the land and its various life forms were so ravingly dangerous that humanity had built its cities under "impervium" domes in the shallow seas.

"Clash by Night" takes place four hundred years before *Fury*, when companies of "Free Companions" are still fighting on the surface of Venus, even though that way of life is doomed by the greater security and opportunities inside the domes. *Fury* focuses on the comfort of that life and what happens to the human species, or any species, when existence becomes too comfortable. It is a novel about an angry man, Sam Reed, but it also, like all science fiction, is about the species, which has regained paradise, lost its restless ambition, and eventually will die unless it can resume its interrupted journey to the stars.

The question for *Fury* is how humanity can be forced from the domes onto the deadly land. The answer is Sam Reed. But, as in life, the answer is not what it seems. *Fury* is complicated by another evolutionary development for human survival: immortality. Among the normal humans on Venus walk tall, slim, aristocratic immortals who live for hundreds, even thousands of years. *Fury* takes up the question of how life would look to someone who faces the prospect of centuries of decades, how they might plan their lives, what they might value.

The novel also faces the question of how humans with normal life spans, as Sam Reed believes he has, would think about their own fates by comparison with those of the immortals. To someone like Sam, tortured by an insane, grief-stricken father, transformed by endocrinological tampering, with his burning ambitions and needs, the answer is "fury." The word that initially is used to describe the surface areas of Venus has come to be applied to the short, bald, thick Sam Reed.

What happens to one of the most fascinating and complex characters in all science fiction, what happens to the best-laid plans of men and immortals, and what happens to the human species are only part of the pleasures of reading *Fury*. One can also enjoy the skillful use of language, the description of the strange and exotic, the interplay between unusual characters, the comparisons to the rest of life, to literature, to mythology, and the imagery . . .

It is a rich experience, and it is a legacy from the Kuttners to other science-fiction writers and readers. Although science fiction was never as much a pulp genre as its format might have suggested, its competition for space on the newsstands and for the scarce coins of the magazine purchaser led to a concentration of ideas, action, and plain language. Up to the 1940s, the SF magazine tradition placed lesser value on characterization, individualization, setting, style, symbol, and myth. The Kuttners made accessible, even popular, the qualities of literature.

And watch out for those last two words.

OUT OF THE SILENT PLANET
C. S. LEWIS

Out of the Silent Planet offers an alternative voice to speak against the dominant trend in traditional science fiction. Its author, C. S. Lewis, is equally set apart from the traditional SF writer. As an Oxford don and in the last decade of his life professor of medieval and Renaissance English at Cambridge, he looked at science fiction from the perspective of the ages and of the literary culture. And yet in his essays he displayed a critical understanding of the nature and value of science fiction.

At its most characteristic, British SF displays a continuity with the rest of literature that American SF, with its origins in the American pulp science-fiction magazines of the 1920s and 1930s, usually lacks. British SF writers were never as isolated as their American counterparts, and mainstream writers often dipped into the divergent waters of SF sometimes without knowing they had done so. H. G. Wells, for instance, may have been surprised by his nomination as the father of modern science fiction, and W. Olaf Stapledon may never have realized that the philosophical novels he was writing were being used as a source of ideas and inspiration by many SF writers.

The tradition continues down to the present. Brian W. Aldiss and J. G. Ballard, for instance, have moved easily between SF and the mainstream, and Doris Lessing has shown no embarrassment at turning frequently to interplanetary romance.

Out of the Silent Planet, originally published in 1938, is part of a trilogy, sometimes called the Cosmic Trilogy or the Ransom Trilogy, completed by *Perelandra* (1943) and *That Hideous Strength: A Modern Fairy-Tale for Grownups* (1945). All belong to the philosophical branch of SF represented by Stapledon's *Last and First Men* (1930) and *Star Maker* (1937). More than Stapledon's works, however, the Cosmic Trilogy addresses the question of good and evil and, more specifically, in terms of Christian theology. The first two volumes particularly operate allegorically, providing a new setting and new names for Christian issues.

Science fiction always has had difficulty dealing with religion. Its premise that the universe is humanly knowable runs counter to religious beliefs in the supernatural or the unknowable, and religions presuppose answers to questions, such as the origin of the universe and the origin and purpose of existence, that SF takes as its major concern. As a consequence, most SF, when it deals with religion, exposes its deleterious effects, treats religion as a superstition to be discarded or outgrown, discovers the reality behind religious beliefs, or creates new religions. Lewis responded by treating SF as if it were myth.

The result in *Perelandra*, which is Miltonian in its retelling of the Garden of Eden story and the temptation of Eve, offers the kind of double-vision reading that allegory requires. Lewis wrote in one of his essays that *Perelandra* was written for Christians only. But *Out of the Silent Planet* retains much more of the concern for the real world that science fiction demands. It offers a spaceship, scientists of both the physical sciences and language, an exploiter of natural resources, an alien planet, and aliens. And even though these are treated for what they represent as much as for what they are, the changed environment and alien existence are dealt with as physical facts to be experienced.

David Lake in *Twentieth-Century Science-Fiction Writers* suggests that "the trilogy . . . defies generic classification: it is very dubiously science fiction, by reason of all those angels (and devils, in the second and third novels), yet it is not exactly fantasy either, for the author firmly believes in the actual existence of his supernatural entities, and is out to convince us, with all the power of his very powerful art, of their reality and supreme importance." In the process Lewis attacks one of the icons of science fiction, the scientist, and what Jack Williamson calls "the basic myth of science fiction," space travel to other worlds.

What Lewis offers as an ideal is the paradisiacal world of Mars, where all creatures live in harmony with each other and with their environment, supported and protected by "eldils," angelic creatures composed of "semi-visible light," and by the archangel supervising the entire planet, Oyarsa. Lewis compares Mars, which the Martians call Malacandra, to Earth. The Malacandrans call Earth "Thulcandra," which means "silent planet"; it is silent because it is presided over by a "bent" eldil and has been quarantined. Part of the Christian allegory may be deduced from Ransom's name, who, like Christ, was taken to Mars to be offered as a sacrifice. Even later, however, Ransom is told that the creator, Maledil the Young, who lives with the Old One and supervises all the planets but Earth, has "dared terrible things" and may have manifested itself on Earth to struggle with the Bent One.

Today Lewis's paradisiacal worlds, though they do not embody current scientific knowledge of Mars and Venus and may not have done so even when they were written, represent a contemporary viewpoint about what

Earth ought to be. They seem like arguments for ecology, and when the scientist Weston is tried by the Oyarsa for murder, his "SF" vision of the expansion of humanity into the universe must confront the angelic "environmental" alternative.

Out of the Silent Planet belongs among the masterpieces of science fiction not simply because it uses SF tropes to make a theological point but because it is the most dramatic and literarily successful expression of a religious viewpoint in science-fiction terms. Its author, Clive Staples Lewis, was born in Belfast, Northern Ireland, in 1898 and died sixty-five years later in 1963. Between those years he had an enviable academic career, beginning with his B.A. from Oxford in 1922, after two years' service in World War I.

His publications began with two volumes of poetry published under the pseudonym of Clive Hamilton and, including his posthumous publications, totaled nearly seventy volumes. His first prose works were, appropriately, allegories or studies of allegory. The work that brought him his early general reputation was *The Screwtape Letters*, published in 1942 as letters from an older devil to a younger one on how to obtain human souls. His most popular fiction was written for children, the "Narnia" novels about a magical kingdom children may enter by means of a door in a wardrobe. They began with *The Lion, the Witch, and the Wardrobe* in 1950 and ended seven books and six years later with *The Last Battle*. They too are filled with Christian allegory but, like *Gulliver's Travels*, are read by children as fantasy adventure.

Out of the Silent Planet can be read in the same fashion, but, like all such readings, the more readers bring to them the more they will take away.

THE MOON POOL
A. MERRITT

A. Merritt and Edgar Rice Burroughs popularized science fiction in the magazines before the science-fiction magazines came into existence, and they helped shape the development of later romantic SF writers. Burroughs, however, is well remembered, while Merritt is almost forgotten.

Burroughs, the older of the two (by nine years), achieved publication earlier and built his popularity on a full-time writing career that turned out one success after another and usually in extended series. Merritt maintained a full-time editing career throughout his writing experience and produced only eight novels and enough stories to fill a single volume. Burroughs specialized in straightforward adventures in exotic locales; Merritt, in exotic adventures narrated in equally exotic prose.

Both began publishing in the Munsey pulp-adventure magazines in the 1910s. Both got their start in *All-Story Magazine*, Burroughs in 1912, with "Under the Moons of Mars," which was published in book form as *A Prin-*

cess of Mars, the first of the John Carter series. His second novel was *Tarzan of the Apes*. Merritt's SF career began with "Through the Dragon Glass" in 1917, followed by "The People of the Pit" and the same year "The Moon Pool," which was so popular that the editor offered Merritt $2,000 for a sequel. *The Conquest of the Moon Pool* was serialized in 1919 and the two were published the same year in book form under the title of *The Moon Pool*.

Abraham Merritt was born in 1884 in New Jersey. His early ambition to become a lawyer got sidetracked at the age of nineteen by a reporting job with the *Philadelphia Inquirer*, where he reached the position of night city editor before he became a staff member for Hearst's Sunday magazine supplement *American Weekly* in 1912 and then editor from 1937 to 1943. He died of a heart attack in 1943 at the age of fifty-nine.

American Weekly had its sensational side, which sometimes included romantic tales of mysterious ruins and peoples in faraway places. Merritt himself had spent a year, including the exploration of ancient Mayan cities, in Mexico and Central America (his expenses paid, Sam Moskowitz has reported, by people interested in his keeping quiet about an event he had witnessed as a cub reporter).

Merritt followed up the success of *The Moon Pool* with *The Metal Monster*, a 1920 serial not published in book form until 1946. Three years later came *The Face in the Abyss*, a 1923 novella reprinted as a novel in 1931 under that title with its sequel *The Snake Mother*, which was serialized in 1930. *The Face in the Abyss* was followed in 1924 by the outright fantasy *The Ship of Ishtar* (1926), which in 1938 was voted the most popular story ever published in *Argosy*. A fantastic mystery, *Seven Footprints to Satan*, was serialized in 1927, published as a book in 1928, and released as a film the same year. *Dwellers in the Mirage* (1932) was followed by *Burn, Witch, Burn!* (1933), which was filmed by Todd Browning as *The Devil Doll*, with Lionel Barrymore, in 1936. *Creep, Shadow!* (1934, sometimes published as *Creep, Shadow, Creep!*) was the last of Merritt's novels.

The Black Wheel was completed by fantasy illustrator Hannes Bok and published in 1947. The incomplete "The Fox Woman" was published in 1949 with an addition by Bok titled "The Blue Pagoda" as *The Fox Woman and the Blue Pagoda*. Merritt's short stories also were published in *Thru the Dragon Glass* (1932), *Three Lines of Old French* (1939), and *The Fox Woman and Other Stories* (1949).

Avon, which published Merritt's definitive collection, also began reprinting his novels beginning in the early 1940s and keeping them in print for many years. By the 1960s the paperbacks all carried the legend "Over 5,000,000 copies of A. Merritt's books sold in Avon editions." Since the figure never increased, the total itself may be untrustworthy, but their remaining in print testifies to their continuing popularity. Moskowitz reported that Liveright's hardcover editions continued to sell steadily in spite of the paperback competition. Although Merritt's romantic subjects and diction fell out of favor in the 1980s, perhaps a result of the more matter-of-fact style adopted by J.R.R. Tolkien in *The Lord of the Rings* trilogy that led a fantasy revival, a recent paperback edition of *Dwellers in the Mirage* may indicate a resurgence of interest in Merritt.

By today's standards, certainly, Merritt's fiction reads like fantasy. Robert H. Wilcox in *The New Encyclopedia of Science Fiction* noted that "Merritt exercised the imagination of his readers over vast distances in time and place, creating weirdly appealing characters, such as a pillar of energy that offers horrid ecstasy, a sentient metal creature, a great carved face that weeps tears of gold, and a snake-mother who shields lovers. Each of his stories describes a battle of good and evil, of outsiders and insiders; the outcome often involves the world and the whole human race."

The lines between fantasy and science fiction, however, were not so firmly drawn in the earlier part of the century. Science was capable of magic, and magic might well become science. *The Ship of Ishtar*, which allows a man to fall onto its deck on the seas near Babylon, can be read only as an exercise of romantic fantasy. But strange secrets being discovered in strange parts of the world were still a possibility, and one could imagine lost races and ancient powers surviving in remote valleys of the far north or in the Himalayas or the jungles of Central America. Or perhaps among "the relics of an early megalithic culture" in the islands of Micronesia that lie north and east of Australia and New Guinea. About them the 1954 edition of *Encyclopedia Britannica* says, "Many of the Micronesian high islands contain remarkably heavy stone ruins suggesting a more advanced and populous civilization than present island culture can explain. Best preserved of these is Nan-Matal in Panape, a Venice-like 'city' of massive basalt structures interlaced by waterways." That is where Dr. Walter T. Goodwin, Larry O'Keefe, and the other adventurers sought the secret of the lost continent and found the Shining One.

Merritt's storytelling may be a bit old-fashioned for modern tastes. His heroes were unswervingly heroic, and they needed to be because they had to face challenges beyond the imaginations of normal men. His heroines were chaste and beautiful, and their courage and steadfastness matched the men fate had intended for them. And there often was a dark beauty whose attractions tempted the hero from his fair one—and his duty. This was standard pulp formula, but Merritt brought something new to it: the marvelousness of the strange and the ambiguity of evil. There is something Homeric in his epics, and in *The Moon Pool* one finds a creation gone astray and the compelling mixture of ecstasy and agony.

Merritt's language, about which much has been made, is Latinate rather than the more earthy Anglo-Saxon of Tolkien, who was himself an Anglo-Saxon scholar. But Tolkien was trying to show the mythological in everyday life, and Merritt was trying to carry his earthbound readers into the ineffable. Like H. P. Lovecraft, his horror-writing contemporary, Merritt used his colorful Latin-derived vocabulary to describe the indescribable, as, for example, in this first glimpse of the Shining One:

> It drew first into sight as a deeper glow within the light. On and on it swept toward us—an opalescent mistiness that sped with the suggestions of some winged creature in arrowed flight. . . .
>
> Closer and closer it drew and now there came to me sweet insistent tinklings—like pizzicati on violins of glass; crystal clear; diamonds melting into sounds!
>
> Now the Thing was close to the end of the white path; close up to the barrier of darkness still between the ship and the sparkling head of the moon stream. Now it beat against that barrier as a bird against the bars of its cage. It whirled with shimmering plumes, with swirls of lacy light, with spirals of living vapour. It held within it odd, unfamiliar gleams as of shifting mother-of-pearl. Coruscations and glittering atoms drifted through it as though it drew them from the rays that bathed it.
>
> Nearer and nearer it came, borne on the sparkling waves, and ever thinner shrank the protecting wall of shadow between it and us. Within the mistiness was a core, a nucleus of intenser light—veined, opaline, effulgent, intensely alive. And above it, tangled in the plumes and spirals that throbbed and whirled were seven glowing lights.
>
> Through all the incessant but strangely ordered movement of the—*thing*—these lights held firm and steady. They were seven—like seven little moons. One was of a pearly pink, one of a delicate nacreous blue, one of lambent saffron, one of the emerald you see in the shallow waters of tropic isles; a deathly white; a ghostly amethyst; and one of the silver that is seen only when the flying fish leap beneath the moon.
>
> The tinkling music was louder still. It pierced the ears with a shower of tiny lances; it made the heart beat jubilantly—and checked it dolorously. It closed the throat with a throb of rapture and gripped it tight with the hand of infinite sorrow!

Merritt's colorful language, romantic imagination, and adventurous plots influenced many aspiring authors. It was no coincidence that Jack Williamson's first story "The Metal Man" appeared in *Amazing Stories* just a year after it had reprinted Merritt's *The Metal Monster* as *The Metal Emperor*. Merritt kept getting reprinted. His work was one of the mainstays of *Famous Fantastic Mysteries*, which reprinted the romantic fantasies of the early Munsey pulp magazines such as *All-Story* and *Argosy* beginning in 1939. The first issue, for instance, featured "The Moon Pool," and the next six issues serialized *The Conquest of the Moon Pool*. Later it would be published in its entirety in a companion magazine *Fantastic Novels* in 1949, and an *A. Merritt Magazine* published five issues in 1949 and 1950.

Many readers who had missed the glory days of the Munsey pulps were able to recapture their romantic appeal in *Famous Fantastic Mysteries*, and to discover a latent love for the remote and the mysterious and the larger-than-life characters who were challenged by them and for the poetic diction in which their adventures were described.

That love for romantic adventures still lies within every reader, waiting only for the opening of the door into the marvelous by a writer with the skills and imagination of A. Merritt.

WHAT MAD UNIVERSE
FREDRIC BROWN

What Mad Universe has two distinguishing characteristics: it is pulp-magazine fiction, and it is a science-fiction novel whose subject is the writing, publishing, and reading of science fiction.

Both characteristics sound uncomplimentary, but they mean something meaningful that I want to discuss at some length. Let me take the second first.

Editors tell writers not to write stories about writers; even teachers of fiction writing, as I am sometimes, tell students that as well. Writers are unusual people with unusual motivations, and the reader is likely to find writers unsympathetic if not incomprehensible. Students, on the other hand, find writers irresistible. With good reason, perhaps: *they* understand them.

Editors fall under the same general prohibition, though writers are less likely to consider them fascinating protagonists. And Keith Winton, hero of *What Mad Universe*, is not only an editor but an unsuccessful writer.

Not only that: Winton is the editor of a science-fiction magazine. Not promising material for a novel. But Fredric Brown, small in stature but big in aspiration, liked challenges. *What Mad Universe* also belongs to a category of novel in the science-fiction field that takes the professionals and fans of that field as its basic world. It was followed in 1951 by *The Case of the Little Green Men* by Mack Reynolds (a friend of Brown's and sometime collaborator)—although this, to be sure, was a mystery set at a science-fiction convention, as was Richard Purtell's more recent *Murdercon*. And it was preceded by Anthony Boucher's 1942 *Rocket to the Morgue*, although this, too, was a mystery novel.

Moreover, to make the situation more incestuous, Winton is editor of *Surprising Stories*, and *What Mad Universe* was first published in *Startling Stories*, one of the two science-fiction adventure magazines published by Popular Publications, a pulp-magazine chain (though probably by no means as profitable) just like the one for which Winton worked. That magazine, edited by a man named Sam Merwin Jr., included letters like the one Winton is editing in the novel and the editor wrote joking responses like the one Winton prepared. Perhaps Brown used *Startling Stories* (and Merwin) as his model because Merwin had already agreed to publish it.

Magazine publication was in September 1948 (book publication came in 1949; that, too, was unusually quick for that period, but Brown had a publisher already for his murder mysteries who was willing to publish his SF as well). Since the magazines came out a month or two before they were dated (to allow them to remain current, or seem current, longer on the newsstands) that was about the time I was receiving a letter from Merwin telling me that he liked my first story, "Paradox," and would pay me $80 for it. This alone would have given me good reason to be favorably disposed toward *What Mad Universe* when it appeared (incestuousness and all).

But the novel needed no special consideration. I loved it for its ideas, and other people, without my reasons, liked it as well. It has been continually reprinted and it has continued to be what it seemed like to many of us at the time: a classic. And that is unusual for pulp-magazine fiction.

Which brings me to the first characteristic. What do I mean by pulp-magazine fiction? The first thing I mean is that the prose is straightforward and the narrative is compulsive. That is, this is a story intended to be enjoyed. It is written with a reader in mind, from its "narrative hook" to its cliffhanger chapter endings and its unrelenting action. It is filled with surprising twists of plot. It is what is today called "a good read" or "a page-turner." Readers will not want to put it down.

When Fred Brown wrote this novel he was a full-time writer, and *What Mad Universe* was intended to pay the bills. It was commercial fiction. Editors wanted from writers the kind of stories that would make a lot of readers buy the magazine. This didn't mean editors had any prejudices against good writing (though "fine" writing was another matter). And what made *What Mad Universe* survive the magazine that published it—indeed, virtually the entire pulp-magazine field, of which a few SF magazines are the only living reminders—was the skill of the writing and imagination contained in what was, in other respects, formulaic.

What is difficult to remember in these days of avant-garde, elitist fiction, experimental in style, often obscure, and frequently disdainful of its readers, is that most great literature has been commercial and even formulaic, from *The Iliad* and *The Odyssey*, through the Greek drama, Shakespeare, and the English novel, up to relatively recent times. What has counted is what the authors have done with the formula, how far they have expanded it beyond the basic need to please their audiences.

Like other SF stories and novels from the SF magazines of the 1940s and 1950s that were written for love as well as for money (the money never was enough to justify the work that went into them), *What Mad Universe* has remained in print because it not only gave the readers what they expected but a good deal more.

Readers will get from *What Mad Universe* an Aristotelian "beginning, middle, and end" and its reminders of a bygone era. Readers also may note that they are reading "historical science fiction." That is an oxymoron like "airline cuisine" and "military intelligence," perhaps, but what else can one call futuristic fiction whose time has come and gone? In spite of popular opinion, science fiction is not prophecy; it is not about "the future" but an infinite variety of possible futures, and if one happens to come close to the truth in large or small detail, that is an accident. Nevertheless readers may be vaguely disquieted by the fact that narratives deal with speculative events that clearly have not happened. All of Jules Verne's *voyages extraordinaires* belong to this category, for instance, as do most of H. G. Wells's scientific romances. And yet they are still eminently readable and enjoyable, as long as one can place oneself in the frame of reference of their original readers and forget, for the time, that the first attempt to send a rocket to the moon did not occur in 1954.

Readers also will find a second and surprising reason for the pulp-fiction style of *What Mad Universe*. In chapter 3, Keith Winton asks himself, "What mad universe was this that took for granted an alien race more horrible looking than the worst Bem that had ever leered from a science-fiction magazine cover?" The fact, as the reader will discover, is that Winton is living in a pulp-fiction universe. It is a universe in which purple-furred monsters from the moon walk into small-town drug stores, in which Arcturan spies are shot down on sight (never mind that one hundred innocent Earth people may die by mistake) and Arcturus plans to wipe out all human life, in which scientists create artificial smog to protect cities and citizens must endure the crime explosion that ensues.

But I will not anticipate any more of Brown's surprises. *What Mad Universe*, so aptly named, is filled with them, and readers should discover them for themselves. What is more, Brown shows an unsuspecting victim, like you or me, thrown into the middle of that crazy world and trying his best to figure it out, and making all sorts of human mistakes as he does so. And finally, Brown produces an explanation that makes sense out of all the insanity—and that may be the most surprising development.

What Mad Universe belongs to one other category of story: the alternate universe. The tradition of the alternate-universe story is closely allied to the alternate-history story, which began in 1819 with a pamphlet by an English cleric named Richard Whately questioning whether Napoleon existed, was revived in 1907 by Sir George Trevelyan's "If Napoleon had won the Battle of Waterloo," and reached its best statements in science fiction with Ward Moore's *Bring the Jubilee* and Philip K. Dick's *The Man in the High Castle*.

The alternate-history story creates a different historical world taking off from a significant event that might have happened differently, such as England not repelling the Spanish Armada, Luther being reconciled with the Catholic Church, the South winning the Civil War, or the Axis Powers winning World War II. Alternate-universe stories, on the other hand, throw characters into worlds where everything is different—or only one small thing is different. And the difference on which that universe depends often is the critical discovery.

Philip Jose Farmer's story "Sail On! Sail On!" appears to be an alternate-history story in which Columbus's first voyage to the New World includes a telegraph and an electric light because Roger Bacon's thirteenth-century scientific experiments were accepted by the Catholic Church, and a monastic order of Rogerians was set up to pursue experimentation; but by the end of the story the reader discovers that he has been reading an alternate-universe story instead, as Columbus and his crew sail off the end of the world.

The reader will discover that *What Mad Universe* is like that: the alternate-history event (in chapter 6) is the discovery of instantaneous space travel in 1903, but the alternate universe . . . That, too, readers will want to learn themselves.

The mind that created all this came in a small body. Fredric Brown was thin, bespectacled, a bit professorial. I met him once when he came to Racine, Wisconsin, where I was working as an editor for a paperback publisher, and he persuaded me to ride back to Milwaukee with him where he was visiting. I was surprised at his appearance, since I had been reading and enjoying his hard-boiled mysteries, but I discovered underneath that unlikely exterior someone who was tough and witty and persuasive.

He had friends in Milwaukee, where he had lived for ten years or so working as a proofreader for the *Milwaukee Journal* while writing stories in his spare time. His first stories were fantasy, published in John Campbell's *Unknown*, but he soon began getting his SF stories published as well, in almost all the magazines including *Astounding*. His five SF novels are well known, but his short stories may be even better known, including "Arena," which was chosen to be reprinted in the *Science Fiction Hall of Fame*, "Etaoin Shrdlu," and "The Waveries." He was the acknowledged master of the short-short story.

His mysteries, beginning with *The Dead Ringer* in 1948, were what enabled him to become a full-time writer in 1947, but even in those one could often trace the mind of a science-fiction writer at work, with its unusual perceptions and special viewpoints. He moved to Taos, New Mexico, for his respiratory problems, went to California to write screenplays without success, and returned to the Southwest, to Tucson, Arizona, where he died in 1972.

He had a special talent and a special vision, some of which can be sampled in *What Mad Universe*.

BLOOD MUSIC
GREG BEAR

Science-fiction writers get credit for their extravagant imaginations. The most popular question asked of them is "Where do you get those crazy ideas?" The answer that is seldom given but may be closest to reality is "from scientists." It is the scientists, particularly contemporary scientists, who have discarded their distrust of speculation, who have the crazy ideas. SF writers simply naturalize them by imagining worlds in which scientific speculations have become reality. SF writers deal in the human implications of innovation.

Scientific concepts seem to occur to scientists about the same time, as if the ideas were in the air and the scientists inhaled them as they breathed. The most famous example is the simultaneous development of the theory of evolution by Charles Darwin and Alfred Russell Wallace. Charles Fort put it this way: "In steam-engine time people invent steam engines." The same situation prevails among science-fiction writers. In their case the explanation might be as simple as the fact that writers read the same scientific journals, *Scientific American*, say, or *The New Scientist*, or *Science*, or even such current popularizers of science as *Discover* or *Science Digest*, or even the daily newspaper.

In the 1920s, for instance, the SF magazines were filled with stories which were takeoffs, in one way or another, of Einstein's theory of relativity; writers of the 1930s were obsessed with the weaponry of war and an impending final war, culminating in the early 1940s with the promise and threat of nuclear war/energy. The postwar period was so dominated by stories about a final nuclear war, or its aftermath, that one editor placed a ban on any more such stories in his magazine and suggested instead a story about J. B. Rhine's work at Duke University on parapsychology, upon which he was promptly flooded with stories about telepathy and telekinesis.

In the 1960s and 1970s, scientific speculation became so much bolder, and so much better publicized, that writers began to convert new ideas into fiction more rapidly. When Freeman J. Dyson speculated about an advanced civilization capturing all the energy from its star by building its total planetary matter into a giant sphere entirely encircled, Larry Niven took a slice of that "Dyson sphere" to construct his *Ringworld*, and Bob Shaw, among others, used the whole thing for his *Orbitsville*.

Dyson's speculation about giant spheres was part of a broad discussion of communication with aliens stimulated in the late 1950s by Giuseppe Cocconi and Philip Morrison, and picked up by a broad range of scientists including Frank Drake, Carl Sagan, and I. S. Shklovskii, and dozens of stories appeared about SETI (as it came to be known), the search for extraterrestrial intelligence, including my own *The Listeners* and Sagan's *Contact*. Robert Thomson and Frank McConnell discovered evidence in planarian worms for what they called chemical memory, followed up by Holger Hyden, George Ungar, and others. Chemical memory became the subject of numerous works, including "The Planners," a Nebula Award story by Kate Wilhelm, and my novel *The Dreamers*.

The list goes on. Heisenberg uncertainty became a feature or the central motif of many works, followed in the 1980s by the paradox of Schrödinger's cat, featured in Frederik Pohl's *The Coming of the Quantum Cats* and George Alec Effinger's "Schrödinger's Kitten," among others. Cloning was the subject of dozens of stories, including Ursula K. Le Guin's "Nine Lives" and Kate Wilhelm's *Where Late the Sweet Birds Sang*. Speculations that the proper place for humanity might be outer space, broached as early as 1929 by J. D. Bernal's *The World, the Flesh, and the Devil*, got new life in the 1970s and produced a flood of stories about space colonies and hollowed-out meteors as habitats, culminating in George Zebrowski's *Macrolife*.

Finally, two marvelous coincidences illustrated the way in which today, new science is translated into fiction almost overnight. The hard-science speculation that new materials might make possible an elevator into space was turned into Arthur C. Clarke's Nebula and Hugo Award–winning *The Fountains of Paradise* and Charles Sheffield's *The Web between the Worlds*, both published in 1979. Information theory, and specifically Kantor's concept of information mechanics, as well as speculation that the final miniaturization of the computer would end up in a biological form, produced Greg Bear's *Blood Music* and Paul Preuss's *Human Error*, both in 1985.

Blood Music, then, comes straight out of yesterday's scientific journals and scientific texts. Frederick Kantor's *Information Mechanics* was published in 1977, and in the early 1980s, K. Eric Drexler's *The Engines of Creation*. *Information Mechanics* suggests that all reality can be reduced to exchanges and interpretations of information; *The Engines of Creation* speculates that machines can be built smaller than living cells and that intelligence of human complexity can be squeezed into one cubic centimeter of space, what he called "nanotechnology."

The science, however, is only the foundation for *Blood Music*; on it Bear builds a striking edifice of imaginative speculation, poetic descriptions of what has been until now unimaginable, and a colorful mosaic of believable human characters. What Bear has created is not so much an extrapolation of a world in which biological computers have become a reality as a universe, and a humanity, radically changed by the development of biological computers. In the process he has written a compelling novel, filled with flesh-and-blood characters in a realistically imagined world and imbued with that feeling of awe, that "sense of wonder," so prized by SF connoisseurs.

Writing this kind of novel, combining the knowledge of science, the imagining of naturalistic detail, and the poetry of vision and language, requires an unusual combination of qualities. Bear is one of the few writers who could have handled it. He earned a bachelor's degree in English from San Diego State University in 1973 and joined that with an interest in science to further a career as a science-fiction writer that had begun six years earlier when, at the age of sixteen, he published his first story, "Destroyers."

Bear's first novels, *Hegira* and *Psychlone*, were published in 1979. His novella "Hardfought" won a Nebula Award in 1984, and the same year the novelette "Blood Music" (upon which the later novel was based) won both a Nebula and a Hugo. He has written fantasy and horror, including *The Infinity Concerto* (1984) and *The Serpent Mage* (1986). He also wrote *Beyond Heaven's River* (1980), *Strength of Stones* (1981), and *Corona* (1984).

The Forge of God explores another potent idea out of today's scientific speculations: the miniature black hole (or something close to it, neutronium, or the stuff of collapsed stars, and anti-neutronium) and its potential for destroying Earth. *Eon* (1985) and *Eternity* (1988) continued the exploration of information theory begun in *Blood Music* through the mechanism of a mysterious hollowed asteroid and an exploration of anomalies in space and time. His close inspection of a near-future (2047) Los Angeles in *Queen of Angels* (1990), an Easton Press Signed First Edition, is a twenty-first-century *Crime and Punishment* that uses a detective-story format to explore the nature of crime as well as the consciousness of self that lies at its heart.

Bear also has published two collections of short stories, *The Wind from a Burning Woman* (1983) and *Tangents* (1989). He served as president of the Science Fiction Writers of America from 1988 to 1990.

Readers who would like to anticipate the next wave of science-fiction speculation might consider nanotechnology, which has been featured in several recent novels including Bear's *Queen of Angels*. Computer-human interfaces, which were central to the "cyberpunk" movement, may already have had their day. Stephen W. Hawking's 1988 best-selling *A Brief History of Time* already has spawned one upcoming novel and may be mined for others. But readers who want to be as current as the writers will have to do what they do: read the latest science books and magazines and let their imaginations soar.

They may have to if they want to keep up with reality. Bear believes that artificial molecular-scale machines will be designed and built within the next decade, and that any scenarios devised by science-fiction writers may be too conservative.

SPEAKER FOR THE DEAD
ORSON SCOTT CARD

Speaker for the Dead is one of fewer than a dozen novels that won both Hugo and Nebula Awards. What may be an even more remarkable distinction is that the book for which *Speaker* is a sequel, *Ender's Game*, also won the Hugo and the Nebula.

Although *Speaker* is a sequel, it can be read entirely without reference to *Ender's Game*; it is complete in itself. The earlier novel deals with the experiences of a child, Ender Wiggin, trying to survive a harrowing military academy experience, only this academy is in orbit and it gathers together the incipient military geniuses of Earth to prepare them for the second onslaught of aliens that threatens the possible future destruction of humanity. How Ender not only survives but also prevails, and how his success leads, unintentionally, to genocide, can be left to those who wish to experience that award-winning novel for themselves.

The Ender Wiggin of *Speaker for the Dead* is a sadder, wiser man, burdened with guilt and the cocoon of the hive queen who bears within herself the possibility of reconstituting her lost species. He has assumed the responsibility of "speaking for the dead," representing those who no longer can speak for themselves, just as his life has become a speaking for the dead "buggers" whom he was responsible for destroying.

About this new custom that sometimes comes into conflict with the more traditional religious burial ceremonies, one character remarks: "The Speakers for the Dead are really quite innocuous—they set up no rival organizations, they perform no sacraments, they don't even claim that the Hive Queen and the Hegemon is a work of scripture. The only thing they do is try to discover the truth about the lives of the dead, and then tell everyone who will listen the story of a dead person's life as the dead one meant to live it."

And a Catholic bishop replies, "And you pretend to find that harmless?"

Speaker for the Dead is also a novel of alien contact.

Science fiction has used the concept of aliens in a variety of ways. They entered science fiction in H. G. Wells's *The War of the Worlds*, poking their horrid heads out of the cylinders that had brought them from Mars, building their tripod-mounted killing machines, and planning to use people as cattle. This use of the alien as the ultimate threat to human survival persists throughout later SF.

Aliens also can stand for the encounter of inferior and superior levels of civilization. In contacts with aliens humanity can take the role of the European conquerors of the Americas, the missionaries to the South Seas, or the bearers of technology and culture, with all the manifold opportunities for choice and self-destruction. Or humanity may find itself in the tragic role of

Tasmanians being discovered by the Europeans, a parallel that Wells drew upon when he conceived the idea for *The War of the Worlds*.

Aliens offer the possibility of ultimate difference. Having evolved in totally different circumstances, possibly with different chemistries and certainly different social organizations, aliens can be used not only to explore the possibilities of other ways of behaving, even other ways of thinking, but they also can give writers the opportunity, by comparison, to discuss and to question human ways of thinking and *behaving*.

Much science fiction, since Murray Leinster's "First Contact" (1945), has been devoted to the question of how widely divergent thinking creatures can find ways of mutual survival, even of mutual assistance. Mike Resnick's *Second Contact*, a volume in the Easton Press Signed First Edition series, plays off that discussion.

The alien also offers metaphorical possibilities: the human condition can be framed as a struggle between self-awareness and empathy, between solipsism and community. The alien represents in its ultimate form "the other" that Ursula K. Le Guin focuses on in her Hugo and Nebula Award–winning novel *The Left Hand of Darkness* (1969).

Sometimes the narrative strategy transforms one image of the alien into another, and the statement of the story may be that the golden rule does not apply, that we should not judge others by ourselves, that we should defer our decisions to the reality of alien difference.

Ender's Game, Card's 1985 novel, uses the alien in several of its manifestations. The military academy and the search for youthful military geniuses are motivated by the possibility of the alien as competition for livable planets, including Earth itself, and even for survival, and is transformed, at the very end, into the concept of the alien as misunderstanding. Meanwhile, in terms of family, in terms of the military academy community, Ender is alienated, turned into an alien himself.

Speaker for the Dead, Card's 1986 novel, deals with human and alien redemption through the medium of understanding, through the ultimate experience in empathy, that exists between alien species. As Speaker for the Dead, Ender's ability to place himself in the position of others leads him finally to comprehend and place in context what originally seems an abhorrent alien practice. It is this ability to suspend judgment, and the imperative to "love thy alien as thyself," that the novel ultimately is about.

Card became a major science-fiction writer in a remarkably short time. A practicing Mormon, he was born in Richmond, Washington, in 1951, and earned a B.A. in theater in 1975 from Brigham Young University and an M.A. in English in 1981 from the University of Utah. He later did further graduate work in English at Notre Dame. He served as a volunteer Mormon missionary in Brazil in 1971–1973 and operated a repertory theater in Provo in 1974–1975. He also has served as proofreader and editor of a university press, as editor of *Ensign* magazine and of Compute Books, and as a teacher at the University of Utah, Brigham Young, Notre Dame, and the Clarion Writers Workshop.

Card's first professional writing experience was as a successful playwright, but he turned to science fiction in 1977 with the publication of "Ender's Game," the novelette that preceded the novel and became a Hugo finalist. That was followed by other award nominees, such as 1978's "Mikal's Songbird," that earned him in the same year the Campbell Award as best new writer.

Card's first novel was *Hot Sleep* (1978), followed by *A Planet Called Treason* (1979) and *Songmaster* (1980). He also has published *Hart's Hope* (1983), *The Worthing Chronicle* (1983), *Wyrms* (1987), and a science-fantasy series about an alternate America of the early 1800s in which folk magic is real, beginning with *Seventh Son* (1987) and continuing with *Red Prophet* (1987) and *Prentice Alvin* (1988). He wrote a well-received novelization of the film *The Abyss* (1989). Some of his short fiction has been published in *Capitol* (1978), *Unaccompanied Sonata and Other Stories* (1981), and *Cardography* (1987).

Of his own work, Card has written:

> Repeatedly my central characters occupy an unsought key position in their community; repeatedly they choose to suffer or cause unspeakable pain or sacrifice in order to save the community.... Often my characters are children or otherwise innocent, forced ahead of time into responsibilities they cannot, but nevertheless do, bear.... They are always isolated from the community they uphold. They tend to have exceptional gifts and exceptional weaknesses; they are introspective enough to notice their weakness and strength and pain, but not enough to notice their virtue.... And all my fiction is infused with a strong belief in the perfect-ability of human beings, at least in part through their own desires and works.

Card is introspective enough to trace what he writes about and how he writes about it to his upbringing and faith as a Mormon, but he brings to that perspective his own unique experiences and his own special abilities to transform his heritage and his experiences into remarkable fiction.

ISLANDS IN THE NET
BRUCE STERLING

Bruce Sterling's work as a codifier and popularizer of cyberpunk threatened to overshadow his own writing reputation, but in 1988 *Islands in the Net* changed all that. Sterling had attracted critical attention with his short stories beginning with "Man-Made Self" in *Lone Star Universe* (1976) and with his novels beginning with *Involution Ocean* (1978), but *Islands in the Net* was his big popular success. It also won him the John W. Campbell Memorial Award for the best SF novel of the year.

Born in Brownsville, Texas, in 1954, Sterling earned a degree in journalism from the University of Texas in 1976, the same year his first story was published in the anthology of Texan SF. His first novel and his second, *The Artificial Kid* (1980), were what Colin Greenland in *The Encyclopedia of Science Fiction* called "moralized extravaganza." Joe Sanders in *Twentieth-Century Science Fiction Writers* describes them as explorations "of the very nature of self-control as his protagonists gain experience and self-knowledge in bizarre future societies."

Sterling followed "the fantastic exorbitance of his early work" (Greenland) with *Schismatrix*, "a 1-volume history of interplanetary expansion and transformation of the human race," written with "a hard-edged and highly detailed realism closely informed by scientific speculation and extrapolation." Closely allied with the novel was a series of short stories about two groups of humans with different prescriptions for coping with the challenges of the universe: the Shapers, who want to alter humanity genetically, and the Mechanists, who want to augment human abilities with prosthetics. A group of the Shaper/Mechanist stories were published in *Crystal Express* (1989).

By this time, however, Sterling's career as a spokesman for cyberpunk had run its course. Cyberpunk generally is dated from the publication of William Gibson's *Neuromancer* in 1984 although foreshadowed by many works including 1950s and 1960s novels and stories by Alfred Bester, Samuel R. Delany, and others, and in the early 1980s by the fiction of such writers as Sterling himself, Rudy Rucker, Lewis Shiner, and John Shirley. Cyberpunk became a movement, however, with the publication of Sterling's critical fanzine *Cheap Truth*, which codified and defended the tenets and ambitions of cyberpunk between 1984 and 1986, and culminated in the publication of *Mirrorshades: The Cyberpunk Anthology* (1986), which Sterling edited and for which he provided a defining introduction that resembled, according to Peter Nichols, "a manifesto."

The characteristics of cyberpunk begin with the name itself. Although the word is now more familiarly used by the media to describe aspects of the real world, it is still, uncharacteristically, attributed to its SF sources, particularly Gibson. Films like *Tron*, *Videodrome*, and *Blade Runner*, all distributed in 1982, preceded it, and others, including the 1992 television miniseries *Wild Palms*, deliberately invoked the cyberpunk genre, including a celebrity appearance in that film by Gibson himself. The word itself was invented by Bruce Bethke in his 1983 *Amazing* story "Cyberpunk," but the term was first applied critically by *Isaac Asimov's SF Magazine* editor Gardner Dozois. "Cyber" describes the fiction's technological background of a massively computerized near-future world; "punk" describes the viewpoint from which this world is approached.

The various works categorized as cyberpunk may differ in their political extrapolations—Gibson's future world is dominated by Japanese firms, while George Alec Effinger's is controlled by Arabs and other oil-rich Middle Easterners—but they all project into the next century a society highly dependent upon information and the computers that can best store and manipulate it. The computers, moreover, assume power of their own, as they aspire not only to the status of artificial intelligences, but to personhood. Traditional political systems have been largely superseded by multinational corporations with their bottom-line amorality. All this is viewed from the bottom: by characters who are often outcasts dwarfed by the powers that control the world in which they live, able to survive only through the use of street smarts, which in this world means the ability to manipulate information. And the style itself reflects the information density of computer data or, even more, of films such as *Blade Runner*.

It is a Dickensian world in which the cybernetic revolution has replaced the Industrial Revolution and the computer hacker stands in for Fagin or, in some instances, for Oliver Twist. As a matter of fact, Sterling and Gibson combined their talents to produce *The Difference Engine* (1990), what some critics called "steam-punk," an alternate-world novel in which Charles Babbage's 1821 design for a mechanical computer was actually built and resulted in a steam-driven, punched-card 1850s Great Britain led by Prime Minister Lord Byron. But in the novel the power of the computer has done nothing for the squalor of everyday life.

What the cyberpunk writers were extrapolating into the twenty-first century were trends that many people see developing today: In the midst of growing power and wealth, ordinary people find themselves increasingly powerless, and their only defense, a knowledge of the way things are and an ability to manipulate information better than the people ostensibly in control. And yet cyberpunk remained essentially "romantic" in that it showed individuals making a difference, like knights charging impregnable fortresses.

Islands in the Net, though it was categorized as cyberpunk, departed from the cyberpunk model in various significant ways. Its protagonist, for instance, is a woman who has it all, a handsome husband who shares the domestic chores including their new baby, a secure future with a multinational conglomerate and the possibility of rapid advancement, and a world in which "peace, prosperity, and profit," according to one jacket blurb, seem assured. It is a world built on information, like those of the cyberpunks, but in this world much of the information is financial or biochemical, and it is a world whose fragility becomes evident by the end of chapter 2 when Laura Webster is launched into a series of crises that allow her, and the reader, to explore the world while it shatters around her.

The basic problem of a world based on information, the "net" that the title alludes to, is the ease with which information can be stolen without a trace and the explosive power of its misuse. As Sterling describes the situation:

> The havens were bootstrapping their way up to Big Brother Status, trading for scattered bits of information, then collating it and selling it back—as a new and sinister whole.
> They made a business of abstracting, condensing, indexing, and verifying—like any other modern commercial database. Except, of course, that the pirates were carnivorous. They ate other databases when they could, blithely ignoring copyrights and simply storing everything they could filch. This didn't require state-of-the-art computer expertise. Just memory by the ton, and plenty of cast-iron gall.

Sterling pursues the information process in his real life as well. He is a lecturer and essayist and an authority on the present-day computer networks and their bulletin boards and programs. He has said that he may put his next novel on one of the networks so that computer people can promote it as well as his status as a lecturer, and his most recent book is the nonfiction *The Hacker Crackdown: Law and Order on the Electronic Frontier* (1992), about computer crime.

Cyberpunk as a literary movement began to merge hack into the general SF scene as its vision of the future became more common in film and more commonly emulated in fiction. Although the general culture still is exploring its implications, the founders and authorities of *cyberpunk* have moved on to other, more individual projects.

That includes Bruce Sterling as well as William Gibson. Sterling already has displayed a remarkable range to add to his virtuosity. "Just wait till the Kid grows up," Joe Sanders quotes from *The Artificial Kid*. Like all writers worth following, Sterling is still growing.

THE POSTMAN
DAVID BRIN

Universal catastrophe has been a familiar theme in science fiction. C. S. Lewis used the word "eschatology" to describe a concern with significant change in humanity's nature or condition. As the literature of the human species, science fiction offers a variety of scenarios about the ways in which humanity may be changed, and one of these—perhaps the most dramatic of them—involves the event that destroys, or nearly destroys, the species and the way in which the remnants of humanity survive and perhaps rebuild civilization. In *The Postman* David Brin offered a familiar event—nuclear holocaust—but a novel concept of what keeps a society from disintegrating and might help it reconstruct something worth preserving.

Early catastrophe stories and novels often depicted a solitary individual or small group wandering through a devastated world before they, too, succumbed. The event that precipitated the devastation usually was natural, as in the plague that killed almost everyone in Mary Shelley's *The Last Man* (1827) or the poison gas that did the same thing in M. P. Shiel's *The Purple Cloud* (1901). Stars or planets or meteorites have been frequent sources of disaster as in Camille Flammarion's *Omega* (1894), H. G. Wells's "The Star" (1897), Balmer and Wylie's *When Worlds Collide* (1933), John Wyndham's *The Day of the Triffids* (1951), Fritz Leiber's *The Wanderer* (1965), and Pournelle and Niven's *Lucifer's Hammer* (1977).

Plagues have been a familiar visitation upon a long-suffering humanity since the beginnings of history. Science fiction picked up the idea as a possible end to humanity with Edgar Allan Poe's "The Masque of the Red Death" (1842), and Jack London made it the precipitating factor in his "The Scarlet Plague" (1912), as J. D. Beresford did in *Goslings* (1913). One of the classic treatments emerged in George R. Stewart's *Earth Abides* (1949). Plagues remain a favorite with writers of eschatological narratives, with some variations suggesting the fragile hold humanity has on existence. One of those was John Christopher's *No Blade of Grass* (1956), which suggested that a plague might strike something upon which humanity was dependent, like the grasses, which includes wheat. In a series of catastrophe novels published between 1962 and 1966, J. G. Ballard suggested a variety of ways (wind, flood, drought, crystalline transformation) in which the natural world might turn against humanity.

After the wartime use of the atomic bomb, the possibility of man-made catastrophe tended to dominate SF authors' nightmares, possibly as a way of warding off racial suicide or cautioning against the strategies, or the human hates and fears, that might lead to an atomic holocaust. H. G. Wells had speculated about the possibility of an atomic bomb as early as *The World Set Free* (1914), and other writers had dealt with the concept throughout the early history of the SF magazine. But its reality brought the grim realization that nuclear disaster was not just a theoretical possibility.

Theodore Sturgeon's "Thunder and Roses" (1947) and Ray Bradbury's "The Million-Year Picnic" (1946) and "There Will Come Soft Rains" (1950) were examples of the concerns, and sometimes the guilt for having imagined the possibility, of many SF writers. In fact, stories such as these were so commonplace that *Galaxy* editor H. L. Gold announced in 1952 that he would henceforward reject all stories of "atomic gloom." As a consequence, nuclear fears migrated into novels such as Judith Merril's *Shadow on the Hearth* (1950) and Nevil Shute's mainstream treatment (and perhaps the best known of all), *On the Beach* (1957) and its film version in 1959, although *Dr.*

Strangelove (1964) is a close rival. Other well-known nuclear holocaust narratives include Pat Frank's *Alas, Babylon* (1959), Walter Miller Jr.'s *A Canticle for Leibowitz* (1960), and the 1983 television film *The Day After*.

Catastrophe stories, then, tended at first to differentiate themselves according to the cause of the catastrophe and the lessons humanity might learn from it. After that, if humanity survived, the stories tended to be similar narratives of human suffering and endurance emphasizing the fragility of human civilization and the superficial nature of altruism when confronted with questions of survival. The number of nuclear holocaust stories, however, demanded differentiation in terms of human response.

That is what Brin's *The Postman* offered. What makes society possible, the novel suggests, is communication, and when a survivor of a nuclear holocaust just happens to come across the remains of a mailman and assumes his role in the disintegrating post-holocaust society, the theme works itself out in a personal and appealing narrative. Its success is indicated by its winning the John W. Campbell Award for the best SF novel of the year and its *Locus* award.

Actually *The Postman is* a bit of an anomaly in Brin's body of work. It is a story limited by a single, unheroic protagonist's viewpoint and his personal interactions. What Brin has become best known for is multiple-viewpoint space epics. In fact, Donald L. Lawlor in *Twentieth-Century Science-Fiction Writers* said that Brin writes in "the Verne tradition, which emphasizes the quest/adventure potentials of scientific technology." Certainly Brin's Uplift series, which includes his first novel, *Sundiver* (1980), and his second, the Nebula and Hugo Award–winning novel *Startide Rising* (1983), belongs to that tradition, and to that one should add the third novel in the series, *The Uplift War* (1987).

The Uplift series also concerns contact with superior aliens and the human struggle for survival in a universe far more complicated than anyone had ever suspected, and an element of mythology in the notion of now-vanished Progenitors, who many millions of years ago "uplifted," or raised to sentience, a myriad of alien species. Add to this an alien suspicion of humans because they "uplifted" themselves and do not have a guiding (and exploiting) patron and because this feral species has actually "uplifted" dolphins and chimpanzees.

In addition Brin has published *The Practice Effect* (1984), *Heart of the Comet* (with Gregory Benford, 1986), *Earth* (1990), and a body of short fiction, some of which has been collected in *The River of Time* (1986). He also is a frequent lecturer and writer on science and scientific philosophy.

This easy movement between literature and science seems to come naturally to a recent group of authors who have solid scientific credentials and who are not reluctant to speculate in the field of their expertise. Brin, for instance, earned his B.A. from Cal Tech in astronomy, his M.S. in applied physics, and his Ph.D. in space science from the University of California, San Diego. He has taught at San Diego State University and San Diego community colleges but now devotes himself to full-time writing.

He promises to be one of the continuing stars of the science-fiction heavens, which seem to burn brighter and longer when they are based on solid scientific reality.

WHEN GRAVITY FAILS
GEORGE ALEC EFFINGER

The history of human civilization is the history of human augmentation. With its own feeble powers of tooth and muscle, humanity might eventually have populated the entire Earth (though some islands or inaccessible or hostile continents might still be free from human habitation), but that gradual spread would have taken tens of thousands of years longer (and would still be incomplete) and humanity would be numbered in the low millions and would be gathered, at best, into tribes. If it had survived at all—without tools.

Arthur C. Clarke remarks somewhere—perhaps he was quoting Robert Ardrey—that rather than man inventing tools, it was tools that invented man. That is, the sticks that primitive hominids picked up placed a premium on better muscular coordination and therefore on a larger and more complex brain: Hominids who were better at using tools survived, prospered, and passed on their characteristics to more, and more successful, offspring.

Tools. By the use of tools humanity has made itself virtually independent of nature—sometimes to humanity's sorrow. But humanity would be only another animal without the tool. Tools and humanity are symbiotes; the tool augments humanity's deficiencies in the natural world. And the process that began with knife and spear and hammer, with plow and scythe, with bridle and stirrup and horse collar, with boat and vehicle, with steam engine and dynamo, has not yet ended—indeed may just have begun.

If the augmentation of human abilities is the history of civilization, speculation about the next and succeeding augmentation and how it will change the lives of the people who use it is the definition of science fiction. Science fiction is the literature of the remarkable change in the way people lived and thought that became apparent shortly after the Industrial Revolution. SF speculates about future change, what advantage it will bring those who experience it and possibly what payment it may exact from them, for nothing comes free.

George Alec Effinger's *When Gravity Fails* suggests that the next human augmentation will be to the brain. Many tools have affected the brain, including, if Clarke is correct, the size and complexity of the primitive brain. But after that first evolutionary leap, tools affected not the brain but the mind—

that is, by changing the conditions in which people live, tools changed the ways in which people looked at themselves and the world they lived in. And through tools for learning—philosophy, logic, mental disciplines including the scientific method, books, schools, scientific instruments, and so on up through computers—tools have augmented the ability of the mind to consider, retain, and organize information.

The next step, according to Effinger and other science-fiction speculators, may be direct augmentation of the brain itself. Rather than absorbing information through the senses, future people may be able to plug information directly into their brains, and in *When Gravity Fails* Effinger suggests that a new kind of plug-in augmentation will change humanity once again, but in a new and remarkable manner.

The new, startling, and sometimes horrifying world in which the computer becomes a controlling factor created a new kind of science fiction called "cyberpunk" to which *When Gravity Fails* has been linked. Ever since the invention of the computer, science-fiction authors have incorporated into their stories its potential for change. Sometimes computers were viewed as intellectual companions or even saviors, as in Robert A. Heinlein's *The Moon Is a Harsh Mistress* (1966) or David Gerrold's *When Harlie Was One* (1972), sometimes as threats, as in Martin Caidin's *The God Machine* (1968), D. F. Jones's *Colossus* (1966), or Harlan Ellison's "I Have No Mouth, and I Must Scream."

The most consistent portrayal of the computer and its mobile variation, the robot, was drawn by Isaac Asimov in his robot stories and novels beginning with the stories gathered into *I, Robot* (1950). But Asimov's world was depicted primarily as a civilization to which computers and robots have been added. The "cyberpunk" vision, first displayed in 1983 by William Gibson in his Nebula and Hugo Award–winning *Neuromancer*, delineated a computer-shaped civilization. The difference was that cyberpunk started with the all-powerful computer and built a world around it. It was a world of multinational corporations, the only organizations powerful enough to exploit the full potential of the computer for gathering, storing, and manipulating information, and people who defined themselves in relationship to the computer. The people that the cyberpunk authors concerned themselves with—which explains the "punk" in the word applied to their work—were the underclass, the street people. Some of them, extrapolated from today's computer hackers, could plug themselves directly into the computer matrix, into what Gibson called "cyberspace," and by their ability to manipulate the information networks get by with what has always stood the underclass in good stead, its street smarts.

Effinger's *When Gravity Fails* differs from cyberpunk in a number of important ways. Rather than plugging into "cyberspace," Effinger's characters plug modules ("moddies") into themselves. Where the majority of cyberpunk narratives deal with the amoral world of national corporations, often Japanese, *When Gravity Fails* describes a world of players at the game of politics and intrigue; an absence of great powers means an opportunity for everyone to strive for advantage, much like Renaissance Europe. Effinger's future world is centered in the Middle East, perhaps shaped by oil reserves, and rather than cyberpunk's creation of new ways of thinking and behaving appropriate to a world based on powerful, innovative technology, *When Gravity Fails* offers new methods shaped by and sometimes in conflict with the traditions of the Middle East.

Rather than identifying *When Gravity Fails* as cyberpunk, then, *When Gravity Fails* and cyberpunk might better be traced, like humanity and the apes, to a common ancestor—the idea of a world shaped by computers, from which no future science fiction can ever entirely be free. The question that Effinger raises, moreover, is not cyberpunk's question of power (and how the powerless will cope) but of morality, which cyberpunk virtually ignores. When almost everything is possible, *When Gravity Fails* asks, what is moral?

Certainly when readers encounter Marîd Audran they find nothing to admire about his pointless, dissolute existence in the ghetto, called the "budayeen," of an unnamed Arabic city. Events force him, however, from his life of drugs and compliant females into a role as a cop and compel him to use moddies to enable him to think and behave in ways that are impossible to him without such augmentation. So it begins—the reluctant hero and the challenging world of change—a mystery to be solved, in the tradition of the hard-boiled detective story. Effinger even uses hard-boiled private eye diction, and consciously—one of his epigraphs comes from Raymond Chandler's famous essay "The Simple Art of Murder."

Such was the success of *When Gravity Fails*—it was a finalist for both the Nebula and the Hugo when it was published in 1986—that Effinger followed it with two sequels: *A Fire in the Sun* (1990) and *The Exile Kiss* (1991). *The Exile Kiss* was a selection of the Easton Press Signed First Editions of Science Fiction series.

Effinger was born in 1947, attended Yale and New York Universities, and then, in 1970, attended the Clarion Writers Workshop that has launched so many successful SF writers. A year later Effinger became a full-time writer. He did much of his early work for Marvel Comics and novelizations of the *Planet of the Apes* TV series, but his own work tended more toward the surreal, beginning with *What Entropy Means to Me* (1972) and continuing with *Relatives* (1973), *Nightmare Blue* (with Gardner Dozois, 1975), *Those Gentle Voices* (1976), *Death in Florence* (1978), *Heroics* (1979), *The Wolves of Memory* (1981), *The Nick of Time* (1985), and *The Bird of Time* (1986). He also has produced several collections of his own special kind of short fiction: *Mixed Feelings* (1974), *Irrational Numbers* (1976), and *Dirty Tricks* (1978).

His most famous short story, "Schrödinger's Kitten," won all the awards—Nebula, Hugo, and Sturgeon—the year (1988) it was published.

A number of years ago Effinger wrote in a fan magazine named *Thrust* that there were two kinds of writing—tap dancing and storytelling—and that storytelling was better. In his budayeen trilogy Effinger has demonstrated that he is a master of both.

DO ANDROIDS DREAM OF ELECTRIC SHEEP?
PHILIP K. DICK

Do Androids Dream of Electric Sheep? was published by Doubleday in 1968, as part of its science-fiction line. Doubleday was publishing between two and three science-fiction books a month and was the only regular publisher of hardcover science-fiction novels. The cover jacket showed the dismantled parts of a mechanical sheep inside a series of boxes enclosed within a larger box, above this the title in larger curly letters, and at the top, in small type, Doubleday Science Fiction and Philip K. Dick.

The novel sold probably no more than five thousand copies, if that. Doubleday limited its print runs to what it expected to sell to subscribing libraries plus a limited bookstore sale and would rather publish a new novel (and sell the paperback rights) than reprint. The novel got no significant critical notice, though it was a finalist for the Nebula Award, won that year by Alexei Panshin's *Rite of Passage*.

Do Androids Dream of Electric Sheep? was Dick's twenty-third novel in thirteen years, most of them written swiftly for a small advance and few royalties from Ace Books. But *Now Wait for Last Year* had been published by Doubleday two years earlier. Ace published Dick's first novel, *Solar Lottery*, in 1955. Before that he had concentrated on short stories, publishing more than sixty (more than one a month) in science-fiction magazines between 1952 and 1955. He met one of his author heroes, A. E. van Vogt, at the 1954 World Science Fiction Convention in San Francisco, and van Vogt told him that books made more money than short stories. Dick was shy—he had to be dragged to the World Convention and would only meet people who came to him and his wife in the lobby—and was known then mostly for the skill and imagination of his stories. After his novels began to appear—sometimes two or three a year—Dick's reputation among his fellow writers was as a talented author with a remarkable, off-center vision who wrote too fast and published unwisely.

Slowly and surely that impression changed. Five years earlier than *Androids*, Dick had won a Hugo Award for *The Man in the High Castle*, and his novels were reprinted frequently, all of them in Great Britain and many in France, where he became as popular as van Vogt. *Androids* was reprinted immediately in mass-market paperback by Signet Books and has seldom been out of print since, sometimes under the title of *Blade Runner*.

Blade Runner changed everything. The first of the big new films made from SF novels and directed as film noir by Ridley Scott, though it did not do well in its initial release, *Blade Runner* has continued to build its reputation over the years and developed a cult following. It has been released in DVD in various director's cuts and still provokes controversy. It resulted in a Hollywood run on Dick fiction (*Total Recall*, *Minority Report*, *Screamers*, *Impostor*, *Paycheck*, and *A Scanner Darkly*).

Unfortunately they came too late for Dick, who died on March 2, 1982, at the age of fifty-three, after a series of strokes accompanied by heart failure, just before the release of the film. He was troubled by many psychological problems, including the death of his twin sister at the age of six weeks, for which he felt guilty. Married five times, he took up various addictions, suspected he had schizophrenia, and had several bouts of what he called "nervous breakdowns" and paranoia about FBI surveillance. All of this, including various supernatural experiences late in life, he turned into fiction—almost all of it concerned with the impermanence and evanescence of identity and reality.

Three sequels to *Androids* and *Blade Runner* were written by Dick's friend K. W. Jeter. *Androids* was one of four Dick novels included in a recent prestigious Library of America edition.

THE HITCHHIKER'S GUIDE TO THE GALAXY
DOUGLAS ADAMS

Don't Panic!

Even when confronted with writing an introduction to a book filled with infinite improbabilities, like a galactic bypass through the space otherwise occupied by the planet Earth, or a galactic president with two heads and three arms, or an alien whose cruelest punishment is making his prisoners listen to his vile poetry.

Or when coping with sentences that start off conventionally and then take a sudden right turn into the unexpected, like: "On Wednesday night it had rained very heavily, the lane was wet and muddy, but the Thursday morning sun was bright and clear as it shone on Arthur Dent's house for what was to be the last time."

Or when the book features an encyclopedia called *The Hitchhiker's Guide to the Galaxy* that tells you everything you need to know about anything and offers the sound advice on its cover: Don't Panic!

Or when a novel full of improbable invention offers the answer to Life, the Universe, and Everything.

Or when the novel is not actually a novel but the print version of a concept that began existence as a radio series that shapeshifted into a television series that transformed itself into a couple of films.

Oh well, as Marvin the paranoid robot would complain, in this life one must do what one is created to do.

According to legend—Adams's own—the idea for *The Hitchhiker's Guide to the Galaxy* came to him while he was drunk in a field in Innsbruck, Austria, looking up at the stars and carrying a book called *The Hitchhiker's Guide to Europe*. But one of Adams's biographies, *Hitchhiker: A Biography of Douglas Adams* by M. J. Simpson, suggests that Adams got the concept after his trip around Europe. Adams's life may have been as much a creation as his fiction.

Adams's first work appeared on BBC television in 1974, the year he was graduated from St. John's College, Oxford, and Adams began working on material for *Monty Python's Flying Circus*. He also contributed material to radio, and in 1977 he and producer Simon Brett pitched the idea of *Hitchhiker* as a science-fiction comedy radio show series. BBC radio broadcast the first series in March and April of 1978. A special Christmas episode was followed by a second series of five episodes in 1980. The first novel, *The Hitchhiker's Guide to the Galaxy*, was published in 1979, followed by *The Restaurant at the End of the Universe* in 1980, *Life, the Universe, and Everything* in 1982, *So Long and Thanks for All the Fish* in 1984, and *Mostly Harmless* in 1992. *Hitchhiker* became number one on the United Kingdom best-seller list and sold more than one million copies in paperback in 1984, a record he equaled twice more with later books. Two years earlier he had three books on the *New York Times* and *Publishers Weekly* best-seller lists.

In the midst of this productivity—although Adams reputedly was a reluctant writer and was quoted by his biographer as remarking, "I love deadlines. I love the whooshing sound they make as they go by"—the radio series was turned into a six-part BBC television series in 1981, later rebroadcast in the United States. All the while Adams was trying to turn the project into a movie, which got filmed and released in 2005 after Adams's death in 2001, at the age of forty-nine, of a heart attack.

On the strength of the script for the *Hitchhiker* pilot radio show, Adams got an assignment to write for *Doctor Who* in 1978, wrote *The Pirate Planet* in Season 16 and *City of Death* under the name of "David Agnew," and, after working as a BBC radio producer for six months, became the script editor for *Doctor Who* in Season 17.

After several trips to Los Angeles to work on a film version of *Hitchhiker*, Adams and his wife, British barrister Jane Belson, moved to Santa Barbara in 1994. They had one daughter, Polly Jane Rocket Adams. Adams had worked on other projects, including computer games and a second novel series, *Dirk Gently's Holistic Detective Agency* (1987) and *The Long Dark Tea-Time of the Soul* (1988). He also was a left-handed guitar player, and his writings exhibited influences from The Beatles, Pink Floyd, and Procol Harum.

Adams was an environmental activist and an atheist, to whom the evolutionary biologist Richard Dawkins dedicated his book *The God Delusion* as "possibly [my] only convert."

Adams was born in Cambridge in 1952. He had a younger sister, Susan, born three years later. Two years after that his parents divorced, and his mother and her two children moved in with her parents. After both his parents married others, Adams had two half-sisters and a half-brother. The young Adams attended school in Brentwood, Essex, until 1971, when he entered St. John's College, Oxford, to study English and was graduated with a B.A. in 1974. Like Kurt Vonnegut Jr., with whose writing Adams's work is often compared, Adams was taller than his photographs made him appear—six feet five. He made jokes about his height as well, recalling, in jest, that his form-master in school, instead of directions to meet under the clock tower, would suggest that they meet under Adams.

In spite of the spoofing tone of *Hitchhiker*, Adams was a technology enthusiast, buying his first computer in 1982 and converting to a Macintosh in 1984, and was reputedly the first or second person to buy a Mac when they became available in the United Kingdom. He, along with such other "Apple Masters" as John Cleese and Gregory Hines, became a spokesman for Apple.

His final book, *The Salmon of Doubt*, was published the year after his death. It was composed of short stories, essays, letters, eulogies, and eleven chapters of his unfinished novel.

His official biography, Nick Webb's *Wish You Were Here*, was published in 2003; a second biography, Simpson's *Hitchhiker*, was published in 2004. Several tribute programs to Adams were broadcast by BBC. His *Hitchhiker* series of novels is available in audio read by Adams; other versions are read by Stephen Fry and Martin Freeman, who played Arthur Dent in the film version.

Adams's other books are *The Meaning of Liff* (1983, with John Lloyd), the original radio series scripts (1985, with Geoffrey Perkins), *The Utterly Utterly Merry Comic Relief Christmas Book* (1986, edited by Adams and Peter Fincham), *The Deeper Meaning of Liff* (1990, with John Lloyd), *Last Chance to See* (1990, with Mark Carwardine), and *The Illustrated Hitchhiker's Guide to the Galaxy* (1994).

The Hitchhiker's Guide to the Galaxy gets much of its appeal from its transformation of science-fiction tropes into comic shorthand. Like "He felt that his whole life was some kind of dream and he sometimes wondered whose it was and whether they were enjoying it." Or "Ah, this is obviously some strange usage of the word 'safe' that I previously wasn't aware of." But *Hitchhiker* isn't all one-liners. It sends up the notion of aliens being smarter or dumber than humans are—they're like us only with more powers and fewer inhibitions. It makes fun of the idea that aliens will act with any more foresight or long-range planning than humans; they will be hogtied by bureaucracy, incompetence, and spite, just like we are. In fact, the entire *Hitchhiker* is human folly played out on a larger stage, and that's what satire has always been good at.

Nevertheless, the reader will find nuggets of gold among the straw of satire and a good laugh on every page. Just don't panic!

Note: The data for this introduction was exhaustively researched on the Douglas Adams website and Wikipedia, which, the reader might note, seems a lot like *The Hitchhiker's Guide to the Galaxy.*

CHILDHOOD'S END
ARTHUR C. CLARKE

Science-fiction classics are created when basic themes are treated innovatively and expressed in engrossing narratives. Good writing helps but may not be essential. *Childhood's End* is one of the classics of science fiction; it has a Stapledonian theme—the purpose of intelligent life and its place in the universe—considered as an unusual form of transcendence and embodied in a story that only begins with the appearance of alien ships in the sky over the Earth. And written with Arthur C. Clarke's skillful use of language and imagery.

The novel began Clarke's transformation into one of the Big Three among science fiction's writers. That was Isaac Asimov's formulation of what was generally recognized throughout the SF world: sometime in the 1970s or early 1980s Asimov, Clarke, and Robert A. Heinlein had, by popular assent, been crowned SF's Triumvirate, whose every new work must be read in order to keep up with what was happening. In 1982, as if in confirmation, Asimov's *Foundation's Edge*, Heinlein's *Friday*, and Clarke's *2010* ranked in the top ten on the *New York Times*'s best-seller list. There may never be another such clearly recognizable group of leaders.

The novel that confirmed what had already been suggested by earlier short stories, articles, novels, and nonfiction books—particularly *The Exploration of Space*, which became a selection of the Book-of-the-Month Club—came about in a peculiarly science-fiction manner. It developed from a novelette, "Guardian Angel," which had been published three years earlier in a minor magazine.

Some ideas in SF appear first in shorter form and then grow into novels, either by accretion or expansion. A. E. van Vogt, for instance, put together several books that way and invented a term for them—"fix-up"—such as *The Weapon Makers* (1947) and *The Voyage of the Space Beagle* (1950). Clifford Simak's award-winning *City* (1952) was one of them; Theodore Sturgeon's

More Than Human, another award winner, was another, as well as Daniel Keyes's *Flowers for Algernon* (1966) and Vonda N. McIntyre's *Dreamsnake* (1978).

What may have inspired Clarke was not only the vision he recounts in his foreword but the image with which "Guardian Angel" concludes, the benevolently satanic Karellan making his first appearance with a child on each shoulder. What cosmic purpose could be served by such a contrast? It would have to be the overwhelming theme of a novel, and in it Clarke would be forced to wrestle with the purpose of existence and the definition of good and evil, and the images burned so powerfully into the human imagination by the King James Bible and Milton's *Paradise Lost*.

The author of this outstanding novel was born in 1917 in England, where he grew up nurtured on American SF magazine as he recounted in his autobiographical *Astounding Days*; went to live in Sri Lanka in his middle years; and produced an unusually large number of successful books, in both SF and nonfiction. The best known of these are *2001: A Space Odyssey*, a novelization of the Stanley Kubrick and Clarke film; *Rendezvous with Rama*; and *The Fountains of Paradise*, all selections of the Masterpieces of Science Fiction series.

DOOMSDAY BOOK
CONNIE WILLIS

It's about time.

Connie Willis has written a great many stories and ten novels. Three of those novels have dealt with the past, two of them by means of time travel. The first of these, *Lincoln's Dreams* (1987), involved a young woman disturbed by dreams, bordering on reality, about the Civil War. It won Willis the John W. Campbell Memorial Award for the best SF novel of the year. The second was *Doomsday Book*, which won both the Hugo Award for best novel, presented by the fans attending the World Science Fiction Convention, and the Nebula Award, voted by her fellow science-fiction writers. The third was *To Say Nothing of the Dog* (1997), a light-hearted romp through Victorian England, which won a Hugo Award. And a short story, "Fire Watch," published in 1982, won both a Hugo and a Nebula. Clearly time is the road to travel. At the end of it lies, if not fame and fortune, at least an award and the approbation of readers and peers.

Doomsday Book was published as a 445-page trade paperback by Bantam Books in July 1992. It had its first hardcover edition two months later by the Science Fiction Book Club and a second hardcover edition (527 pages) by New English Library. The first mass-market edition was published by NEL at 650 pages in August of 1993, and the second at 578 pages a month later by Bantam. It was reprinted by Bantam a year later with a new cover design.

Doomsday Book and *To Say Nothing of the Dog* presume the development of time travel but not in the isolated-inventor mode of H. G. Wells's 1895 *The Time Machine*. Instead, in the Willis novels, time travel has been developed some years or even decades earlier; the procedures and the protocols have been established. These stories are not about paradoxes, which have been ruled out by the nature of time, but about the impact of the past on contemporary human lives, and the present on the past. The process is controlled by university history departments (curiously in Oxford, England), which is both a blessing and a curse—a blessing in that it is used for legitimate research and governed by cautious procedures, and a curse in that it must suffer through academic bureaucracy and incompetence.

Most of the problems in Willis's novels (problems, of course, are what make stories engrossing as well as revealing) occur because of human errors. That's what happens in *Doomsday Book*, when a young woman obsessed with a desire to study medieval England just before it was engulfed by the Black Death is transported without the necessary technical preparation, and discovering what has happened to her and how to retrieve her is handicapped by an epidemic that hits contemporary Oxford. Kivrin Engle struggles to survive in a vividly realized medieval English village, and to get back to the retrieval site, while Kivrin's distraught mentor fights quarantine and circumstances and uncooperative colleagues to rescue her. Both stories are woven together into a gripping counterpoint.

About her preoccupation with time Willis commented for *The St. James Guide to Science Fiction Writers*: "I have always been fascinated by the problem of time and our place in it, and science fiction has allowed me to explore that theme in a variety of ways. . . . Time travel can be a wonderful aid to history, but the lessons to be learned are not always simple or painless ones. The theme of time is one of endless possibilities, and I find the stories unfolding one after the other as if I hadn't begun."

Willis was born in Denver, educated at the University of Northern Colorado in Greeley (B.A. in English and elementary education in 1967), taught elementary and junior high classes in Branford, Connecticut, from 1967 to 1969, and substituted as a teacher in Woodland Park, Colorado, from 1974 to 1981. She has been a full-time writer since 1982 and now lives in Greeley.

She published her first story in 1971, "Santa Titicaca," in *Worlds of Fantasy*, and a scattering of stories in subsequent years. "Fire Watch," however, marked the beginning of her full-time writing career and the onslaught of awards that has accumulated, at last count, to eight Hugos, six Nebulas, a Campbell, and another dozen *Locus*, *SF Chronicle*, and *Asimov's* Readers' Poll awards. Willis also is much in demand as a witty toastmaster at science-fiction and fantasy conventions.

To the casual reader, Willis's career may seem like an overnight success, but to Willis it must seem as if it's about time.

BRUTE ORBITS
GEORGE ZEBROWSKI

Science fiction is a literature of ideas, and nowhere is this better illustrated than in George Zebrowski's *Brute Orbits*. The novel is a meditation upon the subject of crime and punishment: what is a crime, it asks, and what is appropriate punishment? The answers aren't easy. The novel becomes science fiction when Zebrowski speculates about one possibility for solving Western civilization's growing crime rate and the geometrically increasing costs of building and manning prisons. He suggests that society could convert mined-out asteroids into habitats, fill them with convicts, and send them on long orbits (some taking as long as a century) around the sun. What happens to the people in them and what happens to humanity back on Earth provides the drama.

Brute Orbits, whose title reflects not only the savage vengeance (disguised as rational efficiency) that society exacts but also the frequent brutality of the inmates of these space-lost prisons, offers no brief for crime, but it points out that what is criminal depends upon who makes the laws and who benefits from the crime. The novel does not shrink from punishment, but it does point out that so far nothing much has worked as intended. Howard V. Hendrix, in *The New York Review of Science Fiction*, called it "a slim novel fat with speculative ideas about the role of crime and punishment in the shaping of societies and individual lives."

Zebrowski is comfortable with ideas, and with science, too. Born in Villach, Austria, in 1945, the son of Poles displaced by World War II, he earned his bachelor's degree in philosophy from the State University of New York, Binghamton, and, much later, an M.A. He has served as a copyeditor on a daily newspaper, a lecturer in science fiction, editor of the *SFWA Bulletin*, and a consultant for several major publishers, but mostly he has been a full-time freelance writer. He was one of the first alumni of the famous Clarion Writers Workshop and one of the earliest to win recognition in the field. His first story was published in 1970 and his first novel, *The Omega Point*, in 1972. *Ashes and Stars*, published in 1977, and a previously unpublished third part, were published in 1983 as *The Omega Point Trilogy*.

So far, at least, his major work, until *Brute Orbits*, has been *Macrolife* (1979), which, in Stapledonian fashion, tells the story of how humanity discovers its true home in space, as it fashions asteroids into space habitats and takes off to explore the stars and its own evolutionary future. A companion novel, *Cave of Stars*, was published in 1999. Zebrowski also has published

Sunspacer (1984) and *The Stars Will Speak* (1991); *Stranger Suns* (1991), a *New York Times* Notable Book of the Year; *The Killing Star* (1995, with Charles Pellegrino); several Star Trek novels with Pellegrino and Pamela Sargent; and some seventy short stories, some of which have been collected in *The Monadic Universe* (1977 and 1985), and a number of which have been nominated for the Nebula and the Theodore Sturgeon Award.

Zebrowski also has been active as an editor, with four volumes of an original anthology called *Synergy* and such individual volumes, usually in collaboration, as *Tomorrow Today* (1975), *Faster than Light* (1976), *Human Machines* (1975), *The Best of Thomas N. Scortia* (1981), *Beneath a Red Star: Studies in International Science Fiction* (1991), *Creations: The Quest for Origins in Story and Science* (1983), and *Nebula Award Stories 20–22* (1985, 1987, 1988), as well as ten volumes of science-fiction novels for Crown Publishers and two for White Wolf. His most recent anthology is *Skylife: Space Habitats in Story and Science* (with Gregory Benford, 2000).

Of his own work, Zebrowski has written, "I pay attention to the writerly virtues of style, characterization, and lucid storytelling, as much as I do to what makes a work science fiction—its scientific facts, speculative ideas, and philosophical considerations." He has been called "a hard SF writer with literary intent." As if in response to this self-appraisal, Hendrix called *Brute Orbits* "a philosophical meditation on society and its discontents—as if Plato had written his own *Penal Colony* as a companion piece to *The Republic*, and then Olaf Stapledon had revised and adapted the entire manuscript to his own liking."

Brute Orbits, published in 1998, won the John W. Campbell Memorial Award for the Best Science Fiction Novel of the Year.

CITY
CLIFFORD D. SIMAK

Clifford D. Simak was named the third Grand Master by his writing colleagues in the Science Fiction Writers of America. The first two Awards went to Robert A. Heinlein and Jack Williamson. Simak won many awards as a newspaper reporter and editor for the *Minneapolis Star and Tribune*, but that was another part of his life, and the only things that carried over into the science-fiction world were his rural background and Wisconsin roots. Simak, who was born in Wisconsin in 1904 and died in Minnesota in 1988, became SF's "pastoralist," bringing to *Astounding*'s technological fiction a bracing dose of Yankee shrewdness, small-town independence, and agrarian values.

Astounding gave Simak his opportunity. When John W. Campbell Jr. was appointed editor of *Astounding* in 1937, the thirty-three-year-old reporter, who had already written a few stories but had been discouraged by the limited response, turned to his wife and said, "I can write for Campbell. He won't want the same old thing." Campbell welcomed Simak. In return, Simak helped Campbell create what came to be called, much later, "the Golden Age." Simak wasn't as visible as Heinlein or Isaac Asimov or A. E. van Vogt or even Jack Williamson, off in New Mexico. Simak didn't travel far from his Minneapolis home. But his stories traversed the stars, and he became an integral part of that glorious period in science fiction when it was working out the ideas and the methods that became the heart of the SF genre.

Among those stories were "Hobbies," "Lobby," and "Tools," and the novel *Cosmic Engineers*. Later on he would earn a Hugo Award for "The Big Front Yard." In 1950 Simak found a new market for his fiction in *Galaxy* and there published the first of his major novels, *Time and Again*, which launched him on the most visible part of his career. For *Galaxy* he would write *Ring Around the Sun* and his Hugo Award novel *Way Station* (also a Masterpieces selection). Later on, in the twilight of his career, he won a Nebula for his "Grotto of the Dancing Deer." In between he published about a novel a year, bringing forth such solid books as *They Walked Like Men, All Flesh Is Grass, Why Call Them Back from Heaven?, The Werewolf Principle, The Goblin Reservation*, and *A Choice of Gods*.

But it was the stories that were gathered together under the title *City* that made the biggest difference in his career. Horrified by what he saw in World War II as "man's inhumanity to man," as the news of the German concentration camps filtered back to the United States, Simak began writing stories dealing with a return to a pastoral existence made possible by new technologies (such technologies and such a return as are speculated about today). In this vision, Simak saw a downside to the pastoral in the agoraphobia that would cripple humanity's ability to interact with others and the eventual desertion of Earth by humans seduced by the possibility of transferring their minds into the superior bodies of Jupiter's lepers.

In 1952 Simak brought the stories together within a framework of "These are the stories the dogs tell when the fires burn high and the wind is from the north. Then each family circle gathers at the hearthstone and the pups sit silently and listen and when the story's done they ask many questions:

"'What is Man?' they'll ask.

"Or perhaps: 'What is a city?'

"Or: 'What is a war?'"

City won the International Fantasy Award for 1952. It is one of SF's enduring classics.

FLATLAND
EDWIN A. ABBOTT

Flatland is a curious addition to the Masterpieces of Science Fiction series. It seems as much philosophical speculation as fiction, reminding long-time readers in the field of *Coming Attractions*, a collection of articles published in 1957 by Gnome Press with the explanation by editor Martin Greenberg that these should appeal to science-fiction readers because they contained the same kind of speculation that attracted them to SF.

A genre develops when older forms of communication become inadequate to describe a different reality or a different perception of reality. The reality of science fiction was change, and for science fiction readers to accept change the genre had to undermine the reality that readers saw in their everyday world. Writers invented ways to alter perspective, so that readers could see themselves and their ways of life as arbitrary, the result of chance happenings, not some celestial fiat or inevitable progression. As a genre, science fiction insisted that nothing could be taken for granted.

H. G. Wells tried to shake up Victorian complacency with articles as well as stories and novels, all cautioning his readers that the stability they took for granted might be temporary and that humanity's supremacy might be toppled at any moment. Later authors would introduce alternate histories to show that events might have happened otherwise and speculate about alternate physical laws or conditions or different social, political, and even sexual arrangements.

But the ultimate alienation of the readers from their everyday world was to question reality itself, and many authors managed to undermine humanity's confidence in the everyday world or made different interpretations of sensory input just as plausible. One of the earliest works to do this was a curious work by an English clergyman turned teacher and headmaster. Abbott's *Flatland: A Romance of Many Dimensions* (1884) took contemporary theories about dimensions and visualized what it would mean to live in only two of them instead of three.

The work contains, to be sure, a good deal of satire about Victorian society, but its greatest impact was upon the imaginations of its readers as it visualized for them what life would be like if the world were two dimensional, if it had width and breadth but not height. That might not have made the book a classic had it not been for the ingenuity with which A. Square described his existence and the ways of life enforced by the facts of the two-dimensional world.

Part of the impact of the exercise, as in all good science fiction, is its extension to the world of the reader. *Gulliver's Travels* does only half its job if its readers do not see in themselves the pettiness of the Lilliputians, the grossness of the Brobdingnagians, or the ignobility of the Yahoos. If *Flat-*

land's two-dimensional world shapes the lives of its inhabitants and controls their perceptions, how does humanity's three-dimensional world shape its lives and perceptions? In the second part of the book, Square makes that connection when he visits Lineland and, in turn, is visited by a three-dimensional being named Sphere, for whom Square imagines the unimaginable (for three-dimensional beings) four-dimensional world.

FLOWERS FOR ALGERNON
DANIEL KEYES

In 1960, the sixth time the Hugo Awards for fiction were presented, the prize for short fiction went to Daniel Keyes's "Flowers for Algernon." Only two awards for fiction were presented; the novel award went to Robert A. Heinlein's *Starship Troopers*. In his collection, *The Hugo Winners* Volume I, Isaac Asimov made his usual Bob Hope-like complaint about handing out awards to other writers, but he noted about "Flowers for Algernon" that "here was a story which struck me so forcefully that I was actually lost in admiration as I read it. So lost in admiration was I for the delicacy of his feeling, for the skill with which he handled the remarkable *tour de force* involved in his telling the story, that I completely forgot to hate him."

So when Asimov announced the award, he recalled, "My winged words cleft the air impassionedly as I deliver an impromptu economium on the manifold excellences of Daniel Keyes. 'How did he do it?' I demanded of the Muses. 'How did he do it?' . . .

"A hand plucked my elbow and I brought my eyes down to ordinary man-height. And, from the round and gentle face of Daniel Keyes, issued the immortal words: 'Listen, when you find out how I did it, let me know, will you? I want to do it again.'"

Six years later he did it again—in a way. He expanded the novella into a novel with the same title. It shared (with Samuel R. Delany's *Babel-17*) the second Nebula novel award ever presented. The first went to Frank Herbert's *Dune*. It was good company. Interestingly, another novel by Heinlein, *The Moon Is a Harsh Mistress*, which came in third in the Nebulas, won the Hugo Award that year; *Flowers for Algernon* was a finalist.

Flowers for Algernon had two more Hugo nominations in its dramatic forms: the television dramatization, "The Two Worlds of Charlie Gordon" (1962), which lost out to *The Twilight Zone*; and the feature film *Charly* (1968), which was edged out by *2001: A Space Odyssey*, but won the best actor Academy Award for its star, Cliff Robertson.

Flowers for Algernon clearly was an inspired piece of writing, perhaps presided over by the Muses that Asimov invoked. Keyes wrote two other novels but neither of them was science fiction, and although successful as novels and in popular acceptance, neither had the impact of Keyes's masterpiece. Sometimes it happens only once. Of course, if the work is *Flowers for Algernon,* science fiction should be thankful that it happened at all. Better than anything else, it demonstrated to science fiction, and to its authors, the dramatic potential of confessional fiction.

Keyes got his literary start in science fiction, working as associate editor of *Marvel Tales* in 1950–1951 and associate editor of Stadium Publishing in 1951–1952, before turning to photography and then to the teaching of English, first in a Brooklyn high school, then at Wayne State University, and finally at Ohio University, where he was a full professor and sometimes director of creative writing. His other books include *The Touch* (1968), *The Fifth Sally* (1980), *The Minds of Billy Milligan* (1981), and *Unveiling Claudia* (1986).

THE ISLAND OF DR. MOREAU
H. G. WELLS

H. G. Wells was at the beginning of a remarkable literary career when *The Island of Dr. Moreau* was published in 1896. He had struggled through a difficult childhood in an unsuccessful crockery shop. His mother had been an upstairs maid and desperately aspired to middle class for herself and her children; his father had been a gardener and played professional cricket. His mother wanted the young "Bertie" safely apprenticed as a draper or a chemist and "getting on," but Wells saw education as his escape and used his keen intelligence and writing skills as his keys to fame and fortune.

His success in the new schools and credit-by-examination created by the Education Act of 1871 earned him a scholarship to the Normal School of Science and three years of college highlighted by his year of biology under the great Thomas Henry Huxley. After teaching for three years, the young Wells started writing—articles at first (the first was published in 1891) and a biology text. Then, in 1894, the editor of the *Pall Mall Budget* invited Wells to write some "single sitting" stories of science, and Wells found his true vocation. The next year for W. E. Henley, he rewrote as fiction a series of articles about time travel, and *The Time Machine*, and Wells, were well launched into the future.

The Time Machine changed the course of science fiction that had been started on its way by Mary Shelley and Edgar Allan Poe and Jules Verne. Wells's short stories and the novels he wrote between 1895 and 1901 provided a new and more productive source for the science fiction that would be developed in the magazines published between 1926 and 1960. Wellsian fiction would be based on ideas rather than on discovery and adventure.

But all that was uncertain when *The Island of Dr. Moreau* appeared. Always a man at home with passion as well as with ideas, Wells's unhappy marriage with his cousin Isabel had come to separation in 1894 and divorce in 1895, and that same year he had married his student Amy Catherine Robbins, with whom he had experienced the first of a series of affairs that would last his entire adult life. His income from writing had nearly doubled between 1893 and 1894 and would increase by at least 50 percent a year for the next few years, but *The Island of Dr. Moreau* was not the novel Wells might have chosen to solidify the reputation he had initiated with *The Time Machine*. It was not, for instance, the spectacular success of *The War of the Worlds* (1898) or even *The Invisible Man* (1897), *When the Sleeper Wakes* (1899), or *The First Men in the Moon* (1901).

The Island of Dr. Moreau was controversial, stirring up the critics and the antivivisectionists. It was a serious novel, dealing as it did with the forced evolution of animals into people. But it was on a direct intellectual line from Huxley and Wells's articles through *The Time Machine* in its attempt to show the suffering that evolution has inflicted on creatures as they have come through the fires of changing environments and natural selection to their present condition. Looking back upon the novel today, however, it stands as one of Wells's artistic triumphs, and one of the contributions the author made to the continuing meditation of science fiction on the origin and condition of the human species. Even the transformation of animals into people has remained one of SF's most familiar themes, expressing itself in ways as different as Cordwainer Smith's "underpeople" and David Brin's "uplift" process.

THE SWORD OF THE LICTOR
GENE WOLFE

The tetralogy that began with *The Shadow of the Torturer* and continued with *The Claw of the Conciliator* gained new momentum with *The Sword of the Lictor*. Although each of these novels tells a complete story, together they form part of the epic journey of the young man Severian that ends in *The Citadel of the Autarch*. Unlike many series, that are tacked on to one another like Tinkertoys, the four compose the single great novel the author titles *The Book of the New Sun*.

That tetralogy, later extended by popular demand to *The Urth of the New Sun*, became one of the shaping works of the 1980s. The first volume won a World Fantasy Award for 1980; the second, a Nebula Award for 1981; and the fourth, the John W. Campbell Award for 1983. Their subtle blending of fantasy and science fiction traditions prepared a reading public for the intermingling of the two genres that has characterized some of the most significant work of the past half-dozen years, and their success in the marketplace has opened the door to more adventurous stylistic experiments.

Wolfe throws the reader into his far-future world without guide or guidebook. That world is so fantastic that Severian's narrative begins like colorful sword-and-sorcery. Gradually, however, the rationales of science fiction appear, bit by bit, although the difficulties of translating the remote future into contemporary terms remain so great that some mysteries remain teasingly veiled.

Readers caught up in the complex narrative found explanations for the novel's intricacies in the essays published in *The Castle of the Otter*, and those wanting more of the stories embedded in the narrative turned to such chapbooks as *The Boy Who Hooked the Sun: A Tale from the Book of Wonders of Urth and Sky* and *Empires of Foliage and Flower: A Tale from the Book of Wonders of Urth and Sky*.

The creator of this fabulous world was born in Brooklyn in 1931, raised in Texas where he attended Texas A&M and was graduated from the University of Houston with a bachelor's degree in mechanical engineering, and served as a project engineer for Procter and Gamble for sixteen years and then senior editor for *Plant Engineering* for twelve years. His first published story appeared in 1965 and his first science-fiction story, "Trip, Trap," in *Orbit* in 1967. After a series of stories in *Orbit*, Wolfe published his first novel, *Operation Ares*, in 1970, but *The Fifth Head of Cerebrus* (1972) established his reputation for complexity and demands on the reader's attention.

The Book of the New Sun, the first three volumes of which now have been published in the Masterpieces series, brought together Wolfe's stylistic inventiveness and his narrative subtlety into a seamless whole. He became a full-time writer in 1984 and produced, among other stories and novels, a two-volume series, *Soldier of the Mist* (1986) and *Soldier of Arete* (1989), that tells the story of a Greek soldier who cannot remember anything more than twenty-four hours. More recently Wolfe began another four-volume epic, the Starcrosser's Planetfall series, with *Nightside the Long Sun* (1993).

The Encyclopedia of Science Fiction called Wolfe "neither the most popular nor the most influential author" in the science-fiction field, but "today quite possibly the most important." The encyclopedia concludes that Wolfe's "importance does not lie in [the Larry Niven or Greg Bear] kind of originality," but "in a spongelike ability to assimilate generic models and devices, and in the quality of the transformations he effects upon that material."

JEM
FREDERIK POHL

The life of Frederik Pohl is like a history of American science fiction. In fact, Pohl titled his memoirs *The Way the Future Was*. Although he was born in 1920 and the science-fiction magazine was not created until 1926, they grew up together and Pohl and science fiction have reflected each other ever since the middle of the 1930s.

The first stage was fandom. The founder of *Amazing Stories*, Hugo Gernsback, in 1934 announced in *Wonder Stories* the formation of the Science Fiction League, an organization for that developing group of involved readers who became known as SF fans. One of the first to respond was Brooklyn-born Pohl, who joined one group of fans and then another until he became part of the Futurians, which also contained such other future writers, editors, agents, and publishers of science fiction as Isaac Asimov, Cyril Kornbluth, Joseph Dockweiler, James Blish, Judith Merril, Damon Knight, Robert A. W. Lowndes, Richard Wilson, and Donald A. Wollheim.

In 1939 Pohl became an editor. He was nineteen years old, and his wages were $10 a week plus all the stories he could buy from himself. That was how he and a number of his fellow Futurians got their first publications, under a variety of pseudonyms. After World War II, in which Pohl served as a weatherman for the U.S. Army, he worked for an advertising agency and then took over the Dirk Wylie Literary Agency founded by his Futurian comrade, the late Joseph Dockweiler. At one time Pohl served as agent for 90 percent of the science-fiction writers in the world.

But Pohl was too tender-hearted with his writers to make a living as an agent, and his own writing had taken off with the first work under his own name, the classic *The Space Merchants* (1953) written in collaboration with Kornbluth and serialized as *Gravy Planet* in *Galaxy*. Pohl sold a good many stories and novels to *Galaxy* in his witty, satirical style, many in collaboration with Kornbluth (until Kornbluth's early death in 1958). Later Pohl edited the magazine he had helped put out, *Galaxy*, and added *If* and *Worlds of Tomorrow*, and won three consecutive Hugo awards for best magazine. After *Galaxy* was sold and he gave up the editorship, he served as science-fiction editor for Ace Books and then for Bantam.

Pohl has been president of the Science Fiction Writers of America and of the international organization, World SF, but mostly he has been a writer. His early work brought satire firmly into the SF repertoire. In the 1970s he replaced the quizzical eyebrow with a more serious gaze and won a Nebula Award in 1977 for *Man Plus* and a Hugo, Nebula, and Campbell Award in 1978 for his win-everything *Gateway*. He has won two Hugos for his short fiction and the Campbell Award again in 1985 for *The Years of the City*. In 1992 he was presented the Grand Master Award of SFWA. He has written three dozen SF novels, a dozen-and-a-half collections of stories, more than half-a-dozen other novels, and edited nearly two dozen anthologies.

As science fiction has become a respectable member of the literary community, so has Pohl. He became a much-in-demand lecturer on SF and futurist topics, and the only time the American Book Award presented an award for a science-fiction novel, it went to Pohl's *Jem: The Making of a Utopia*.

THE LOST WORLD
ARTHUR CONAN DOYLE

Sir Arthur Conan Doyle, one of a sizable number of physicians who turned to writing as a second career, is best known for his creation of the incomparable detective Sherlock Holmes. He was fondest, however, of his historical novels such as *Micah Clarke* (1889) and *The White Company* (1891). In the third decade of his writing career he turned to science fiction. He began with a flourish in 1912, writing about dinosaurs discovered on a nearly inaccessible plateau in South America, *The Lost World*. It was filmed twice, one of them a classic silent film in 1925, with Wallace Beery as the irascible Professor Challenger, a second time in 1960 with Claude Rains.

Born in Edinburgh in 1859, Doyle was educated in Lancashire and Austria before studying medicine for five years at the University of Edinburgh. He practiced medicine for eight years in Southsea and for three years as senior physician in a field hospital in South Africa during the Boer War. But he already had made a good start in fiction, publishing half-a-dozen novels by 1891, including the first two Sherlock Holmes novels, *A Study in Scarlet* (1887) and *The Sign of Four* (1890). It was the success of Holmes in short story form, however, that encouraged Doyle to turn to full-time writing in 1891; *The Strand Magazine* was founded that year, and the publication of six Sherlock Holmes consecutively between July and December made Doyle's reputation.

Doyle had written something like science fiction earlier in his career, with *The Doings of Raffles Haw* (1891), about the making of gold, and such short stories as "The Los Amigos Fiasco" (1892) and "The Great Kleinplatz Experiment" (1894), but he put that aside for two decades while he was busy with other writing. The success of *The Lost World*, however, encouraged Doyle to produce other work in the category, most featuring Professor Challenger, such as *The Poison Belt* (1913), *The Land of Mist* (1925), "When the World Screamed" (1928), and "The Disintegration Machine" (1929). He also wrote some SF stories in which Professor Challenger did not figure, such as "The Maracot Deep."

The Lost World was every SF reader's favorite, combining all the elements of intrepid explorers venturing into the unknown to discover the marvelous that has eternally attracted young readers. "There are heroisms all around us waiting to be done," one character remarks, and another, the newspaper reporter Edward Malone, remarks, "Our eyes have seen great wonders." Experiences such as these helped identify science fiction with the emotional response that critics have called "sense of wonder."

The Lost World also may have helped reinvigorate the lost-race, lost-world genre that had been created, almost singlehandedly, by H. Rider Haggard (1856–1925) with *King Solomon's Mine* (1885) and *She* (1886). Edgar Rice Burroughs had already begun his Mars novels with *Under the Moons of Mars* (1912), but *At the Earth's Core* would not be serialized for another year and *The Land That Time Forgot*, for another decade. Meanwhile, the lost-world story would flourish in the pulp magazines in the hands of authors such as A. Merritt, Charles B. Stilson, J. U. Giesy, Ray Cummings, and Austin Hall and Homer Eon Flint.

Doyle died in 1930.

THE DEAD ZONE
STEPHEN KING

Stephen King is the most popular author of contemporary times and maybe, considering the rapidity and dedication with which he writes and the audience his work has reached, the most successful of all time. That kind of judgment is easy to defend. The criteria are quantifiable: eighty million books in print by 1992, and if one added his film and TV viewers (most of his books have been filmed and the rest are under option), the total audience for King's work would surpass the number of the world's population that can read English. The more difficult task is to analyze the reasons for King's success.

To raise the question is not to suggest that King's writing skills aren't evident in everything he publishes. But writers don't reach his eminence by craftsmanship alone. Some of his contemporaries may write as well. And, although his gifts as a spinner of tales are considerable, other writers also tell engrossing stories. Part of what makes King, as David J. Skal wrote in *The Monster Show*, "the most successful storyteller in human history," must lie in what he writes about.

Every generation has a dream that touches its most profound hopes and aspirations, and a nightmare that exposes its guilts and terrors, and those writers who put into words those dreams or nightmares find an audience that takes the stories to its heart. Readers may not know why they respond; many know only that the stories speak to their inmost concerns. Skal went on to say about King and the 1980s, "by day Ronald Reagan told people stories about their social prospects they wanted to hear. By night, King told very different stories people didn't want to hear directly, but would devour if presented in the veiled images of vampires, werewolves, rabid dogs, demonic automobiles, geeky outsiders with vengeful psychic abilities, and the omnipresent favorite, the walking, rotting dead."

The book-review editor for *The Kansas City Star*, Steve Paul, asked in an article about "Violence in the Arts," "Is Stephen King our Homer, our Dante? Has he captured the history, the anxieties of late 20th century life and fed them back to us, morsel by rotting morsel?" At least this much is undeniable: No one becomes a best-selling author without writing about those things that a great many readers consider important in their lives. The oddest aspect of King's success is that his subject has been the horror lurking in the neighborhood. Or maybe not so odd considering the omnipresence of casual violence in today's world. Perhaps by attributing such acts to evil, even irresistible evil, readers can find some meaning in their everyday world or purge their fears of pointless death.

One of King's seminal predecessors in contemporary horror, H. P. Lovecraft, labored long in the dark cellars of ancestral guilt. Like Poe, who pioneered the horror story as so many others, Lovecraft had many admirers but, like Poe, earned no Kingly rewards. Most of Lovecraft's literary success came when his work was reprinted in books, many years after his death in 1937. Lovecraft's horror, however, like Poe's, depended upon special places and unusual circumstances; King's happened in the light of day and just around the corner from where his readers lived. King brought horror into everybody's everyday existence.

That was part of King's success, making his readers see the potential for horror in the places they knew and the things they did. But that wasn't all the answer. Perhaps it takes a combination of characteristics: the horror in everyday life, the believable characters who seem much like his readers' neighbors, King's ability to spin tales that made compulsive page turners of every King reader, and, the aspect seldom noticed by readers and critics, King's writing skills.

In his writing, King has the eye of an artist, which sees all the small details that ordinary observers miss, and the voice of a storyteller. Not for him the restrictions of a single viewpoint or a detached observer. King is the omniscient narrator, knowing everything, including the secret stories in the hidden places of everybody's mind, and choosing what to reveal and how to arrange the incidents for greatest impact.

Among his intimate observations is the way in which contemporary reality is shaped by inventions and the brand names given them by manufacturers eager to achieve product loyalty. When Johnny Smith wakes from a fifty-five-month coma, the clearest evidence that time has passed is the introduction of a new technology. A simple one: his doctor is using a fiber-point pen. And not just any pen: it is a Flair. King's observation is minute; such day-by-day innovations that pass the average citizen unnoticed would seem miraculous to an awakened sleeper. That insight is underscored by the brand name. The American mind shuns the generic; it calls all cola drinks "Cokes," xerograph copies, "Xeroxes," tissues, "Kleenex."

A bit later Johnny describes the ephemeral nature of possessions: "Your kid clothes were handed down or packed off to the Salvation Army; your Donald Duck watch sprung its mainspring; your Red Ryder cowboy boots wore out. The wallet you made in your first camp handicrafts class got replaced by a Lord Buxton . . ." The brand names, the specificities, are important in placing the story in a contemporary context; in a work of imaginative fiction not only the brand names but the other closely reported aspects of scene convince the reader of the reality of what might otherwise be dismissed as too fantastic to be believed.

Perhaps as little noticed as King's other writing skills is his artfulness with word and phrase. He demonstrates a particular fondness for the unabashed metaphor, a bit of imagery phrased in poetry of the streets, like a contemporary Raymond Chandler. "Struck in the chest with an invisible sledge hammer while jogging," King writes in *The Dead Zone*, and "the colossal demolition derby of Job's life." The rapid reader, pulled irresistibly along by King's story, might do well to slow down and smell the flowers—of speech.

King has made his greatest reputation and attained his greatest following in the field of horror, most of it dealing with the fantasy elements of possession and the supernatural. But the graduate of the University of Maine began his career as an admirer of science fiction, in which the events all have natural explanations, and King's first novel, *Carrie*, published in 1974 when its desperate author was twenty-seven, is a horror story told in science-fiction terms. Since then King has written many stories and novels that would have been published as science fiction if the name of the author were not more important than the genre. Although he does not restrict himself in his storytelling, King does narrow his range when he deals with the subjects traditionally classified as science fiction. Not for him the far-flung depths of space and time; King sticks to the here and now, and mostly to those kinds of changes that require little technology and little knowledge of science. King writes in that area known as science fantasy, where the unknown powers that people acquire—telekinesis in *Carrie*, pyrokinesis in *Firestarter*, precognition in *The Dead Zone*—are rationalized as possible abilities for which science has not yet come up with an explanation. But the here and now is King's arena, and the simply understood phenomenon, with all its manifold human implications, is far more likely to reach King's far-flung audience.

Even in such science-fiction scenarios as *The Dead Zone*, however, King's intent scrutiny manifests itself. He makes Johnny Smith's ability plausible by raising every conceivable objection to it; Johnny is surrounded by skeptics. In fact, the novel is more about the difficulty of having an unusual, inexplicable ability accepted than about the wonders one might achieve with it. Like much good science fiction—H. G. Wells's *The Invisible Man* is a case in point— *The Dead Zone* takes a familiar wish, in this case the ability to foresee the future, and exposes its drawbacks.

In the process King deals with all the problems: How does one recognize the future when one sees it? How would such a vision work? What previsions should be revealed to the people they affect? Johnny's physician even offers a medical explanation for the changes in Johnny's brain that create, on one hand, a "dead zone" and, on the other, "an awakening of a section of the cerebrum within the parietal lobe." King considers the questions of prevision with the same intensity that he considers the scene that he is describing. The only issue that he chooses not to explore is the logic of foreknowledge: If the perceived future can be changed, then what is it that is foreseen? Possibilities? Probabilities? Alternate timelines?

But these are technicalities for others that would only distract King's readers from his primary focus: the exploration of the contemporary human psyche as it is revealed by the stresses of extreme circumstances treated as part of everyday reality. At that King is the undisputed master, no less in *The Dead Zone* than in his more celebrated horror novels.

Masterpieces of Fantasy

THE OTHER SIDE OF THE MIRROR

In the middle of the 1990s Easton Press decided to add a Masterpieces of Fantasy series to its two science-fiction series. But fantasy is a different genre than science fiction—some students of genre, notably the late Damon Knight, disagree—and their audiences overlap but do not coincide. For reasons that may have had little to do with the nature of genres, Easton decided to treat the fantasy series differently: introductions would not be included. I felt that was a mistake—a masterpieces series needed the statement of a principle that distinguished these books from others and individual justifications for why these works had reasons to be called "masterpieces."

But Easton's collective mind was made up, and I volunteered to write "expanded collector's notes" for the series. "Expanded" meant that the notes were twice as long—four pages rather than two—about the length of one of my introductions—printed on both sides of a separate sheet and included between the cover and the front sheet. Moreover, I decided to begin each "note" with an essay about the nature of fantasy and how it distinguished itself from other genres. Then—after a break—I discussed the virtues of the work at hand.

I gave a general title to the series of collector's notes: The Other Side of the Mirror—a metaphor for fantasy from Lewis Carroll's *Through the Looking Glass*—and began each note with "The subject is fantasy." I've omitted that sentence from most of collector's notes reprinted here, as well as the general title that preceded each one. That would soon grow tiresome. But I hope that my ruminations about fantasy do not.

NINE PRINCES IN AMBER
ROGER ZELAZNY

As a way of introducing the books that will make up Easton Press's Masterpieces of Fantasy, these pages and the ones that follow will discuss various aspects of the genre of fiction that we call fantasy. Questions will be addressed that might reasonably arise when a series called "Masterpieces of Fantasy" is offered to subscribers. What is fantasy? How do we recognize it? How do we distinguish it from other kinds of nonrealistic fiction? How does it affect its readers and how are these effects achieved? By what criteria do we recognize excellence in the genre? How does the work at hand qualify as a "masterpiece"?

Some subscribers may be attracted only to the enjoyment of the reading itself, or the collecting, and find discussions of it at best a waste of time and at worst a detraction to their pleasure in reading. If that is the case, they may skip the discussion, if they have not already done so, and, if they wish, come back to the information about the book and its author after they have finished the book.

But I believe that collectors have a deeper involvement than ordinary readers and that they want to think about what makes a particular kind of fiction important to them. If that is true, they may enjoy discussions about what makes fantasy what it is.

A scholar named Darko Suvin once suggested that a genre is a set of collective expectations created in readers by their previous reading experience. We recognize genres, that is, just as we recognize food or people or places, because we have encountered them before. That recognition sets up expectations that, as readers, we see fulfilled or frustrated or, in some cases, expanded or altered in ways that we find surprising and often pleasurable. By such means do genres grow, and by such means do genre works distinguish themselves from one another.

Another scholar, Brian Attebery, has suggested that a genre may be thought of as a gigantic single volume; the more a person has read in that volume the more he or she will get from further reading in it. An introduction to a genre work, then, may be considered a substitute for greater experience in the genre or a reminder to readers of their previous experience; it identifies the characteristics that the work shares with other works in the genre and suggests how the work at hand distinguishes itself from the rest.

What is this genre called fantasy? How do we recognize it?

The process starts at an early age when we begin to distinguish between statements of fact, or those believed by their speakers to be fact, and statements of fiction, or those clearly not fact and intended to be recognized as such. "All poets are liars," Aristotle wrote.

Further discrimination divides fiction between that intended to represent the real world, or "the way things are," and that which takes the reader into unreal worlds, where "things are not as we know them to be." As children we encounter fairy tales and quickly learn that "once upon a time" is prelude to an encounter with princes and princesses and fairy godmothers and witches that now do not exist and, indeed, never existed in this fashion.

"Once upon a time" is a ritual beginning that creates a world of expectations. It is our open sesame to the worlds of make believe and what if. Expectations are our guide to reading a work. We read genres in different frames of mind; indeed, if we are to read them correctly (that is, to get out of them everything they have to offer), we must learn how to read them; we must learn the protocols that open them for our enjoyment.

A good author helps by including instructions. Unobtrusively, of course. "Once upon a time," for instance, tells us to read the story as a fairy tale. When we enter another world through a rabbit hole or a looking glass or a cupboard or a whirlwind or a witch's curse or a magic broomstick or a star to wish upon, the author is telling us by this fanciful translation to the unknown to leave the everyday world behind, with its practical considerations and skeptical questions. Different rules apply. Be open to strangeness. Hold on to your seats for a wild ride of imagination.

So, to conclude this first brief essay on the other side of the mirror, let me suggest that our initial response to fantasy is intuitive. Damon Knight once said that science fiction was what we meant when we pointed at it. That may be the best definition of fantasy as well: we recognize it when we see it. What we see and how we recognize it is a subject for later discussion. Take *Nine Princes in Amber*, for instance.

Roger Zelazny was born in Cleveland in 1937 and died, tragically early, in 1995. Although he earned his greatest fame and fortune from fantasy, that part of his distinguished career began relatively late. After a start as a poet in college, he turned to science fiction and published his first story, "Passion Play," in 1962. He soon was earning award nominations. In his poetic hands, the skillful use of language and development of character began to match the genre's exciting ideas. Within a year Zelazny got a Hugo nomination and within four years won a Hugo for *This Immortal*. The same year he won two Nebula Awards for "He Who Shapes" and "The Doors of His Face, the Lamps of His Mouth." Two years later, in 1967, he published what he, and many others, considered his best novel, *Lord of Light*.

In 1969 he published three novels—*Creatures of Light and Darkness*, *Isle of the Dead*, and *Damnation Alley*—gave up a job with the Social Security Administration, and became a full-time writer. Eight years later *Damnation Alley* was adapted as a feature film. He published another personal favorite, *Doorways in the Sand*, in 1976 and won both the Nebula and the Hugo

Award the same year for "Home Is the Hangman." He won two later Hugo Awards for short fiction.

Even though Zelazny published exclusively in the science-fiction field for his first eight years, much of that work was based on mythology and exotic religions and internal conflicts. Moreover, his interests in Jungian psychology and internal realities should have suggested his metamorphosis into a fiction based on something other than the explainable. Nevertheless, it came as a surprise to many when Zelazny published *Nine Princes in Amber* in 1970.

The fantasy novel was an immediate success, much more than his earlier science-fiction novels; *Nine Princes in Amber* and its sequels gave Zelazny financial independence and led to his incorporation as The Amber Corporation. Eventually he would write ten Amber novels. Five of them feature Corwin and have been assembled as the Chronicles of Amber; the other novels in that sequence are *The Guns of Avalon* (1972), *Sign of the Unicorn* (1975), *The Hand of Oberon* (1976), and *The Courts of Chaos* (1978). Five more feature Corwin's son Merlin: *Trumps of Doom* (1985), *Blood of Amber* (1986), *Sign of Chaos* (1987), *Knight of Shadows* (1989), and *Prince of Chaos* (1991). *A Rhapsody in Amber* (1981) and *Roger Zelazny's Visual Guide to Castle Amber* (1988, with Neil Randall) are associated publications.

By the time of his death, Zelazny had published thirty-six novels, sixteen collections of short stories, and three volumes of poetry, and edited two anthologies. He completed a novel just three days before he died and left a novel manuscript unfinished.

Nine Princes in Amber begins realistically enough with an accident victim in a hospital bed, but we soon realize that the patient is keenly suspicious of his attendants and displays unusual powers of strength, martial skills, and self-healing. The hero experiences the loss of memory that is frequently encountered in fantasy, but he displays an uncanny ability to track down those who might be able to help him recover his past and to conceal his condition in the process. His powers are not simply superhuman—they are magical.

He is, in fact, a Prince of Amber. Amber, we later discover, is the "one true world" and everything else, including the reality with which we readers are familiar, belongs to shadow. Zelazny plays off the reader's expectation that the fantasy world will be subordinate to the real world in which the reader lives. "Amber had always been and always would be, and every other city, everywhere, every other city that existed was but a reflection of the shadow of some phase of Amber."

Nine Princes in Amber can be characterized as high fantasy, which offers a fully realized alternate reality, as opposed to low fantasy, in which the supernatural element enters the real world. Zelazny's novel exhibits some of the characteristics of high fantasy, heightened color, for instance, and sometimes heightened diction. Readers turn to high fantasy to experience brighter scenes and more intense emotional experiences. Virtually every high fantasy narrative offers at least one scene of mind-bending, sense-distorting drama such as the scene in which Corwin walks the Pattern, an experience enhanced by the knowledge that failure is death and only a Prince of Amber can walk the Pattern and live.

There is more, of course, to *Nine Princes in Amber*, just as there is more to the Masterpieces of Fantasy, and more discussion of fantasy to come. Welcome to the other side of the mirror.

MAGICIAN
RAYMOND E. FEIST

The rise of a fantasy genre to widespread popularity among young people (and some not so young) coincided with the creation and broad participation in fantasy role-playing games. It was inevitable, perhaps, that role-playing, much of which was inspired by fiction, would cross-fertilize the fiction itself. Role-playing has produced such science fiction works as Larry Niven's *Dream Park* series with Steven Barnes, as well as others, some utilizing the convention of human translation into computer worlds. The concept of being trapped into real-life games has spread to films like the 1982 *Tron* and, more recently, the adaptation of actual games to film. But the influence of games is most evident in the fantasy from which they sprang. One of its most adept practitioners is Raymond E. Feist, who enjoyed a career as a designer of fantasy role-playing games before he turned to fiction.

The Encyclopedia of Science Fiction traces fantasy games to the late 1960s. It followed on the heels of modern fantasy itself. As David Pringle pointed out in *Modern Fantasy: The Hundred Best Novels*, the U.S. editions of J. R. R. Tolkien's *The Lord of the Rings* came in 1965 and 1966, Robert E. Howard's Conan was revived at almost the same time, Ira Levin's *Rosemary's Baby* was published in 1967, Fritz Leiber's "Fafhrd and the Gray Mouser" stories were collected and began to be published in paperback in 1968, and Ursula K. Le Guin's first Earthsea novel and Peter S. Beagle's *The Last Unicorn* were published the same year. The first important fantasy game, *Slobbovia*, based on Al Capp's "Li'l Abner" was released in 1969. Other fantasy games followed: *Armageddon, Midgard, Battle of Helm's Deep, Siege of Minas Tirith, Sorcerer,* and even *War of the Rings*, based on The *Lord of the Rings*. The first fantasy role-playing game, *Dungeons and Dragons*, developed by Gary Gygax and Dave Arenson, came out in 1974, and soon proliferated into a variety of games, often based on particular novels or mythologies, and a number of money-making spin-offs, such as rule books, character packs, special dice, posters, CDs, magazines, and other products, including novels based upon the games. These, in turn, have branched into game books with decision trees, storytelling games, board games, and, most recently, collectable card games, which have made Wizards of the Coast in Seattle so profitable that it has bought TSR, the owners of *Dungeons and Dragons* and its publishing empire.

Some of the companies that rode the role-playing game wave branched out into general publishing, like TSR, White Wolf, and, for a while, Wizards of the Coast. And the creators of these games, that often consume years of effort, have sometimes turned to the similar, but less exhausting, challenge of writing fantasy novels.

Among them was Raymond E. Feist. His first novel, and still perhaps his best, was *Magician*, published in 1982 and subsequently, in paperback, in two volumes in 1986 as *Magician: Apprentice* and *Magician: Master*. Ian Nichols, in *The St. James Guide to Science Fiction Writers*, compares Feist to mainstream author James Clavell; where Clavell researches his historical novels in great detail, Feist imagines his fantasy worlds with equal detail.

Magician is part of a Riftwar series that continues with *Silverthorn* (1985), *A Darkness at Sethanon* (1986), *Prince of the Blood* (1989), *The King's Buccaneer* (1992), *Shadow of a Dark Queen* (1994), and *Rise of a Merchant Prince* (1995), all placed in the same fantasy world when armies and magicians from another dimension invade the world of Midkemia. The "rifts" between dimensions serve as portals between the worlds.

The fantasyland of Midkemia is medieval, dominated by the castle of Crydee, where two young friends, Tomas and Pug, are apprenticed to the sword master and the court magician, respectively, until they are separated by the invasion from the oriental, militaristic Kelewan. In some ways it is a typical bildungsroman, as Tomas learns to be a hero and Pug to be a wizard, and both learn that they must play vital roles in the upcoming battle, but it also is a struggle of realities, as the reader learns that underneath the immediate conflict is an ancient war between the Valheru and the gods who have established their own domains upon Midkemia.

Feist's narrative technique is to feature several protagonists rather than one and to follow each in turn to a cliff-hanging conclusion at the end of each chapter. It is a technique older than its earlier master, Edgar Rice Burroughs, but nobody does it better than Feist. The fantasies also feature many of the characteristics classified by John Clute in *The Encyclopedia of Fantasy*.

Much of what Clute has to say about fantasy is drawn from the example of J. R. R. Tolkien's *The Lord of the Rings*, which Clute considers "the paradigm 20th-century text." Clute writes, "When set in this world, [fantasy] tells a story which is impossible in the world as we perceive it; when set in an otherworld, the otherworld will be impossible, though stories set there may be possible in its terms." Clute traces the "otherworld" concept to a statement on "The Fantastic Imagination" by George MacDonald in his 1893 *A Dish of*

Orts: "The natural world has its laws, [which] themselves may suggest laws of other kinds, and man may, if he pleases, invent a little world of his own, with its own laws." The "natural venue" for what Clute calls "the self-coherent impossible tale" is "an internally coherent impossible world in which that tale is possible." Finally, Clute says that "a fantasy text may be described as the story of an earned passage from bondage—via a central recognition of what has been revealed and of what is about to happen, and which may involve a profound metamorphosis of protagonist or world (or both)—into the eucatastrophe, where marriages may occur, just governance fertilize the barren land, and there is a healing."

In his 1939 essay "On Fairy-Tales" (later twice expanded), Tolkien himself described fantasy as a tale set in the enchantment known as Faerie, and which tells of marvels. He laid down four elements he considered essential to the fairy tale (i.e., fantasy): Fantasy, Recovery, Escape, and Consolation. "Fantasy" involves the "secondary world" that Tolkien did so much to establish as the primary place of fantasy and whose creation in *The Lord of the Rings* provided the modern example that shaped so much of what has subsequently been published. "Recovery" includes "recovery of freshness of vision," which Clute interprets as "a capacity to see things as we are meant . . . to see them." "Escape" is the "escape of the prisoner"—that is, from the modern world into the secondary world. "Consolation," Clute says, means the "eucatastrophe" or happy ending.

Clute differentiates fantasy from those categories often associated with it, supernatural fiction and horror. "Fantasy stories are defined here as stories which require completion, and which can be distinguished from their siblings . . . by this requirement." Supernatural fictions and horror have plots that "often terminate—shockingly—before any resolution can be achieved." "Genre fantasy," he points out, "is normally structured so as to defer completion indefinitely, to lead readers into sequel after sequel."

In a sense Feist fits Clute's definition of an author of genre fantasy, and Clute concludes the entry on Feist in *The Encyclopedia of Fantasy* with the description of Feist as "an adept manipulator of standard materials." In the sense that almost all of Feist's novels have been placed in the secondary world established in his first novel, this judgment has some validity. As Ian Nichols has pointed out, "The initial triad of the Riftwar series, *Magician*, *Silverthorn*, and *A Darkness at Sethanon*, remain Feist's strongest works. Perhaps this is because these were the works which introduced the twin worlds of the Tsurani and Crydee to us, and in which Feist's imagination was given freest rein." But a richly imagined "secondary world" is like a good fantasy role-playing game; the players can produce an infinite number of satisfying variations upon their individual adventures. And Nichols continues: "In the first series, Feist challenged some of the prescripts of the Fantasy genre, and this contributed to the interest which that series held."

The exceptions to the novels placed in the Riftwar series are the books of the Empire series, written in collaboration with Janny Wurts: *Daughter of the Empire* (1987), *Servant of the Empire* (1990), and *Mistress of the Empire* (1992) in which a female protagonist must battle various families to win wealth, husband, and heirs. This series also is structured like a game and includes magicians who flout its laws. Feist also has written a stand-alone novel, *Faerie Tale*, about a house haunted by warring supernatural forces, the abduction of a child, and the quest of his twin to the land of Faerie to obtain his release.

Feist, born in 1945, continues to produce significant work that has reached a sizable audience. As Nichols observes, "What remains to be seen is whether Feist can pull off the trick of creating a fascinating world more than once. He has certainly done so with what he has written so far."

THE MALACIA TAPESTRY
BRIAN W. ALDISS

Fantasy and science fiction share many identifying characteristics; some critics claim that drawing distinctions between them is impossible. Both postulate worlds that differ in some meaningful way from the everyday reality of the here and now. Both are literatures of difference, but fantasy is the literature of disjunction and science fiction is the literature of change. Fantasy exists in a world other than our own, but science fiction exists in a world that our world might become or from which it has developed.

Science fiction lets the reader know how the present world has been changed to its new condition; the reader knows how we got here from there, by spaceship, by the passage of time, by a natural phenomenon or discovery or invention, by time machine. Fantasy's connection to the real world is magical, a passageway that can be traversed only by special people, or only at special times or in special circumstances. Science fiction exists in a world transformed by new knowledge; fantasy occurs in a world in which ancient wisdom still prevails or has been rediscovered or elder powers reveal themselves or are unleashed, or in a world to which one or more persons from the real world have been admitted and whose natural laws are different, or whose natural laws or phenomena find a way into our world.

All this would be unimportant were it not for the fact that people read science fiction and fantasy in different ways and therefore a reader's first necessity is to identify the genre. If the difference in the world from the here and now has been created by a natural process, the story is organized around the way people have responded to the change in their physical and social environment, and the reader must question the text to discover what the change is and how it has occurred. Science fiction demands a skeptical reading to get from it the best of what it has to offer.

In fantasy, however, where the difference has been created by some supernatural passage or transformation or manifestation, to focus on the mechanism of the passage, transformation, or manifestation is to misread the work, or even to make a fantasy reading impossible. Fantasy concerns itself with the manner in which people would behave, and even more in the ways in which they would feel and think, if the events of the world were shaped by desire and will rather than thought and action. The skeptical reading required by science fiction destroys fantasy.

After the transportation of the reader to a world changed by some natural process, the characteristic structure of a science-fiction novel is the exploration of that world and of the way in which people respond to the change in their environment. After the translation of the reader to a world that operates by different principles, the characteristic form of a fantasy novel is the attempt to restore order in a world in which something has gone seriously awry.

Science fiction is about change. Fantasy is about tradition.

A good example is Brian W. Aldiss's *The Malacia Tapestry*, originally published in 1976. Malacia is a city-state somewhat like Florence or Venice during the Renaissance. In fact, *The Malacia Tapestry* shares many characteristics with Renaissance Italy, including a threat of attack by the Ottoman Empire. One historic event referred to in the novel is the death of Suleiman. Suleiman (or Soliman I) was the Ottoman sultan who reigned from 1520 to 1566, was called "the Magnificent" and "the Law Giver," conquered Belgrade and Budapest and other cities, and died in 1566, at the age of seventy-one, while besieging Szigetvar.

The historic placement of Malacia fades into insignificance beside the fact that it has existed for thousands of years in its present condition—which fits no city in history—and has devoted itself to remaining unchanged. According to legend, the founder of Malacia was granted one wish by the First Magician, that the city being created "as a monument to the two religions should forever remain unchanged." The granting of that wish became known as the Original Curse. Since then the duty of the Supreme Council has been to protect Malacia from change.

The timeless quality of Malacia, described by Perian de Chirolo, the narrator of the novel, as "the mellow flow of existence," is what confers on the novel the characteristic concerns of fantasy, tradition and the absence of change. Around the forces pushing for change and the efforts of the establishment to keep things as they are the action of the novel revolves.

Malacia is also a city of privilege and poverty, of opportunity for advancement by good fortune or recognition or marriage, of street merchants and taverns—like any Renaissance city. It also is a city that places reliance on astrologers and fortune-tellers and even on the practice of magic. All of this pales beside one enormous fact: Malacia and the world in which it exists trace their origins to reptilian ancestors. Its inhabitants believe that they descended from dinosaurs. This might be dismissed as mere myth were it not for the fact that "flighted people" and "lizard-men" and "ancestral animals" continue to exist in and around Malacia, as well as mythological creatures such as satyrs. The ancestral animals have strange names such as slobber-gobs, shaggy tusks (mammoths?), marshbags, tyrant-greaves (tyrannosaurus rex?), casque-bodies, hauberks, halberd-heads, and wattle-tassets.

What kind of world is it in which the dinosaurs were not eliminated by a change in climate or, as has been postulated more recently, a meteor strike? Does *The Malacia Tapestry* offer an alternate history in which the dinosaurs survived, like Harry Harrison's later Eden trilogy? At one point Perian's scholarly father speculates "that our world is only one of a number of alchemaically conceivable worlds. In some other worlds of possibility, to take an extreme case, *homo saurus* may have been wiped out entirely—say at the great battle of Itssobeshiqueta-zilaha, over three million, one thousand and seven hundred years ago. The result would be a nightmare world in which one of the other human races had supremacy and Malacia never existed."

If the reader is to accept all these aspects of Malacia as significant to the understanding of the novel, the reader might be forced to find some logical explanation for the historical development of this world in ways that replicate, in many ways, our own. Is the author saying that history would have occurred in almost identical fashion no matter what the origins of humanity or the crucial events of the past? But this would be to read *The Malacia Tapestry* as alternate history and science fiction, and that is to misread it. The saurian ancestors, the satyrs, the historical parallels—these are threads in the multicolored tapestry that is Malacia. Unravel it at your peril.

Gary K. Wolfe in *St. James Guide to Science Fiction Writers* offers the suggestion that the author of this remarkable novel may be "the most significant English writer of science fiction since H. G. Wells." Born in East Dereham, Norfolk, in 1925, Aldiss served in Burma and Sumatra during World War II and on his return to England worked in Oxford bookshops. Fictionalized sketches about bookselling, collected as *The Brightfount Diaries* in 1955, began his writing career. He turned to science fiction in 1954 and to the mainstream best-seller in 1970 with his autobiographical novels *The Hand-Reared Boy*, *A Soldier Erect* (1971), and *A Rude Awakening* (1978). His Squire Quartet was launched in 1980 with *Life in the West*. He became associated with the British New Wave when it was created in the pages of *New Worlds* beginning in 1964, but he retained his appreciation for traditional SF.

Aldiss's bibliography runs to nearly ninety books and plays and the editorship of another thirty volumes. Among his most honored novels have been

Hothouse (Hugo, 1962), *Barefoot in the Head* (1969), *Frankenstein Unbound* (1973; filmed by Roger Corman in 1990), and, most especially, his thoroughly researched hard-SF Helliconia trilogy, based on a planet with an eccentric orbit around two suns that gives it a cycle of seasons lasting for millennia and corresponding adaptations to which its population is forced. The first of these, *Helliconia Spring* (1982), won the John W. Campbell Award for the best SF novel of the year and was followed by *Helliconia Summer* (1983) and *Helliconia Winter* (1985).

Aldiss also has been productive at the shorter lengths. His "The Saliva Tree" won a Nebula Award for 1965, and he has published more than twenty-five collections of short stories. In addition to his other contributions to SF, he has been an active scholar and critic, editing *SF Horizons* with Harrison in the early 1970s, putting together collections of essays and reviews, and writing a carefully considered history of science fiction, *Billion Year Spree* (1973), revised (with David Wingrove) in 1986 when it won the Hugo Award. He has received the Pilgrim Award of the Science Fiction Research Association, the J. Lloyd Eaton Award, and the IAFA distinguished scholarship award. He was guest of honor at the World Science Fiction Convention in 1965 and 1979, and was a founding trustee, and later president, of World SF.

The Encyclopedia of Science Fiction called *The Malacia Tapestry* "a love story with fantastic elements." That could also be a description of Aldiss's relationship with science fiction.

MYTHAGO WOOD
ROBERT HOLDSTOCK

"Some places cry out for a murder," and sometimes murder seeks out a place to happen. So it is, too, with fantasy. Most fantasies require special circumstances. Those that do not, that happen in the glaring light of day, have the unique quality of reconciliation with the everyday world, the kind of quality that John W. Campbell's *Unknown* pioneered and James Blish's *Black Easter* and *The Day After Judgment* exemplified. But fantasies, like alchemy and psychic powers and mushrooms, thrive best in the dark cellars of the world.

All of this, of course, is an aspect of the romantic notion that humanity has a special relationship to the universe, that, indeed, the universe was created to provide a home for humanity and that it responds to human needs or apprehensions or emotions—or, alternatively, that the universe was created by or for some other kind of beings, usually creatures older, wiser, and more powerful, and humanity is a latecomer or an interloper. The extreme form of this romantic notion was called by John Ruskin the *pathetic fallacy*, in which nature reflects human emotional states, the heavens weeping when we grieve, the sun beaming when we are joyful.

Since fantasy is basically romantic, the relationship is understandable. Science fiction is the literature of the rational mind and focuses on the ability of intelligence to shape the resistant world through the manipulation of natural law.

Fantasy is the literature of the human will and deals with the ability of chosen people to shape the malleable world by means of ancient wisdom.

Fantasy does not require the plausibility of science fiction. Fantasy assumes a hierarchical world governed by supernatural powers, and that those powers surrender their secrets to those who place themselves in the proper relationship with it. And yet fantasy must explain why the world seems to be governed by natural law rather than by supernatural whim.

Sometimes the explanation is that the world only *seems* to be governed by natural law, that this is a surface reality covering a deeper reality, as in Roger Zelazny's *Nine Princes of Amber*. Sometimes the everyday reality that seems to operate without magic or miracles is the result of the abandonment of the world by the supernatural forces that once controlled it, as in the mythology created by H. P. Lovecraft, or by the gods and goddesses, or demons, who have been lost to the modern world because they have been displaced by science or offended by contemporary skepticism. Most often the explanation offered by the fantasy is that the supernatural still can be found in our modern world—*but only in special places.*

Some places, of course, cry out for fantasy: a dark closet, an ancient castle, a dusty attic, a creepy cellar, a cemetery, a mortuary, a cloud kingdom, a magic pool, an enchanted forest . . . These are the locations where people can be alone with their dreams and their fears, and, alone, they can indulge their imaginations and create their own worlds of maybe or might have been. Childhood is the time when fantasy begins, when perceptions have not yet been conditioned to see things the way the world sees them, when the mind has not yet been taught to discriminate between the things that are real and the things that *might* be real or *ought* to be real, or could be willed into existence. Fantasy may be the recollections of such childhood uncertainties, and its truths may reflect the psychological adjustments the child makes to the adult world.

Some scholars of the fantastic have divided fantasy into two major types: high fantasy, which offers a fully realized alternate reality, such as that in *Nine Princes in Amber*, and low fantasy, in which the supernatural element enters the real world. Low fantasy is what we are concerned with here. The entrance of the supernatural element into the real world must be psychologically appropriate if readers are to yield their necessary suspension of disbelief.

Sometimes the supernatural is summoned by magical spells or incantations, or simply wished into existence by lonely or angry or frightened people. Sometimes it enters without invitation, sneaking into the world or into the lives of special people, or bursting through the flimsy wall that separates the world from creatures that lurk outside.

But mostly they require special circumstances: a pentacle engraved in just the right way, midnight of some special day in some special place, an unhallowed altar and an unholy sacrifice, unspeakable rites . . . How would the reader respond to Frankenstein's monster without the storm gathering above the lonely castle and the electrical apparatus laddering its discharges while a mad scientist glares down at a monstrous shape upon his operating table stirring into life? Shakespeare wrote about such matters in *A Midsummer Night's Dream*: "As imagination bodies forth / The form of things unknown, the poet's pen; Turns them to shapes, and gives to airy nothing / A local habitation and a name."

One of the persistent places of mystery and enchantment have been forests. Dante began his descent into hell with the lines: "In the middle of our life I came to myself in a dark wood where the straight way was lost." In Pilgrim America forests were the places that had not yet been tamed or brought to plow and still belonged to savagery and savages, and authors such as Nathaniel Hawthorne, in "Young Goodman Brown," made it a site for witches' sabbaths. Robert Holdstock, in *Mythago Wood*, explains the human distrust of forests as the conflict between people pushing back north at the end of the last ice age and forced to clear the forest for farmland: "There would have been a bitter struggle for survival. The wood was desperate and determined to keep the mastery of the land. Man and his fire had been determined that it should not. The beasts of that primal woodland had become dark forces, dark Gods; the wood itself would have been seen to be sentient, creating ghosts and banshees to send against the puny human invader."

Holdstock, the author of *Mythago Wood*, was born in Hythe, Kent, England, in 1948. He earned a bachelor of science degree in applied zoology from the University College of North Wales and a master of science in medical zoology from the London School of Hygiene and Tropical Medicine, but he soon turned to writing, publishing "Pauper's Plot" in *New Worlds* in 1948 while still a student and a number of other short stories collected in *In the Valley of the Statues* (1982).

After serving as a research student for London's Medical Research Council from 1971 to 1974, he turned to full-time writing and produced a number of novels and novelizations under the pseudonyms of Ken Blake, Richard Kirk, Robert Black, Chris Carlsen, Steven Eisler, and Robert Faulcon. Under his own name, he began publishing science-fiction novels, notably *Eye Among the Blind* (1976) and *Earthwind* (1977), but it was the publication of

Mythago Wood in 1984 that gave Holdstock major stature among readers and critics and won the World Fantasy award. It was followed by such sequels as *Lavondyss: Journey to an Unknown Region* (1988) and *The Hollowing* (1993) and the title story of the collection *The Bone Forest* (1991).

Mythago Wood is as archetypal as the creatures that inhabit it. "Mythago" is a word created by Holdstock by combining "myth" and "imago," in the "portmanteau" fashion invented by Lewis Carroll. An "imago" is the term given to a portrait in wax, often of ancestors, of Roman times; in psychoanalysis, it is the conception of the parent retained in the unconscious. Holdstock uses "mythago" to describe the archetypes of ancestral memory. Just as myth is a story of forgotten origins that narrates some ostensibly historical events and embodies the "truth" about gods or peoples, "mythagoes" are the physical survival of ancestral needs, such as King Arthur and Robin Hood, Arthur to protect the Celts from the invading Saxons, Robin to protect the Saxons from tyrannical Normans.

They survive in Mythago Wood, a forest that has remained untouched since the last ice age, a wood that casts its spell upon the family that lives in an isolated dwelling nearby. The forest has the magical quality of being far bigger on the inside than the outside and of protecting itself against casual exploration by confusion and misdirection. In this fashion Holdstock casts over Mythago Wood an aura of mystery, magic, and suspense, as well as an explanation for how it could continue to exist unknown and untouched in the modern world.

Unknown and untouched by all but the family that lives in Oak Lodge and to whose eyes and minds and hearts come the evidences of something otherworldly emanating from the forest that stretches nearby. In Mythago Wood the figures of ancient myth may still survive, and people's desires may take actual form. The novel is an exploration not only of the nearly infinite woods existing within three square miles, but of the depths and heights of human desires and fears and hopes.

John Clute in *The Encyclopedia of Science Fiction* says of the novel and its sequels, "In transforming the Matter of Britain into archetypal sf, [Robert Holdstock] has re-assembled old material, and old generic devices, into a new territory for fiction."

THE UNPLEASANT PROFESSION OF JONATHAN HOAG
ROBERT A. HEINLEIN

The subject is fantasy.

That is what the late John W. Campbell Jr. told himself in 1938, not long after he had become editor of *Astounding Stories*. He would change the name of the eight-year-old magazine to *Astounding Science Fiction* and would transform science fiction, through his own editorial influence and the judicious application of the economic power of his publisher, Street & Smith, into what later would become known as "the Golden Age." But what about fantasy?

Fantasy, of course, was the older form of imaginative fiction, dating back to the beginnings of storytelling itself, with narratives like *Gilgamesh* and *The Odyssey*. But with the arrival of the Industrial Revolution and the Age of Science, science fiction had become the more popular form of fiction that took as its initial premise some significant departure from everyday reality. Of course, a good number of fantasy novels and stories remained popular: the works of Lord Dunsany, for instance, or such children's classics as *Water Babies* or *Peter Pan*, the romantic comedies of Thorne Smith, the planetary fantasies of Edgar Rice Burroughs, the immensely popular romantic fantasies of A. Merritt, and the other science fantasies of the Munsey pulp magazines, a number of which would be reprinted, beginning in 1939, in *Famous Fantastic Mysteries*. But by 1938 no one had been able to create a successful fantasy magazine. In fact, the publishing wisdom of the time was that fantasy simply didn't sell.

Street & Smith experimented with *The Thrill Book* in 1919, and *Weird Tales* had been offering a broad mixture of science fiction, fantasy, and horror since 1923. But *Weird Tales* paid its authors poorly and irregularly, and although it had its faithful readers and survived from month to month and year to year, it never seemed to thrive.

Campbell imagined a different kind of fantasy magazine, one that would combine science fiction's plausibility with fantasy's freedom, and convinced his publisher that he should be allowed to create a companion magazine to *Astounding*. It would be called *Unknown*, and it would publish what might be called "rationalized fantasy." Brian Stableford and Peter Nicholls in *The Encyclopedia of Science Fiction* comment that "fantasy is sf-like when it adopts a cognitive approach to its subject matter, even if that matter is magic." They go on to say that "supernatural fantasy approaches the condition of science fiction when its narrative voice implies a post-scientific consciousness" and science fiction "approaches the condition of fantasy when its narrative voice implies a mystical or even anti-scientific consciousness." This suggests that what Campbell determined to publish in *Unknown* was fantasy written as if it were science fiction. Campbell announced the new magazine in the February 1939 issue of *Astounding*: "It has been the quality of the fantasy you have read in the past that has made the very word anathema.... *Unknown* will be to fantasy what *Astounding* has made itself represent to science fiction. It will offer fantasy of a quality so different from that which has appeared in the past as to change your entire understanding of the term."

The new magazine attracted some of the same writers who were contributing to the young editor's science-fiction magazine: British writer Eric

Frank Russell (whose *Sinister Barrier* was credited by Campbell as "starting in motion the already-laid plans" for *Unknown*), L. Sprague de Camp, L. Ron Hubbard, Theodore Sturgeon, H. L. Gold, Fritz Leiber, Henry Kuttner and C. L. Moore, Jack Williamson, and Robert A. Heinlein.

The magazine was an instant critical success and published a number of classic stories and novels, most of which have been reprinted in book form and persist as part of this masterpieces of fantasy series. The late Thomas D. Clareson in Marshall Tymn and Mike Ashley's *Science Fiction, Fantasy, and Weird Fiction Magazines*, credited *Unknown* with "a major impact on the development of the fantasy genre, and, perhaps more so, on the broader field of science fiction."

Unfortunately, it lasted for only thirty-nine issues. It changed its name to *Unknown Worlds* in 1941, and in 1943 it ceased publication, killed by the wartime paper shortage, although its sales had never been substantial, certainly not as substantial as those of *Astounding*, for whose monthly publication *Unknown Worlds* may have been sacrificed. Its demise is still lamented.

Robert A. Heinlein was just starting his science-fiction career when the first issue of *Unknown* appeared in March 1939. His first story, "Lifeline," would be published in the July 1939 *Astounding*. By September of the following year he had published in *Unknown* a novella called "The Devil Makes the Laws," which he would later reprint as *Magic, Inc.* In May of 1941 Heinlein contributed the classic paranoia story "They," and in October of 1942 the novella "The Unpleasant Profession of Jonathan Hoag." This one he would publish under the pseudonym of John Riverside. The only other out-and-out fantasy he wrote was the 1963 novel *Glory Road*.

Born in 1908 in Butler, Missouri, Heinlein graduated from the Naval Academy in 1929 and retired because of physical disability in 1934. After trying various other occupations, including silver mining, he turned to his old love, science fiction, and discovered the mother lode. He became an instant favorite of science fiction readers and led the field, like SF's own Moses, into one promised land after another (unlike the biblical Moses, Heinlein got to cross his Jordan): his narrative innovations made it possible to write more sophisticated and more effective SF, he broke the SF barrier in the slick magazines, he initiated a tradition of SF juveniles with his series for Scribner's, he wrote and advised on SF films, and finally he made a breakthrough onto the best-seller lists with *Stranger in a Strange Land*. He became one of the first of the full-time science-fiction writers and the first of its millionaires, and for all of these reasons and more he was named the first of the Science Fiction Writers of America's Grand Masters. He has been called "the most influential science fiction writer of all time." Since his death in 1988, his work, which created an SF film renaissance with *Destination Moon* (1950), has been translated into such films as *Robert A. Heinlein's The Puppet Masters* and *Starship Troopers*, with perhaps more to come.

If Heinlein's first love was science fiction, his fantasies all became classics of their kind, and the collection brought together as *The Unpleasant Profession of Jonathan Hoag* has been called, by George Zebrowski, "one of the great collections of short fiction by an American writer in contemporary times." Published originally in 1959 in hardcover by Gnome Press, it has often been reprinted in paperback. It includes not only the title story but "They" and "All You Zombies" (an SF time-travel story published originally in *Fantasy and Science Fiction*), as well as "The Man Who Traveled in Elephants" (published as "The Elephant Circuit" in a short-lived magazine called *Saturn Science Fiction and Fantasy*), "Our Fair City" (published, ironically, in *Weird Tales*, possibly because *Unknown Worlds* had died and there was no other market), and "And He Built a Crooked House," which was one of Heinlein's 1940 *Astounding* stories.

The glue that binds these stories together is their difference. They are all unique specimens of their kind: nothing quite like "And He Built a Crooked House," for instance, appeared in *Astounding* before or has appeared since. "All You Zombies" is the classic time-travel story, involving all of its paradoxes. Even the two stories from *Unknown* were special for that magazine. Perhaps most special. They involve the two basic themes that obsessed Heinlein throughout his writing career: paranoia and solipsism. Solipsism also is the basic question of "All You Zombies."

Solipsism, which is the philosophy that the only thing that anyone can be certain of is the self, is closely allied to paranoia. Solipsism, however, is what drives "All You Zombies" into its intricacies of relationships, and paranoia is what imbues "They" and "The Unpleasant Profession of Jonathan Hoag" with their particular frissons that vast forces may be aligned against their protagonists and the apprehension that even worse revelations may lie ahead. What is Jonathan Hoag to make, for instance, of the discovery that what has been found under his fingernails is not blood, as he suspected, but something so much worse that the doctor tears up the analysis and asks him to take his business elsewhere? And that is only the first of a series of developments that lead to a shattering revelation.

The novel that launched *Unknown*, Russell's *Sinister Barrier*, was based on the notion, suggested by that connoisseur of the outrageous occurrence, Charles Fort, that people are property, owned by mysterious and powerful aliens who collect some of them from time to time. *The Unpleasant Profession of Jonathan Hoag* takes that concept to its ultimate conclusion. It represents the best of what *Unknown* had to offer, the matter-of-fact irreverence to the paranormal that finally reveals vast forces manipulating the universe. It is a great deal of fun, and behind that fun lie some unsettling truths about the human condition.

THE BELGARIAD: PAWN OF PROPHECY
DAVID EDDINGS

In *The Craft of Fiction*, Percy Lubbock wrote, "The whole intricate question of method, in the craft of fiction, I take to be governed by the point of view—the question of the relation in which the narrator stands to the story." In fantasy, the author has a similar choice: in what relation does the story's fantasy world stand to the real world? Upon that decision rests much of the effect the story will have on the reader.

The fantasy world may exist alongside but isolated from the real world and people may pass through some portal into it, like *Alice in Wonderland*, find exotic adventures, and emerge wiser and more experienced. Or the fantasy world may enter the real world, like the elder gods in Lovecraft's horror stories, and awaken the characters, and the reader, to the implications of ancient ways and forbidden knowledge. And sometimes the real world and the fantasy world may interact in unexpected ways, as in Roger Zelazny's Amber novels.

A second decision is *when* the fantasy world exists. Sometimes it is contemporary. Sometimes it is a past when people believed in magic and, perhaps as a consequence, magic may have worked for them. In those scenarios, our world is descended from those earlier worlds, and we have lost the magic that they once employed for reasons that have to do with faith or science or the nature of magic. Or some forms of magic may survive in protected pockets or among people who remember what the rest of us have forgotten, as in Fritz Leiber's *Conjure Wife*. In other scenarios, as in Randall Garrett's Lord Darcy stories, magic abilities exist in an alternate history, and we compare our world to what it might have been.

But sometimes the fantasy world has no relationship to the real world, as in J. R. R. Tolkien's *The Lord of the Rings*, and the only lessons to be learned from it are what comparable creatures may feel and do in comparable circumstances; hobbits, like humans, can be cautious and curious, cowardly and brave, and faced with difficult choices between good and evil.

This kind of high fantasy, which offers a fully realized alternate reality, may have achieved its most complete creation in *The Lord of the Rings*, but had its predecessors. The prolific turn-of-the-century Irish author Lord Dunsany wrote many fantasies (the most famous may have been *The King of Elfland's Daughter*) placed in "a pseudo-medieval never-never realm," as David Pringle described them. Dunsany was followed by the British writer David Lindsey and his remarkable *A Voyage to Arcturus* (1920), the Yorkshireman E. R. Eddison and his epic novel *The Worm Ouroboros* (1922), and such American writers as James Branch Cabell, Clark Ashton Smith, and Robert E. Howard.

Howard created a new mythology of gods and ancient heroes in his Conan and Kull stories published in the 1930s *Weird Tales*, which were revived and extended in the 1950s and after by L. Sprague de Camp. Fritz Leiber's Fafhrd and the Gray Mouser stories and novels, starting in 1939, opened up still newer kingdoms for fictional adventure. Howard placed his Conan in the prehistoric land of Cimmeria, but Leiber put his heroes in Nehwon, which perceptive readers transposed into Nowhen.

The advantage of Nowhen is its existence outside the historic context. Deprived of even Greek and Roman civilization, characters must depend upon brawn and wile and hand-to-hand combat; intimate relationships undistanced by technology and uncomplicated by contemporary psychology; a milieu in which magic and witchcraft are credible; and a hierarchical system in which the rise and fall of greatness offers classical tragedy and in which good and evil can contend for the universe. Perhaps the greatest advantage of Nowhen is that its events *never* have to conform to historical accuracy or to lead, in some fashion, to contemporary realities, and thus the reader is freed to enjoy a narrative, like such adult fairy tales as the *Star Wars* films, without consequences in the real world. One of the characteristics of Nowhen stories is that they are usually found in multiple volumes; another is that their imaginary landscapes require maps.

Often such scenarios offer gods who intervene in human affairs, as in ancient Greek mythology, or some alternative cosmological system. Events are set in motion by some disturbance in the natural or rightful order of things, and the essential task of the protagonist or protagonists is to restore order. Alternatively, an imbalance exists that must be restored by the overthrow of evil, with all its unprincipled power, and the ascension of righteous good. Most Nowhen narratives are morality plays. The characters may exhibit some confusion about the proper course of action and may have to learn how to function in a world of magic, particularly if they are young and must be taught adult responsibilities and the way the world works, but are seldom confused about the difference between right and wrong.

That is what David Eddings offers in his Belgariad epic fantasy, which begins here with the first volume, *Pawn of Prophecy*. In *Pawn of Prophecy* the reader is introduced to a world of gods and sorcery and of kingdoms that have no historic parallels. Unlike the Greek gods, the seven gods of the Belgariad world were brothers (who their parents were, or how the gods came into existence, remains a mystery). Like the Greek gods they quarreled over power and their favorites among the races of the world. One of the gods, Torak, stole the Orb of his brother Aldur and used it to aid the Angaraks, but when his brothers and their followers were defeating him in battle, Torak used the Orb to split the Earth asunder. In the process he maimed himself. All the gods but Torak retired lest the world be destroyed by a new war. The sorcerer trained by Aldur, Belgarath, stole back the Orb so that Torak would be held in check. The Orb was given to Riva and his heirs, for only they could hold it without being destroyed, to preserve the world against the return to power of Torak and his followers. As *Pawn of Prophecy* begins, however, an apostate student of Belgarath has stolen the Orb, and Belgarath must marshal his few forces and, with the boy Garion, set out to find the Orb and restore it to its proper place. And, one suspects, Garion himself, who does not know, though the reader suspects, that he is the only living descendant of Riva. Eddings has chosen to tell his story through Garion, whose youthful innocence and native skepticism make him an ideal guide for the reader to follow through the world Eddings has invented.

David Eddings began his remarkable writing career with *High Hunt* in 1973, but his current success began with *Pawn of Prophecy* in 1982. A dozen years later he had completed seventeen novels and had become a familiar name among fantasy readers. Born in Spokane, Washington, in 1931, he earned a B.A. in literature from Reed College in 1954 and an M.A. in English from the University of Washington in 1961, interspersing that with two years in the U.S. Army in 1954–1956. He worked as a buyer for the Boeing Company and has taught college English.

The Belgariad continues with *Queen of Sorcery* (1982), *Magician's Gambit* (1983), *Castle of Wizardry* (1984), and *Enchanter's Endgame* (1985). They were published in two volumes in 1985 as *The Belgariad*. Eddings started a second series in the same world, *The Mallorean*, in 1987 with *Guardians of the West* and continued it with *King of the Murgos* (1988), *Demon Lord of Karanda* (1988), *Sorceress of Darshiva* (1989), and *The Seeress of Kell* (1991). A third series, *The Elenium*, consists of *The Diamond Throne* (1989), *The Ruby Knight* (1990), and *The Sapphire Rose* (1992); and a fourth series, *The Tamuli*, of *Domes of Fire* (1992), *The Shining Ones* (1993), and *The Hidden City* (1994).

Michael Cule in *The St. James Guide to Science Fiction Writers* comments that The Belgariad stays in memory because it entertains: "It concentrates to great effect on character and action, the twin keys to storytelling." And he calls attention to Eddings's enjoyment in exploring "the issues of predestination, of responsibility and of moral choice in a universe where the gods are almost embarrassingly immanent and interfere regularly in human affairs."

"The focus of the books," Cule continues, "is on the comedy of character. The contrasts among the members of the band of heroes, between the toweringly noble (and not-too-bright) knight Mandorallen, and the berserker warrior Barak, between the grim horse-lord Hettar and the spy Silk, the centuries old battling between the sorcerer Belgarath and his daughter Polgara, the developing love between Garion and the Imperial (and imperious) Princess Ce'Nedra and the growth of a sense of responsibility in the two adolescents: these are what Eddings concentrates on."

Eddings himself has commented: "I've tried to create realistic, believable characters to function in an unrealistic, unbelievable world. I left the warts on them, allowed them to be silly from time to time and to bicker with each other when they felt that way. I can only hope that the reader has half as much fun with the books as I did."

From the feel of *Pawn of Prophecy*, that would be a great deal of fun, indeed.

THE CHRONICLES OF THOMAS COVENANT THE UNBELIEVER: LORD FOUL'S BANE
STEPHEN R. DONALDSON

The subject is fantasy, the kind of fantasy called "high fantasy."

"High fantasy," as *The Encyclopedia of Fantasy* defines it, takes place in a "secondary world," like the Middle-Earth of J. R. R. Tolkien's *The Lord of the Rings*, that is autonomous, impossible, and self-coherent. The actions in high fantasy affect the destinies of these secondary worlds.

Stephen R. Donaldson's *Lord Foul's Bane* is a high fantasy that is often compared with *The Lord of the Rings* from which, scholars say, it draws a good part of its structure and some of its characters. But Donaldson's approach to his secondary world, the Land, differs in remarkable ways.

By "impossible" the encyclopedia means that the world cannot exist "in terms of our normal understanding of the sciences and of history," and in this respect *Lord Foul's Bane* qualifies. By "self-coherent" is meant that "the world . . . is governed by internally consistent rules to which the reader gives credence, and in terms of which anything can be believed . . . as long as that which is believed in is *livable*." That certainly applies to *Lord Foul's Bane*. By autonomy the encyclopedia categorizes a world that can exist independently of what the reader calls the real world, "without any lingering need to 'normalize' . . . secondary worlds by framing them as traveller's tales, or dreams (entered via portals), which prove exiguous at dawn, or timeslip tales, or as beast-fables." Here is where *Lord Foul's Bane* departs from traditional high fantasy.

The overall title of the six-volume series *The Chronicles of Thomas Covenant the Unbeliever* and *The Second Chronicles of Thomas Covenant the Unbeliever* reveals one important distinction: the protagonist (at least in the first three volumes) doubts the reality of the secondary world. As John Clute observes in *Survey of Modern Fantasy Literature*, "His chill refusal to go along with the world constantly violates the delicate decorum of shared belief that makes most fantasies work for their creators, the characters, and their readers. Covenant violates the sense of awe."

Moreover, Covenant is an unlikely and unlikable protagonist. "Woebegone, diseased, haggard, obsessed, self-pitying, weak, violent, ungrateful, and choked with ire, he is anything but a willing and usable vessel or conduit for immanence on the cheap," Clute continues. The world into which Covenant is thrust, the inhabitants believe, has been created out of Nothing, but evil was introduced by the Creator's eternal Opponent. Cast out of Heaven by the Creator and bound to existence, the Opponent, Lord Foul, can escape only by dissolving the Law that binds existence. Only Covenant can destroy the Creator's prison, but it will not work if his action is coerced. He must be brought to his own Despite. "That this prison also represents to Covenant the humanity he must constantly refuse," Clute writes, "is the underlying paradox, the underlying dilemma that causes him such extraordinary anguish, making him in the end, despite his repellent personality, a figure with whom the reader must sympathize deeply."

The novel begins with Covenant's discovery of his leprosy and the process by which he learns to live with it, including the world's fear of him and his disease. His wife, fearing contagion, divorces him while he is in a leprosarium; his neighbors shun him; eventually the world itself rejects him, as he is drawn through a "portal," by being knocked down by a car, into the Land where Lord Foul hopes to use Covenant to gain his own freedom. Leprosy involves the numbing of the extremities and Covenant has been taught VSE, the Visual Surveillance of Extremities, to check for damage that he cannot feel. It is this model of perception, VSE, that stands as a central image throughout the Chronicles and leads continually to Covenant's questioning of his interactions with the secondary world.

Of his own writing, Donaldson has said:

> Virtually everything I write is about *redemption*: most of my characters are caught up in a vital and necessary struggle to "work out their own salvation, with fear and trembling." ... Of course, to claim that redemption is one of "the fundamental questions to life," puts me in conflict with much of modern philosophy.... If one accepts—in any form—Sartre's postulate that "Man is a futile passion," then the whole concept of *redemption* becomes something of a joke. Clearly, I reject that postulate. But I'm also intelligent enough to understand its relevance, and recognize its power. (Hence the grimness of much of my work).

Grimness exists in *Lord Foul's Bane*, to be sure, but also power and relevance as well, and perhaps even redemption. Individual readers will have to discover that for themselves as they follow Covenant's tortured path through the Land whose growing disease reflects his own condition in the real world.

Stephen R. Donaldson, whose entry into published fiction came at the age of thirty, in 1977, with *Lord Foul's Bane*, was born in 1947 in Cleveland, the son of a physician. His father specialized in the treatment of leprosy, and it was this familiarity that Donaldson used to such good effect in characterizing Covenant and his disease as well as the metaphors of affliction that pervade the Chronicles. Donaldson earned his B.A. in English from the College of Wooster and his M.A. in English from Kent State University. He served as a teaching fellow at Kent State, as an acquisitions editor of Tapp-Gentz Associates, and for two years as an associate instructor for Ghost Ranch Writers Workshops.

Lord Foul's Bane, The Illearth War, and *The Power That Preserves*—the three volumes of the First Chronicles—all were published in 1977. For these he earned the British Fantasy Society award and the John W. Campbell Award as best new writer, both in 1979. The Second Chronicles followed more slowly: The *Wounded Land* in 1980, *The One Tree* in 1982, and *White Gold Wielder* in 1983. He published a collection of short stories in *Daughter of Regals and Other Tales* in 1984, and began a second fantasy series, *Mordant's Need* with *The Mirror of Her Dreams* and *A Man Rides Through*, both in 1987. He turned to science fiction, as Donaldson himself put it, "toward more 'realistic,' objectively real, modes of expression," with the Gap sequence: *The Gap into Conflict: The Real Story* (1990), *The Gap into Vision: Forbidden Knowledge* (1991), *The Gap into Power: A Dark and Hungry God Arises* (1992), *The Gap into Madness: Chaos and Disorder* (1994), and *The Gap into Ruin: This Day All Gods Die* (1996). He has written three detective novels under the name of Reed Stephens and a nonfiction book, *Epic Fantasy in the Modern World: A Few Observations* (1986), and has published a second collection of short stories, *Strange Dreams* (1993).

Donaldson's fantasy novels are not only a tribute to the rising tide of fantasy that lifted all boats with the success of *The Lord of the Rings* and other novels in the mid to late 1960s; they are a critique of them as well. As Clute has commented in *The Encyclopedia of Fantasy*, Covenant's "unbelief is perhaps [Donaldson's] most original single invention, for it radically transfigures every moment of the first sequence and profoundly contradicts the reader's normal expectations about the relationships between the Hero and the Land, the Quest and his Companions, plus the overall relationship to the decorum and moral requirements that define the condition of being a hero. It thoroughly exposes the artifact of the normal fantasy secondary world as a stage-set for the deeds of protagonists whose every act is deeply patriotic, deeply land- and folk-affirming."

At the same time, as Sonya Cashdan and Barbara C. Stanley pointed out in *Survey of Science Fiction and Fantasy Literature*, "From both Tolkien and medieval lore Donaldson draws the motifs of hidden identity, prophecy, sacred or profane objects, Christ figures and Satan figures, enchanted places, enchanted or magical animals, words of power, and help unlocked. From medieval literature, he incorporates the motifs of a land's health being tied to human health, of moral decay being reflected in physical decay, of earthly struggles carrying eternal consequences, of evil disguised as good, and of fate calling the chosen to fulfill tasks upon which the destiny of many depends." To this one might add the names given to characters; in medieval epics and Renaissance allegories, names are powerful and reflect the nature of the inner self.

While he brings to his work the vast resources of literature and the experience of high fantasy, Donaldson also contributes his own sense of values: the only direction to move is forward, never out. Aaron Rosenberg sums up Donaldson's attitude toward life and the appropriate human response to it in the conclusion of the entry in *The St. James Guide to Science Fiction Writers*: "As one Morn Hyland realizes in *The Gap into Conflict: The Real Story*, 'Vast space was deadly: it called for valor, determination, and idealism.' The same can be said for life itself; Donaldson himself supplies most of the idealism, but his characters demonstrate the courage and persistence that it takes to change, and far beyond simple redemption, they give themselves to the effort of changing their world, our world, for the better."

High fantasy can have no higher calling.

THE MISTS OF AVALON
MARION ZIMMER BRADLEY

Fantastic worlds are either invented or co-opted; that is, authors either make them up or they take them over. All fantasy, of course, has its origins in objective reality as it is interpreted by individual minds and transformed by the creative imagination. Some of it, however, is a new construction intended to reconcile anomalies in traditional interpretations of the real world or to provide fanciful explanations for the curiosities of the human mind or simply to entertain the willing reader with appealing romantic adventures in lands of make-believe.

Roger Zelazny's *Nine Princes in Amber* was an invention. Peter Beagle's *The Last Unicorn* transformed the material of fairy tales. Elizabeth Moon's *Sheepfarmer's Daughter* took much of its substance from the historical world before translating it into imaginary geography and peopling it with *real* magicians.

Some fantasies, however, adopt existing mythologies, or occasionally historical realities, for their stories, sometimes retelling myths and folk tales in familiar ways, sometimes reinterpreting them in the light of subsequent events or to bring their psychological power to bear on contemporary problems or sensibilities. Of these by far the most common source of stories has been the Bible, not only the narrative of Jesus himself but the many incidents and parables of the Old and the New Testaments, which resonate differently for each generation. Not only is the basic document itself frequently retranslated, but the individual stories provide the material for new stories and novels. Take the stories of Adam and Eve, for instance, or Cain and Abel or Job or the Great Flood or Salome or Judas . . .

Perhaps the second most common source of narrative material is Arthurian legend, called "the matter of Britain," because it deals with the mythical defining qualities of the British nation. The Arthurian cycle actually reached its fullest development in France, where the legends may have been brought by Celts fleeing the Saxon invaders. An irony exists in the fact that the legendary hero of the English was the king given credit for turning back invasions of the people the English consider their ancestors, the Saxons, just as Sir Thomas Malory may have brought back into English the Arthurian legend in order to give substance to the past of the Normans who had conquered the Anglo-Saxons, even to the point of having Guinevere flee from Mordred to the Tower of London, whose construction was not started until 1078, a dozen years after the Norman Conquest.

The great Arthur himself does not appear in British histories until the year 800, when a Welsh chronicler named Nennius used the name in his *Historia Britonum* in referring to a leader against the Saxons. Gradually, in additions over the centuries, Arthur became identified as a Welsh or Roman military leader of the Celts in Wales against Germanic invaders in the fifth century. When he became king, he surrounded himself with great knights whose chivalric deeds filled the most popular cycle of medieval romance.

Geoffrey of Monmouth added a great deal to the Arthurian legends about 1136, with his *Historia Regum Britanniae*. The French poet Wace contributed some additional detail, and a little later Chretien de Troyes gave the legends their first literary treatment, in Old French, in his romances. In the next decade, the English poet Layamon dealt with Arthur in *Brut*, as did many other authors of medieval romances. Sir Thomas Malory wrote the definitive version for later generations in his 1485 *Le Morte d'Arthur*, published some years after Malory's death. Spenser based his *The Faerie Queene* on it, Milton considered writing a national epic using it, and Tennyson mined it for his *Idylls of the King*. Since then it has been used by composers, poets, and authors for innumerable variations, including Mark Twain's comic *A Connecticut Yankee in King Arthur's Court* and most recently T. H. White's *The Once and Future King*, which was adapted for the animated Disney film *The Sword and the Stone* and the musical *Camelot*.

Little is known for sure about the translator and compiler of what has been called "the first English prose classic" and "one of the chief foundations of English prose" except that he died in 1471. *Le Morte d'Arthur* was the name given the book (the original title was *The Book of King Arthur and the Knights of the Round Table*) by William Caxton, the printer who published the book in 1485. Literary historians have identified Malory as a knight who served in France and was on the wrong side of the War of the Roses, was refused amnesty and threatened with arrest, and may have compiled his manuscript in prison. In a preface to the first edition, Caxton wrote that he printed the book "after a copye unto me delivered whyche copye Syr Thomas Malorye dyd take oute of certeyn books of frennsshe and reduced it in Englysshe." To Malory certainly and to Caxton should go much of the credit for putting the stories into the form in which they descended to the readers and writers who came after them, and in such "simple, direct, idiomatic, yet musical and dignified" style that it has kept its hold on the imagination of succeeding generations.

Marion Zimmer Bradley in *The Mists of Avalon*, like every author before her, has retold the Arthurian story in her own way and for her own purposes. In the acknowledgments to the first edition of 1982, she expresses her gratitude to her husband, Walter Breen, for saying, at a crucial moment in her career, "that it was time to stop playing it safe by writing potboilers," and for providing "financial support so that I could do so." The result was a best-seller that created a new audience for Bradley—and for Arthur.

Up to that time Bradley had been known mostly for her Darkover series of science-fantasy novels, which she launched in 1958 with the publication of *The Planet Savers* in *Amazing Stories* and *The Sword of Aldones*, both published as books in 1962. Born in Albany, New York, in 1930 and educated at New York State College for Teachers and (a decade and half later) Hardin-Simmons University, Bradley began publishing stories in 1953 and novels in 1957. The Darkover series, set on a planet settled by Terrans, began in action and adventure and developed into a study of contrasting cultures created by the wide use of telepathy on Darkover, of the resistance of anti-technological Darkover to efforts by the human Empire to integrate it into a political and economic union, and of questions of sexual politics that expressed itself in part through the Free Amazons, who later became known as Renunciates.

The series attracted so many dedicated readers that a special fandom grew up around it, and Bradley allowed her world to be shared by other writers, through Darkover anthologies and through the *Marion Zimmer Bradley Magazine*. So far the "matter of Darkover" has been developing for more than thirty-five years and over more than a dozen novels, more than a dozen anthologies and collections, and numerous issues of her magazine.

Some of these same concerns about culture conflicts and gender issues show up in *The Mists of Avalon*. What gives this Arthurian treatment its special character is that Bradley chose to tell familiar stories from a different viewpoint. The key elements of the medieval romance, Professor George Saintsbury wrote, were war, love, and religion. There always is a quest; often the love interest is directly connected with the quest, although in some cases it is a distraction from it; and the war interest always is connected. The religious interest is almost universally "an inseparable accident. But everything leads up to, involves, eventuates in the fighting. The quest, if not always a directly warlike one, always involves war; and the endless battles have at all times, since they ceased to be the great attraction, continued to be the great obloquy of romance."

The quest, war, battle—all these are the almost unique province of men. Even love, often that idealized form known as "courtly love," is present largely to motivate men to quests and battle. The romance, therefore, is largely an account of the doings of men, told about men from the viewpoint of men. Bradley decided to tell her version of the Arthurian legend from the viewpoint of the women who are affected by the concerns and actions of men but who have their own concerns: Arthur's wife, Guinevere (Bradley calls her, in a more Celtic fashion, Gwenhwyfar); his mother, Igraine; Viviane, the Lady of the Lake; but mostly Morgan of the Faeries, who is also known as Morgan (here Morgaine) le Fey.

Morgan, sorceress, witch, sister, and lover (in Bradley's version) of Arthur, who assists him to the throne and becomes his greatest enemy, tells the story as it seems to her, and indeed, introduces it through a prologue. And Bradley frames the story, not only in the prologue written by Morgan but the epilogue written about her, in terms of conflict between the old religion—the goddess-centered religion of Avalon—and the new religion of Christianity. Bradley identifies the old religion with the land of Faerie and suggests a kind of doorway between worlds that once could be opened by the power of people's beliefs and slowly faded through silence and misunderstanding and the victory of Christianity. But perhaps, Bradley suggests, Avalon still can be reached by mortals. Perhaps the Holy Isle of Avalon still is where it always was, if only we can believe and step through the mists.

THREE HEARTS AND THREE LIONS
POUL ANDERSON

Fantasy, like the daydream, allows the imagination to explore without limitations. While traditional fiction limits itself to the world of experience and historical fiction to our experience of the past, and even science fiction submits its speculations to the censorship of the possible, fantasy acknowledges no restrictions, and the fantasy reader will accept any premise if it is the "open sesame" to a fascinating world. Fall down a rabbit hole, open a door in a wardrobe, get hit on the head by a crowbar, be struck by lightning, or recite a magical verse—all these are doorways to adventure and like any doorway diminished by the rooms they reveal.

Yet even fantasy has its traditions, and Poul Anderson's *Three Hearts and Three Lions* follows the path first opened by Fletcher Pratt and L. Sprague de Camp in their Incomplete/Complete Enchanter series. The Harold Shea stories began in 1940 in *Unknown* with "The Roaring Trumpet" and "The Mathematics of Magic" and continued with *The Castle of Iron*, "The Wall of Serpents," "The Green Magician," and others. But Pratt and de Camp themselves had predecessors. De Camp himself was one, with his 1939 *Unknown* novel *Lest Darkness Fall*, and that was preceded by Mark Twain's 1889 *A Connecticut Yankee in King Arthur's Court* and dozens of imitators. Each of these, though in the tradition of the person or persons translated to a past or mythical world and finding a place in it, sometimes changing it dramatically, differs from the others in significant ways.

The common elements are the translation into the other world, usually by accident, occasionally by design; the discovery of the nature of that world; and the challenge of surviving in it and then coping with it. In *A Connecticut Yankee*, for instance, Hank Morgan is hit on the head by a crowbar and wakes up in King Arthur's time; in *Lest Darkness Fall*, Martin Padway is struck by lightning and wakes up in sixth century Rome. But where Twain's sixth-century Britain is half myth and half pop history and Morgan attempts to create the Industrial Revolution a millennium early, de Camp's Italy is historically accurate and Padway recognizes an opportunity to forestall the coming Dark Ages. In a sense, *Lest Darkness Fall* is a critique of *A Connecticut Yankee in King Arthur's Court*.

The Harold Shea series, on the other hand, represented a new departure. First of all, Shea and his professor reach the fantasy world by means of a formula, and the fantasy worlds they enter are alternate realities in which established mythologies have been realized—Norse mythology, for one, and then the world of Edmund Spenser's *The Faerie Queene* and Ariosto's *Orlando Furioso*. In those worlds magic actually works according to hardand-fast rules; the residents of these alternate realities acquire the rules by rote, but contemporary minds are able to analyze their mathematical structure and perfect them.

Anderson takes his models and uses them for his own, more serious purposes; his novel, while adventurous and even comic, focuses more on the nature of heroism than the pragmatism of Hank Morgan and Martin Padway. Like both of the earlier characters, Holger Carlsen is knocked unconscious. He has returned to Denmark in 1941 to join the anti-Nazi resistance. In a desperate hand-to-hand battle with Nazis who have occupied Denmark, Carlsen gets shot. When he awakes, like Harold Shea he finds himself in a fantasy world where magic works. The title of the novel refers to the design of three hearts and three lions Carlsen finds on the shield that is awaiting him in a forest, along with a suit of armor and a horse. In *Three Hearts and Three Lions* the land of Faerie is real. Fantasy is always a battle between good and evil, between order and chaos, and as Carlsen gathers allies and discovers enemies he learns that a battle is in preparation. Humans are on the side of

Law and the Faerie Folk, who are gathering an army to attack, are on the side of Chaos.

Thus begins an epic adventure that David Pringle lists among his *Hundred Best Novels of Modern Fantasy*. *Three Hearts and Three Lions* would have enjoyed an honored place in the pages of John Campbell's short-lived and long-lamented fantasy magazine *Unknown*. First published in 1939 and killed in 1943 by the wartime paper shortage, *Unknown* (which later expanded its title to *Unknown Worlds*) published "rationalized fantasy" in which the supernatural was bound by laws like those by which science operates in the natural world. It created a renaissance in fantasy similar to the Golden Age that Campbell inaugurated when he became editor of *Astounding Stories* in 1937. *The Encyclopedia of Fantasy* comments that *Unknown* "published more quality fiction per issue than any other magazine."

Alas for Anderson, like Miniver Cheevy he was born too late for fantasy's greatest magazine but just right to catch the end of the Golden Age of science fiction. Anderson was born in 1926 in Bristol, Pennsylvania, and earned a bachelor's degree in physics from the University of Minnesota, where he met a man who would become another famous science-fiction writer, Gordon Dickson, also a 1948 graduate. Anderson beat Dickson into print, in part because Dickson pursued a graduate degree in creative writing for a couple of years. They collaborated on Dickson's first published SF story in 1950 and later on a series of stories and a novel about mischievous aliens known as Rokas, *Earthman's Burden* (1957), *Star Prince Charlie* (1975), and *Hoka!* (1983).

Meanwhile Anderson got his first story published in *Astounding* in 1947 and published sixteen stories, mostly in *Astounding*, through 1950. His first novel, *Vault of the Ages* (for juveniles), was published in 1952. His second and third, *Brain Wave* and *The Broken Sword*, a seminal science-fiction novel and a significant fantasy novel, were both published in 1954. Since then he has published at least one novel a year, and sometimes two or three, most of them science fiction; he also has published many stories and collected them into several dozen volumes; and he has written a half-dozen mysteries. His work in science fiction has earned him almost a dozen Hugo and Nebula Awards, a British fantasy award, and a Tolkien Memorial Award. He was guest of honor at the 1959 World Science Fiction Convention and president of the Science Fiction Writers of America in 1972–1973.

His fantasy may have seemed more like a break from science fiction, but it has been important in its own right as well as extending the tradition of rationalized fantasy inaugurated in *Unknown*. His fantasy also is tinged with what *The Encyclopedia of Fantasy* calls, in W. H. Auden's words, "the northern thing," a focus on the Scandinavian myths with their (perhaps sunlight-deprived) melancholy that is relieved in Anderson's work by SF's technological optimism. The encyclopedia refers to the "Nordic-twilight hue" that "permeates much of [his]" fiction.

The Broken Sword, which also ranks among David Pringle's *Hundred Best Novels*, tells the story of changeling half-brothers, one human-born, one elf-born, who grow up to take different sides in a violent war between elves and trolls. "Despite its general neglect [it remained out of print for a dozen and a half years] it has become an influential work," Pringle wrote, "thanks to the enthusiasm of Michael Moorcock and a few other latter-day practitioners of Sword and sorcery." Pringle concludes that "Poul Anderson . . . remains true to the essential spirit of those Old Norse sagas which have inspired his remarkable novel."

Operation Chaos (1971), like many of Anderson's books a combination of stories originally published in magazines (in this case *Fantasy and Science Fiction* between 1956 and 1959), is a more light-hearted approach to the war between Law and Chaos. *Hrolf Kraki's Saga* (1973) deals more directly with Icelandic myth in the reworking of Norse saga. *A Midsummer Tempest* is set in an alternate world in which Shakespeare's plays are based on fact, particularly the fantasies *A Midsummer Night's Dream* and *The Tempest*. *The Mermen's Children* (1979), another collection of previously published stories, deals with Christianity's triumph over Faerie.

Anderson's *The Devil's Game* (1980) is more of a horror story about a pact with the devil set in the framework of a thriller. More recently he has written, with his wife, Karen, a series of novels based on Celtic fantasy beginning with *The King of Ys: Roma Mater* in 1986 and continuing with *The King of Ys: Gallicenae* (1987), *The King of Ys: Dahut* (1988), and *The King of Ys: The Dog and the Wolf* (1988). The city of Ys is a Greek-Punic outpost in Brittany that has an influence on late-Roman politics, according to *The Encyclopedia of Fantasy*. The encyclopedia concludes its summation of Anderson's influence on fantasy with the comment that "most of his fantasies have been cast as requiems, though sometimes disguised as romps; and perhaps [Anderson] now feels that the Northern way of life they mourn has—as he has told us more than once—indeed passed away."

But in the passing they have left behind the sagas and Anderson's recollections of them in his contemporary fantasies, and particularly in one of the classics of modern fantasy, *Three Hearts and Three Lions*.

THE COMPLETE COMPLEAT ENCHANTER
L. SPRAGUE DE CAMP AND FLETCHER PRATT

The subject is fantasy.

One approach to the subject was taken by *Unknown*, published as a companion fantasy magazine to John W. Campbell's science-fiction magazine,

Astounding. Campbell hoped to restore the good name of fantasy by obtaining stories written with rigor and humor. In the first issue, published in March 1939, he wrote, "It will offer fantasy of a quality so far different from that which has appeared in the past as to change your entire understanding of the term." The magazine fulfilled his promise, publishing stories that retain their charm to this day and even creating a new fantasy field as important, perhaps, as the science fiction he is credited with transforming. The magazine changed its name to *Unknown Worlds* in 1941, and then, sadly, was killed by wartime paper shortages in 1943, but it is still wistfully remembered and its stories and novels remain in print.

What was their charm?

Campbell tried to explain it in a foreword to a 1948 retrospective, *From Unknown Worlds: An Anthology of Modern Fantasy for Grownups*: "The old 'Unknown Worlds' believed that fantasy was intended for fun; it used the familiar creatures of mythology and folklore, but treated them in a most disrespectful fashion. Fantasy—and the Things of fantasy—are, we felt, much more fun than anything else, if you'll just take off those traditional wrappings of the 'grim and gharstly.'"

The *Weird Tales* kind of fantasy, the Lovecraftian Gothic with its special conditions of darkness and isolation, evoked feelings of terror and sometimes of loathing; it used archaic language to remind its readers of the long-past eras when a belief in witchcraft and magic was commonplace, or to describe the indescribable. But what if modern humans, in the midst of their everyday occupations, were confronted by the supernatural, or ordinary people, with ordinary sensibilities, were thrown into worlds in which magic worked? The result might be surprising: adventure, sure, of a kind that the reader might well identify with by the light of day, but often funny, too.

One analyst, Les Daniels, has commented that "the typical [*Unknown*] tale recognized the humorous incongruity of the supernatural in urban life and demonstrated that even magical intervention in the affairs of men was unlikely to relieve the frustration of the human condition." The stories weren't all like that, of course—some of them dealt with urban horrors and contemporary paranoia, and some of them helped develop the kind of sword-and-sorcery category that Robert E. Howard had already pioneered—but the majority of the stories had an element of the comic.

The language was different, too. The ordinary characters spoke ordinary, colloquial English, and the contrast with their supernatural encounters made the situations even more hilarious. As David Drake has pointed out, L. Sprague de Camp was one of the first to defend the use of contemporary speech in heroic settings when he wrote a letter to the editor of *Argosy* concerning *The Harp and the Blade* by John Myers Myers. But de Camp and Fletcher Pratt already had practiced such usage in their Harold Shea novels, adopting it, perhaps, from Mark Twain's *A Connecticut Yankee in King*

Arthur's Court. Twain's novel, like Thorne Smith's *The Night Life of the Gods* and his other comedies of the supernatural reappearing in today's world, has not been given sufficient credit for providing a precedent for *Unknown*'s new approach.

The same authors who were creating the Golden Age for Campbell's *Astounding* readers were drawn to the challenge of this new fantasy genre. *Unknown* assembled a remarkable roster of contributors: L. Ron Hubbard supplied *Slaves of Sleep*, "The Indigestible Triton," "Fear," and "Typewriter in the Sky"; Robert A. Heinlein, "The Devil Makes the Laws," "The Unpleasant Profession of Jonathan Hoag," and "They"; Fritz Leiber, eight stories including "Two Sought Adventure" and the unforgettable *Conjure Wife*; Theodore Sturgeon, sixteen stories, including "It," "Shottle Bop," and "Yesterday Was Monday"; A. E. van Vogt, *The Book of Ptath*; Jack Williamson, *The Reign of Wizardry* and *Darker Than You Think*.

But the uncrowned king of *Unknown* was L. Sprague de Camp, who published fifteen stories in the magazine; even more remarkable, ten of those were novels. He published as many stories in *Astounding* during the same period, but only *The Stolen Dormouse* was a novel; still, one of his *Unknown* novels, the classic *Lest Darkness Fall*, was a great alternate history treatment (and is classified today as science fiction) and would have been published in *Astounding* had *Unknown* not existed.

De Camp, who was born in 1907 and, like another Golden Age marvel, Jack Williamson, is still writing at the age of ninety, earned a degree in aeronautical engineering from the California Institute of Technology and a master's degree from Stevens Institute of Technology. He worked for the Inventors Foundation and International Correspondence Schools and held other positions while he was breaking into the writing business. He published his first story, "The Isolinguals," in *Astounding* in 1937, and he collaborated on a novel with P. Schuyler Miller, *Genus Homo*, that didn't get published until 1941, but his career blossomed under the editorship of John W. Campbell, who took over at *Astounding* in late 1937.

World War II, in which de Camp served as a lieutenant commander, working alongside Heinlein and Isaac Asimov at the Philadelphia Navy Yard, interrupted de Camp's writing career. He returned in 1949 with a series of future-history stories and novels based around the concept that Brazil would become the dominant world power and Portuguese, the dominant language: The *Queen of Zamba, Rogue Queen*, and *The Hand of Zei* are the leading examples of his Viagens Interplanetarias series.

In the mid-1950s de Camp was attracted to Howard's Conan stories and devoted much of his later career to resurrecting, restoring, and adding to the Conan legend. He also contributed his own novels to the sword-and-sorcery genre as well as nonfiction books such as *Literary Swordsmen and Sorcerers* and *Blond Barbarians and Noble Savages* and anthologies such as *Swords and Sorcery* and *Warlocks and Warriors*. He has written well-regarded historical works such as *Lands Beyond* (with Willy Ley), *Lost Continents, The Ancient Engineers*, and *Great Cities of the Ancient World*, as well as historical novels such as *An Elephant for Aristotle* and biographies of Howard and H. P. Lovecraft, *Dark Valley Destiny* and *Lovecraft*. He also wrote the *Science Fiction Handbook* in 1953 and revised it, with Catherine Crook de Camp, who has collaborated on much of his later work, in 1975.

De Camp won the International Fantasy Award in 1953 for his nonfiction book with Ley, *Lands Beyond*; SFWA's Grand Master award in 1978; and the World Fantasy Life Achievement award in 1984.

But it is his Harold Shea stories, written with Fletcher Pratt, and published over a series of years, that provided impetus to de Camp's early career. The idea itself, of a psychologist projected by symbolic logic into a series of fantasy worlds, originated with Pratt. An SF and fantasy writer who also was a prominent naval historian, Pratt died at the age of fifty-nine in 1956. His best-known novels are *The Well of the Unicorn* (1948) and *The Blue Star* (1969). In addition he published three dozen historical books, most of them about the U.S. Navy, particularly its role during World War II. He also wrote about spaceflight and was cofounder of the American Rocket Society.

The Harold Shea novels got started in the May 1940 issue of *Unknown* with *The Roaring Trumpet*, in which Shea projected himself into the world of Norse mythology, and advanced to *The Mathematics of Magic* (Spenser's *The Faerie Queene*) in the August 1940 *Unknown* and *The Castle of Iron* (Ariosto's *Orlando Furioso*) in the April 1941 issue. *The Wall of Serpents* (the Finnish *Kalevala*) was published in the June 1953 *Famous Fantastic Novels* and *The Green Magician* (Irish myth) in the No. 9 issue of *Beyond Fantasy Fiction* in 1954.

One of the sources for the Harold Shea adventures, and for other uses of magic in *Unknown*, was Sir James Frazer's *The Golden Bough* (1890, rev. 1911–1915), which suggested that magic recognized "immutable laws" just like science, and that these laws could be systematized as the Laws of Sympathy, the Laws of Similarity, and the Laws of Contact. As Reed Chalmers, a fellow psychologist, suggests in the early pages of *The Roaring Trumpet*, "Medicine men ... believe they are working through natural laws. In a world where everyone firmly believed in such laws ... the laws of magic could conceivably work. ... Frazer and Seabrook have worked out some of these magical laws."

In addition, the novels incorporate ideas about multiple universes that have more scientific persuasiveness now than they did in the 1940s: "There is an infinity of possible worlds, and if the senses can be attuned to receive a different series of impressions, we should infallibly find ourselves living in a different world," Chalmers points out. Well, Shea tries it, and it works. The result is a series of delightful adventures (often described as "rollicking") in which the laws that govern those particular worlds may vary (the trick is to discover what the laws are before they prove fatal) but the comedy never does.

DARKER THAN YOU THINK
JACK WILLIAMSON

If science fiction is physics, fantasy is psychology. If science fiction is outer space, fantasy is inner space. If science fiction is rocket ships and formulas, fantasy is broomsticks and spells. If science fiction is the there and then, fantasy is the nowhere and nowhen.

Distinctions like these between science fiction and fantasy lead to a novel, *Darker Than You Think*, that combines elements of both genres in a form that has been called "rationalized fantasy." As David Pringle wrote in *Modern Fantasy: The Hundred Best Novels*, "This is one of those novels that occupy the uncertain zone between science fiction and the supernatural horror story." The novel was written by a science-fiction writer who started publishing stories in the SF magazines in 1928 at the age of twenty and is still publishing them seventy years later. His name is Jack Williamson, and a 1997 novel, *The Black Sun*, was voted onto *Locus Magazine*'s "recommended reading" list, and a Williamson short story, "The Firefly Tree," was included in David Hartwell's 1998 *Year's Best SF*.

As amazing as Williamson's longevity in the SF-writing profession (and perhaps an explanation for it) has been his adaptability: science fiction changes every decade, and Williamson has adjusted to each new direction in writing styles and subject matter. Born in 1908 in Bisbee, Arizona, Williamson grew up on an isolated, near-desert New Mexico homestead and found companionship among books, particularly science fiction and fantasy. His discovery of the pulp magazines led him to *Amazing Stories* and that magazine inspired him to try writing science fiction and fantasy.

Williamson's first story, "The Metal Man," published in *Amazing Stories* in 1928, showed the influence of the romantic concepts and lush descriptions of science-fantasy master A. Merritt. In the 1930s, Williamson apprenticed himself to an older writer, Miles J. Breuer, and learned to "curb [his] tendencies toward wild melodrama and purple adjectives." Among other notable space adventures, he published *The Legion of Space* trilogy between 1934 and 1939 and *The Legion of Time* in 1938. During the 1940s Williamson adapted to the demands of John W. Campbell's Golden Age for greater scientific rigor, and produced the "Seetee" antimatter series *Seetee Ship* (1942–1943/1951) and *Seetee Shock* (1949/1950) and, most important, "With Folded Hands" and *The Humanoids* (1949; 1948 as " . . . And Searching Mind").

The 1950s brought a writer's block and a return to academia to finish up an undergraduate degree that he had abandoned in 1930 to pursue his writing. He followed that with an M.A. in English in 1957 and a Ph.D. in 1964. Most of his writing during this period was in collaboration, with James Gunn on *Star Bridge* (1955) and with Frederik Pohl on a number of novels, a partnership that has lasted into the 1990s. In the 1960s, however, Williamson adapted even to the extremes of the New Wave emphasis on style and adoption of entropy as its major metaphor. Although his production was slowed by the academic demands of his position at Eastern New Mexico University, he continued to produce fiction publishable in every decade.

In addition, Williamson turned his energies toward teaching and scholarship. He led in the development of courses to teach science fiction, cataloged courses offered around the country, edited *Teaching Science Fiction: Education for Tomorrow* (1980), and published his dissertation, *H. G. Wells: Critic of Progress* (1973), for which, in addition to his other scholarly work, he received the Pilgrim Award of the Science Fiction Research Association. He was named the second Science Fiction Writers of America Grand Master (after Robert A. Heinlein). He has served as president of SFWA and as guest of honor at the World Science Fiction Convention. Although he retired from teaching in 1977, he still teaches a course at ENMU every year.

Darker Than You Think was published as a novella in the December 1940 *Unknown*, John W. Campbell's companion fantasy magazine to *Astounding Science Fiction*. The story was one of the most popular of those published in the thirty-nine issues of *Unknown*, and the reason was not only the tense adventure and the occult mystery, and what John Clute in *The Encyclopedia of Fantasy* called "a tortured (and still haunting) erotic frankness unusual in genre literature of the 1940s"; its psychological reverberations touched a responsive chord in thousands of readers.

The reasons for the psychological underpinnings for the story and the psychological validity of the details lie in Williamson himself. In 1936, "deeply troubled" and going through his own "private depression," according to his autobiography, *Wonder's Child*, Williamson enrolled in a year-long analysis with a psychiatrist at the Menninger Clinic in Topeka, and in 1940 he renewed his analysis in Los Angeles. As psychologist Alan C. Elms has noted in articles and his book *Uncovering Lives: The Uneasy Alliance of Biography and Psychology* (1994), Williamson's therapist was suggesting that he abandon his focus on fantastic literature in order to improve his grasp on reality and adjust to greater social normality. The therapist argued that SF and fantasy allow authors to take leave of their conscious egos and that in Williamson's writing "the value of fantasy was constantly increasing and ... in many ways [Williamson] was ignoring reality in order to maintain this ever-increasing interest in [unrealistic] thinking." Even earlier, in Topeka, one psychiatrist had commented "that writing science fiction was symptomatic of neurosis. His casual promise that I could be cured of that became one more mental problem."

Fortunately for his career and his readers, Williamson wanted no remedy for writing, but the experience enriched the novel that Fantasy Press published in 1948. "Though books are like children, too different for any fair comparison," Williamson wrote in *Wonder's Child*,

> Darker has always been close to my heart, perhaps because of what it let me say about myself. Dr. Glenn, the analyst in the story, has hints of Dr. Tidd, and it strikes me now that the novel can be read as a comment on my own inner conflicts as I discovered and grappled with them under the analysis. In the story, Will Barbee is at first bewildered and horrified by the emerging strangeness in himself; at the end he has come to accept himself. . . . I think it reflects my own growing willingness to accept bits of myself that I had always feared or hated.

Fantasy Press was one of the first of the fan publishers that sprang up after World War II to rescue from the moldering pulp magazines the serials that had remained uncollected since the beginning of magazine SF and fantasy in 1926. Doc Smith's "Skylark" and Lensman series were among them, and Williamson's own *Legion of Space* trilogy, Heinlein's early work, and dozens more. Most of the publishers failed after a few years because of undercapitalization (although their early books are valued by collectors at many times their original cost), but their success in selling books to faithful fans ultimately led to the establishment of SF lines by such old-line publishers as Simon & Schuster and Doubleday and by such new paperback publishers as Ace and Ballantine.

In the expansion of the "Darker Than You Think" novella into a novel, the scene of the story was shifted from New York City to the small town of Clarendon (Williamson suggests that it has some aspects of Topeka), psychotherapy and sanitarium scenes were added, as well as the hallucinatory transitions between Will Barbee's sleeping and waking. In addition, Barbee (is the resemblance to Williamson's birthplace a coincidence, or his first name, Will?) is better developed and his transformation is more effectively handled. The virtues of the original, however, are retained; *Unknown*'s preference for rationalized fantasy produced that unique tension between the supernatural material and its naturalistic presentation. The theme of lycanthropy has seldom been more skillfully handled (and may be compared to Richard Matheson's use of vampirism in *I Am Legend*), and the concept of *homo lycanthropus* provides a provocative explanation for much that is obscure in myths and legends as well as modern crime and insanity and creative genius.

Darker Than You Think was not Williamson's only venture into fantasy. His *Golden Blood*, which featured a lost race and a golden tiger in the Arabian desert, was published in *Weird Tales* in 1933 and a revised version reprinted as a paperback novel in 1964. Another novel, *The Reign of Wizardry*, which dealt with the survival of magic in Minoan Crete until it was killed by the rise of science, was serialized in *Unknown* in 1940.

Williamson was primarily a science-fiction writer, however, and even his fantasy was carefully researched and the supernatural elements "explained" in some rational fashion. He received a World Fantasy Award in 1994 for Life Achievement, but to have done what Williamson has done and for the length of time that he has done it is, without a doubt, a life achievement of an even higher order.

Darker Than You Think is the fantasy novel that dramatizes the conflict at the heart of a life that took a boy from a lonely New Mexico farm and carried him to the stars through the unlikely medium of the pulp magazines.

BLACK EASTER AND *THE DAY AFTER JUDGMENT*
JAMES BLISH

Fantasy exists in as many different varieties as authors have dreams and readers have the imaginations to follow. Even more than other forms of fiction, fantasy emerges from the inside of an author's mind unfettered by the bonds of what is real and what is possible. In a literature as free as this, distinctions may seem meaningless, but determining why fantasies resemble or differ from each other can provide not only more informed reading but greater enjoyment.

What shapes the reader's engagement with a fantasy is the way the fantastic world relates to the real world. In fact, the first challenge a reader faces in a fantasy is to determine whether the actions described are real and ordinary, real and fantastic, or unreal and maybe the delusions of a disturbed mind. Until that determination is made, the reader must suspend judgment on the correct interpretation of the story's events. Sometimes the author even withholds information or deliberately confuses the issue.

Relationships between the fantastic and the real world range from almost none to almost all. "Almost" is a necessary qualification, since without any relationship, a fantasy would be incomprehensible; and if the fantasy is congruent with the real world there is no fantasy.

Take the first few selections of the Masterpieces of Fantasy series. Roger Zelazny's *Nine Princes in Amber* posits a world "more real" than the one we know and to which our world is only one of many subsidiary realities. Peter S. Beagle's *The Last Un icorn* relates to the real world only in the comparisons to be drawn from its use of human types as characters and familiar fairy tale motifs as the mechanism for their relationships. Elizabeth Moon's *Sheepfarmer's Daughter* is an alternate reality in which a world resembling Renaissance Europe occupies unfamiliar geography but obeys all the laws of nature and of human psychology except one: magic works. Marion Zimmer Bradley's *The Mists of Avalon* plays out its feminist interpretation of the Arthurian story within the world of myth; some readers may believe the people and events once existed in some form but most think they were invented by poets to provide people with heroes and establish a national identity.

In other stories, the fantastic element exists as an isolated part of the real world, exhibiting itself so infrequently that only those fortunate enough or unlucky enough to encounter it become aware of its existence. Often the fantasy world requires special circumstances to summon it forth. One such example is Robert Holdstock's *Mythago Wood*, which casts its spell only on those who live adjacent to a primeval forest. The Masterpieces of Fantasy series also will offer imaginary worlds separated from the real world by such a vast chasm of time or reality that its relevance to our here and now exists only by inference. Such worlds are described in J. R. R. Tolkien's *The Lord of the Rings* and in Mervyn Peake's *The Gormenghast Trilogy*.

The second factor shaping the reader's engagement with the fantastic story is the attitude of the characters toward the fantastic element. Are they skeptical at the start but gradually become convinced of the existence of magic or witchcraft or of other supernatural forces acting upon them or the world? Are they believers trying to convince a population of atheists? Are they sensitive, special people singled out for magical favors or malign mistreatment? Are they ordinary people caught up in mysterious circumstances? Or do they accept the fantastic element as being an everyday aspect of their world?

John W. Campbell, the editor of *Astounding Science Fiction/Analog* who presided over science fiction's "Golden Age," provided a new alternative when, in 1939, he created a companion fantasy magazine called *Unknown* (later *Unknown Worlds*). *Unknown* featured stories written like science fiction in postulating a single departure from the real world with everything proceeding logically from that premise, but in this case the departure was fantastic rather than plausible. The result was a magazine with a special feel (and a special hold on the loyalties of its readers, who lamented its demise because of the wartime paper shortage, in 1943). That feel was reality; whether comic or deadly serious, the stories represented a close approximation of the real world and the acceptance of that world by the characters who peopled it. Several selections of the Masterpieces of Fantasy series were first published in *Unknown*, including L. Sprague de Camp and Fletcher Pratt's *The Compleat Enchanter*, Robert A. Heinlein's *The Unpleasant Profession of Jonathan Hoag*, and Fritz Leiber's *Conjure Wife*.

James Blish's *Black Easter* and *The Day After Judgment* came along too late to be published in *Unknown*, but they might have been if *Unknown* had still been in existence. In fact, they were even too late for *Beyond*, the fantasy magazine created by H. L. Gold, that occupied the same relationship to *Galaxy Science Fiction* as *Unknown* to *Astounding* and lasted from 1953 to 1955. *Black Easter* was published in 1968 and *The Day After Judgment* in 1971. In their matter-of-fact acceptance of magic as a part of everyday life and business, the two novels cast their spell of plausibility over the reader. In fact, the world of the late 1960s is represented so accurately, in all its Cold War neuroses, political competitions, and financial dealings, that the reader must think twice when the fantastic enters, even though the first sentence should be a guide: "The room stank of demons."

That sentence illustrates the strategy of the narrative, to link the commonplace with the extraordinary and thereby obtain a skeptic's temporary acceptance of the supernatural: By changing only three letters the sentence can be made to read: "The room stank of onions." But, although Campbell and Gold might have been tempted by *Black Easter* and its sequel, they might finally have rejected its serious metaphysical intent and its literary ambitions.

Blish, who was born in East Orange, New Jersey, in 1921 and died of cancer in Oxford, England, in 1975, was better known as a science-fiction writer. He had begun publishing stories in the lesser magazines while still a student at Rutgers University (he earned his B.Sc. in 1942 and he studied at Columbia toward a master's degree in zoology). Even before his college days, however, he had become associated with the Futurians, a New York fan group made up of enthusiasts, such as Isaac Asimov, Frederik Pohl, Donald Wollheim, and (later) Damon Knight, who went on to earn fame and influence in science fiction.

Blish's reputation was established in the 1950s when his novelette "Surface Tension" was published in *Galaxy* and *Earthman, Come Home* in *Astounding*. Both were reprinted in *The Science Fiction Hall of Fame*. Both became part of longer works (Blish had a habit of recycling earlier materials), "Surface Tension" in *The Seedling Stars*; *Earthman, Come Home* in the four-volume *Cities in Flight*. "A Case of Conscience," published as a short novel in *If* in 1953, was expanded into a novel in 1958 and won a Hugo Award. "Beep," a 1954 *Galaxy* novelette, was reworked into the 1973 novel *The Quincunx of Time*. "Beanstalk," a 1952 novella, became the 1961 *Titans' Daughter*.

Although he loved science fiction, Blish also had a healthy skepticism about its flaws, and another aspect of his career was exhibited in a series of reviews published mostly in fan magazines in which he held the field to the standards of all good literature. An admirer of avant-garde fiction and poetry (Blish was an authority on the work of James Joyce), he wrote most of his critical articles under the pseudonym of "William Atheling, Jr.," the pen name used by Ezra Pound for the music criticism he wrote for *The New Age*. Later those articles were collected in *The Issue at Hand* (1964) and *More Issues at Hand* (1970). Along with Damon Knight's articles and reviews (published as *In Se arch of Wonder*, 1965/1967), they provided the theoretical background for much later scholarship.

Blish was a many-talented man filled with ambitions that he had difficulty fulfilling. Scholar David Ketterer, in *Imprisoned in a Tesseract*, called him a "serious Renaissance man, a relentless and driven worker . . . rationalistic, meticulous and scholarly, even monkish . . . well informed about a number of diverse subjects including musicology . . . ruthlessly honest intellectually and possessed by a scrupulous sense of integrity." He tried full-time writing several times before he succeeded—he was more productive as a part-time writer; freedom seemed to induce writer's block—and then, ironically, it was made possible by a contract to turn *Star Trek* episodes into novelettes, by which he gained his greatest general recognition. He wanted to break away from science fiction, but he kept returning. Perhaps his best non-science-fiction work was a historical novel about the life of Roger Bacon, *Doctor Mirabilis*; he claimed that this, *Black Easter* and *The Day After Judgment* (considered as a single novel), and *A Case of Conscience* formed a thematic trilogy under the overall title After Such Knowledge. They were all concerned, he thought, with one of the oldest problems of philosophy: Is the desire for secular knowledge, let alone the acquisition and use of it, a misuse of the mind, and perhaps even actively evil?

GATHER, DARKNESS!
FRITZ LEIBER

Sometimes the genre is difficult to identify. In some novels the fantastic enters the real world so gradually that for a while the story seems like a mainstream novel of character and its everyday problems; in others the fantastic and the subjective are so inextricably mixed that the reader can never be sure if the correct interpretation of events is the supernatural or illusion, or even insanity. Such authorial strategies carry a message: the fantastic lies all about us unseen and usually unsuspected; or the supernatural, because it is not bound by the laws of everyday reality, can never be ruled out; or since the human mind is self-contained and subject to delusion, illusion, and psychosis, we can never finally know the nature of the world, or the reality of what seems inexplicable.

In more contemporary fiction, fantasy and science fiction have often been intertwined in various subtle ways. Once that would have been considered heresy. The science-fiction magazines rigorously excluded fantasy on the assumption that science-fiction readers wanted their genres pure (and that fantasy did not sell or, at least, did not sell as well), even though some of the secondary magazines regularly published adventure stories placed in space or on alien planets or on fantastically changed Earths, stories that were sometimes classified as science fantasy. And even the purest of the SF magazines, *Astounding*, published the science-fantasies of A. E. van Vogt. But it was not until *The Magazine of Fantasy and Science Fiction* was created in 1949 that the genres were displayed within the same covers.

The publication in 1980 of *The Shadow of the Torturer*, the first volume of Gene Wolfe's tetralogy (later expanded into a quintology) called *The Book of the New Sun* marked a daring departure in genre misdirection. *The Shadow of the Torturer* and its sequels evoked the reading responses of fantasy: the richly imagined and colorful far-distant future with its medieval political structures and guilds, its ancient buildings and rigid traditions, its baroque characters, its acceptance of magic, and its archaic and sometimes elevated diction, combined with a picaresque plot and a narrative reticence to encourage that acceptance of the mysterious and the inexplicable that we associate with heroic fantasy.

It was only when the series was complete that a science-fiction interpretation could be overlaid on the fantastic events—and even then some readers were confused. All of this, of course, could be rationalized in terms of Arthur C. Clarke's third law: "A sufficiently advanced technology is indistinguishable from magic." We might further surmise an authorial message: Your inability to understand the principles underlying phenomena does not mean that the cause must be supernatural. Take religion, for instance. Some critics have suggested that *The Book of the New Sun* is Christian parable.

Other writers have used the contradictory protocols for reading fantasy and science fiction to suggest alternative readings of future events. Jack Williamson, for instance, in *Demon Moon* (1994) provided a fantasy setting for what turned out to be a science-fiction situation, as if to illustrate the process by which reality is transmuted into myth when the past is lost. Michael Swanwick in *Stations of the Tide* (1991) offered a science-fiction novel that turned into fantasy, and in *The Iron Dragon's Daughter* (1993), a fantasy novel that turned into science fiction. Perhaps what these authors are trying to tell us is that we live in a world in which fantasy and science fiction have become inextricably intertwined and that it behooves us to suspend our judgment until all the evidence is in. And: If you think you know what's going on, you're probably mistaken.

None of this, of course, is without precedent. In 1939, John W. Campbell, editor of *Astounding Science Fiction*, created a companion fantasy magazine, *Unknown*, which was much loved until it was terminated in 1943 because of the wartime paper shortage. For *Unknown*, Campbell wanted fantasy stories written as if they were science fiction—that is, granted one fantastic premise, everything proceeded rationally. In that magazine in 1939 Fritz Leiber published his first story, "Two Sought Adventure," a tale of Fafhrd and the Gray Mouser, whose deeds Leiber would trace for the rest of his life and for whose subgenre Leiber would invent the term "sword and sorcery."

In fact, Leiber was better known as a fantasy writer than a science-fiction writer, although it was not until the late 1960s, with the success of Tolkien's *The Lord of the Rings,* of Le Guin's *A Wizard of Earthsea,* of Beagle's *The Last Unicorn,* and particularly of Howard's *Conan* novels, that the Fafhrd and the Gray Mouser stories began to appear in book form. The series would eventually be published in ten volumes. *Conjure Wife,* a novel about the subtle emergence of witchcraft in a college setting, was more acceptable to a general audience at the time and was reprinted in book form in 1953. First published in the April 1943 issue of *Unknown,* it was followed the next month by the initial installment, in *Astounding,* of Leiber's first important science-fiction work, *Gather, Darkness!*

Gather, Darkness! reads like fantasy, with its powerful priesthood, its medieval setting and serfs, and its religious miracles and accusations of witchcraft. Throughout the novel the reader finds scientific trickery masquerading as traditional religious ceremonies and supernatural manifestations. Almost immediately, however, the reader discovers, in the denunciation by Brother Jarles, that the scientists of the Golden Age, afraid that humanity was slipping into barbarism and ignorance, established a new religion whose miracles are performed by science and controlled by a priestly hierarchy that resurrected the Middle Ages for the common people.

The only force suitable for fighting this new "religious" tyranny is the traditional supernatural opponent of the established religion, witchcraft—or, in this case, superior technology in the guise of witchcraft. Part of the fun of *Gather, Darkness!* is the way in which Leiber manipulated the traditional imagery of the supernatural to show the machinery working behind the scenes, from haunted houses, halos, angels, and manna to gods coming to life.

All of this, it turns out, came naturally to Leiber, both the ritual and the theater. Born in 1910 in Chicago, the son of a Shakespearean actor and himself a sometime stage and motion-picture actor, Leiber earned a bachelor of philosophy degree from the University of Chicago and studied at the Washington, D.C., Episcopal General Theological Seminary. He served as an Episcopal minister at two New Jersey churches in 1932–1933 before working as an actor, editor, college instructor, airplane inspector, and associate editor of *Science Digest* for twelve years.

He won six Hugo Awards for *The Big Time* (1957), *The Wanderer* (1964), "Gonna Roll Them Bones" (1967), "Ship of Shadows" (1969), "Ill Met in Lankhmar" (1970), and "Catch That Zeppelin" (1975); "Gonna Roll Them Bones," "Ill Met in Lankhmar," and "Catch That Zeppelin" also won Nebulas. Leiber was presented the World Fantasy Award for "Belsen Express" (1975) and *Our Lady of Darkness* (1977) and the Lifetime Achievement Award in 1976; he was presented the Gandalf Grand Master award in 1980 and the SFWA Grand Master award in 1981. He was guest of honor at the World SF convention in 1951 and 1979 and of the World Fantasy Convention in 1978. He died in 1992.

The church, or witchcraft, to harbor subversion has a science-fiction tradition. As Don A. Stuart, the pen name he used for his more philosophic stories, John W. Campbell wrote two stories dealing with the effort of humanity to rid itself of alien conquerors by the use of a mystical figure, "Out of Night" (1937) and "Cloak of Aesir" (1939), later published as part of a collection under the latter title. In 1941 *Astounding* serialized *Sixth Column* by Robert A. Heinlein, writing as Anson MacDonald, about the overthrow of a conquering pan-Asian horde by American scientists disguised as a religious cult. Since Campbell was famous for suggesting story ideas to his authors, it seems likely that he recommended to both authors the use of a religious front for revolution.

Campbell was a notorious gadfly, and one of his favorite devices was to ask authors to imagine a situation contrary to traditional belief. Religion is traditional and conservative; to use it for revolution is the kind of mind-altering concept that Campbell liked to spring on his readers. The conjunction also provoked the reflection that religion and science may be different in their interpretations of the world but the "miracles" they perform, or claim, are indistinguishable. As Campbell liked to remark, "Science is the magic that works."

Each of the uses of Campbell's insight was different. In *Gather, Darkness!*, called by Alva Rogers in *A Requiem for Astounding* "one of the top ten, or at least top twenty favorites of all time," religion assumed its traditional role, with technology as its tool, and witchcraft became the force for revolution. In the process Leiber anticipated such later developments as holographic projections, which he called "telesolidographs," and mind-altering techniques years before Orwell's more celebrated *Nineteen Eighty-Four*. He also suggested that "to the truly skeptical mind, diabolic forces are just as reasonable building blocks for the cosmos as mindless electrons."

GORMENGHAST
MERVYN PEAKE

Some fantasies are one of a kind; others are the first of their kind; still others are adaptations or extensions of familiar narrative patterns. Fairy tales, ghost stories, horror stories, myths, quests, journeys, Gothics—all these are traditional ways of delving into the fantastic for particular purposes, and a reader turns to them in the expectation of remembered responses and the hope for something more. The best of them satisfy expectations and offer, in addition, skill in execution, novel insights, or the extension of the pattern into new shapes or new territories.

Of course even familiar patterns began somewhere, but those origins were mostly long ago, in the dim, forgotten stirrings of story itself. Tracing that is the work of scholars. Some of the familiar patterns have their origins in historic times, however, like the Gothic novel. Horace Walpole got that started in 1764 with *The Castle of Otranto*, and people have been elaborating ever since on the idea of haunted castles and endangered heroines.

Other celebrated works have been the first of their kind or at least picked up previous myths and folktales and gave them a shape and a form so special that the process is difficult to differentiate from invention. Bram Stoker's *Dracula*, published in 1897, was like that, and to its persistent appeal, including the various film versions of the novel or those based on the films rather than the novel, we can trace the current morbid fascination with the vampire in all its permutations. Another seminal work was Mary Shelley's 1818 *Frankenstein*, which combined the appeal of the Gothic with early nineteenth-century potential for creating life. A third such work was J. R. R. Tolkien's 1954–1956 *The Lord of the Rings*, which proved to skeptical publishers that best-sellers could emerge from fantasy and was succeeded by hundreds of what Tolkien called "subcreations" and others called "invented fantasy worlds." Tolkien revived "high fantasy" as a genre, but it isn't the genre that is at issue here (although the Gothic novel might fall into that category) but works whose concepts or style created imitators and successors, like Robert E. Howard's *Conan*, which launched an entire category of "sword and sorcery" or "heroic fantasy."

The remaining group contains those creations whose originality permits no imitation and engenders no offspring. They are sui generis, one of a kind, unique, peculiar. These are the terms that describe Mervyn Peake's Gormenghast trilogy—indeed, they describe Peake himself.

Born of missionary parents in Kuling, China, in 1911, Peake was educated in the Tientsin Grammar School and Eltham College, Croyden College of Art, and the Royal Academy Schools, graduating in 1933. He lived on Sark, one of the Channel Islands, from 1933 to 1935 and 1945 to 1949. Between those spans of years he taught at the Westminster School of Art and served in the British Army from 1941 to 1943 and then as military artist for the Ministry of Information. His early career was as an artist; he worked as a book and magazine illustrator and had one-man shows in 1943 and 1944 and the following year toured Europe as staff artist for *The Leader*. He taught at the Central School of Art in London from 1949 to 1960.

As a writer, he published the first volume of his masterpiece, *Titus Groan*, in 1946. The second volume, *Gormenghast*, was published in 1950, and the final, unfinished volume, *Titus Alone*, was published in 1959. A revised edition, reconstructed from the manuscript by Langdon Jones, was published in 1970. All three were published together, as *The Gormenghast Trilogy*, in 1988. The 1988 volume includes pages from a planned fourth volume, *Titus*

Awakes, but even the third volume was found in draft form only, as the author had already suffered the onset of the encephalitis that finally killed him in 1968.

John Clute, in *The Encyclopedia of Science Fiction*, wrote that the trilogy "was never in its author's mind a complete entity." And "it remains a series of texts whose power is remarkable, and the definition of which in generic terms is loaded with difficulties. Although couched in language which might point towards fantasy, it contains no fantasy elements; though redolent of a dying-Earth venue in its sense of belatedness and in the person of Titus's father—a fidgety, crochet-ridden, entropy-exuding manic-depressive aristocrat whose like has haunted the dying-Earth habitats of writers from M. John Harrison to Richard Grant—the first 2 volumes cannot be thought of as [SF]."

The National Observer, which called the trilogy "an eccentric, poetic masterpiece," asked the reader to "speculate for a moment. Suppose you are a novelist, seeking to dramatize a great theme, perhaps the most durable and engaging of all themes in imaginative literature. It is the theme of discovery: the discovery of self, of choice and independence, of what man is and the world is. The theme of Homer, Virgil, and Dante; of Cervantes and James Joyce. The theme of giants . . ."

The books themselves are dominated not so much by the narrative but by the image of Gormenghast castle and the densely pictorial way it is presented. Written by an artist (and illustrated with his own drawings), the first volume is (in Clute's words) "the most intensely painterly books ever crafted." It deals with the birth of the new heir to the castle, Titus, the seventy-seventh Earl of Groan, and the first two years of his life, and its greatest accomplishment is the depiction of the great, sprawling castle, virtually a world in itself, and the gallery of grotesques who populate its endless corridors.

"There would be tears and there would be strange laughter," Peake wrote. "Fierce births and deaths beneath umbrageous ceilings. And dreams, and violence, and disenchantment." And: "Over their irregular roofs would fall throughout the season, the shadows of time-eaten buttresses, of broken and lofty turrets, and, most enormous of all, the shadow of the Tower of Flints. This tower, patched unevenly with black ivy, arose like a mutilated finger from among the fists of knuckled masonry and pointed blasphemously at heaven. At night owls made of it an aching throat; by day it stood voiceless and cast its long shadow."

The central portion of the trilogy, *Gormenghast*, is Titus's bildungsroman, his coming-of-age story. But it is also the story of the Machiavellian Steerpike (Titus's alter ego?), who murders and burns and hopes to marry his way toward the usurpation of the castle. In the final book Titus leaves the castle to explore the strange, futuristic world outside. Robert Irwin in *The St.*

James Guide to Fantasy Writers suggested that "the enclosed and ritual-driven Forbidden City of Peking may have served as a partial model for Peake's castle." But he also offers the possibility "that the castle is an image of the labyrinth that is the human mind, with all its unexplored corridors and cellars. Towards the end of *Titus Alone,* Titus has the sensation that 'the earth wandered through his skull . . . a cosmos in the bone; a universe lit by a hundred lights and thronged by shapes and shadows; alive with endless threads of circumstance . . . action and event. All futility; disordered; with no end and no beginning.'"

As an author Peake was remarkable in other ways: he had, for instance, as many art books as novels: *The Craft of the Lead Pencil* (1946), *Drawings by Meryyn Peake* (1950), *Figures of Speech* (1954), *The Drawings of Meryyn Peake* (1974), *Meryyn Peake: Writings and Drawings* (1974), and *Sketches from Bleak House* (1983). In 1953 he published a non-Titus novel, *Mr. Pye,* about a visitor to the island of Sark who is so good he finds himself growing the wings of an angel and tries desperately to rid himself of them. Peake published an early book for children, *Captain Slaughterboard Drops Anchor* (1939), and a later one, *Letters from a Lost Uncle* (1948). Two volumes of short stories were published after his death, including *Peake's Progress: Selected Writings and Drawings of Mervyn Peake* (1978), and nine volumes of poetry: *Shapes and Sounds* (1941), *Rhymes Without Reason* (1944), *The Glassblowers* (1950), *The Rhyme of the Flying Bomb* (1962), *Poems and Drawings* (1965), *A Reverie of Bone and Other Poems* (1967), *Selected Poems* (1972), *A Book of Nonsense* (1972), and *Twelve Poems 1939–1960* (1975). He had two plays produced, *The Connoisseurs* (1952) and *The Wit to Woo* (1957), and several radio dramatizations, including one for *Titus Groan* in 1956.

Somehow they all seem overshadowed by Gormenghast itself, this monumental creation that consumed much of Peake's creative imagination and perhaps Peake himself. As *New World* said of him, "To discuss the work of Mervyn Peake presents a special difficulty; the reviewer is faced by the incredible diversity of his wide-ranging talents. Illustrator, painter, poet, novelist and playwright, he represents a creative phenomenon, a man with an intense and individual inner vision."

Clute summed up, "Throughout, the wealth of detail of the work makes Gormenghast one of the most richly realized alternate worlds in all the literature of fantasy or [SF]."

THE LAST UNICORN
PETER BEAGLE

Last time we looked into the other side of the mirror, I suggested that fantasy takes place in the worlds of "make believe" and "what if" and that our first response is intuitive: we know it when we see it. We open a book, and there it is, as Keats wrote in his "Ode to a Nightingale": "The same that oft-times hath / Charmed magic casements, opening on the foam / Of perilous seas, in faery lands forlorn."

But what is it we see, and how do we know it?

What we recognize today as fantasy started in preliterate days as myth. Myth is a collection of anonymous stories that have their origins in the folk-beliefs of races or nations; myth offers supernatural explanations for the natural world that fit a group's concept of what it means to be human or how and why the universe began and the place of humanity in it. Myths survive today, however, not as belief-systems but as stories and as images imbedded in the language. We speak, as Erik Rabkin has pointed out in his *Fantastic Worlds*, "of Herculean feats and Procrustean beds and the Oedipus complex."

Rabkin believes that myth developed into folktales, as a culture begins consciously shaping its myths. Folktales are offered first as entertainment and only secondarily as explanation; they are clearly man-made.

Some familiar stories get surrounded by narrative conventions aimed at particular audiences. The fairy tale, for instance, offers a set of recognizable conventions directed at children. Sometimes, when those conventions are shaped in an artistic fashion, a familiar story can be reimagined for another audience—a children's story for adults, for instance.

Rabkin sees myth, folktale, and fairy tale forming "a sliding scale along which the stories become more conventionalized, the audience becomes more limited, the teller becomes more sophisticated, the truth value becomes more symbolic and less literal, but in all of which the issues remain the same."

After the Industrial Revolution and the advent of the Age of Science, supernatural explanations for the way things are became less necessary and less plausible. The literature of the Industrial Revolution and its emerging middle class was realism and, in particular, the realistic novel, which portrayed the changing world in pragmatic terms and offered the middle class instruction in how to behave, the way myths and folktales provided lessons for children.

Rather than performing a social function like myth, modern fantasy may be antisocial. The Austrian critic Franz Rottensteiner has written that "modern fantasy is a reaction to industrial society and its pressures. . . . It is not chance that this kind of fantasy arose in nineteenth-century England, the country that first felt the full pressure of industrialization; that its main practicioners, whether Morris, Lord Dunsany, C. S. Lewis, E. R. Eddison, or J. R. R. Tolkien, all profoundly disliked their own time; or that this literature reached its greatest popularity in the scientifically and industrially most advanced country on Earth (the US) and then spread from there to foreign countries. Modern fantasy is a literature for a discontented city population."

The Gothic romance, with its haunted castles and supernatural apparitions, sprang up in the middle of the eighteenth century, beginning with Horace Walpole's *The Castle of Otranto* in 1764. After the turn of the nineteenth century, the Gothic novel drew upon the sciences to nurture early science fiction, as in Mary Shelley's *Frankenstein* (1818). By the end of that century, authors such as George MacDonald and William Morris deliberately tried to evoke an earlier era with their fairy tales and magical romances. At about the same time Bram Stoker was writing *Dracula* and the ghost story was becoming popular; such narratives brought the supernatural into everyday life to evoke emotions of awe or terror at the unseen or the unknown, or even sometimes at what lurked in the subconscious mind.

Otherworldly fantasy was created early in the twentieth century, as David Pringle has pointed out in *Modern Fantasy*, by authors such as "Lord Dunsany, E. R. Eddison, David Lindsay and—in America—by James Branch Cabel, A. Merritt, H. P. Lovecraft and Clark Ashton Smith." That eventually led to Tolkien and the world of the hobbits, and in the United States to Robert E. Howard and Conan's Hyperborea.

And they, in turn, led to the great boom in modern fantasy, which up to the 1960s was a minor publishing category. In the 1960s new possibilities emerged from rival U.S. paperback editions of *The Lord of the Rings*, from the book versions of Conan retrieved and edited by L. Sprague de Camp, from Ira Levin's *Rosemary's Baby*, from the first paperback editions of Fritz Leiber's Fafhrd and the Gray Mouser sword-and-sorcery stories, and, as Pringle notes, from two books issued in 1968, Ursula K. Le Guin's *A Wizard of Earthsea* and Peter Beagle's *The Last Unicorn*.

Beagle was born in New York City in 1939 and earned a bachelor of arts degree from the University of Pittsburgh twenty years later. While still a student he was writing *A Fine and Private Place*, which got published while he was studying at Stanford University in 1960–1961. In *The Fantasy Worlds of Peter Beagle* (1978), he recalled writing his first novel at the age of nineteen about a real cemetery in the Bronx. He wrote it sitting in his dormitory room, trying to type softly at two in the morning. He also commented that there were only two important things to know about his fiction: that he is a born hider who cultivates an air of guileless candor; and that he has always been a singer, even a writer and public performer of songs. Of course he also says that he is "an old professional liar" and nothing he says is to be trusted.

But Beagle's most remarkable aspect may be that at the age of twenty-eight he published one of the fantasy novels that helped turn a generation into readers of fantasy. *The Last Unicorn* is a modern fairy tale—that is, it takes the characters and narratives of classic children's stories and adapts them for adult reading by adding real-world sensibilities, while retaining their appeal to children. It is also, in a sense, meta-fantasy—that is, it comments about the nature of fantasy and fairy tales while it is spinning its web of enchantment. It discusses the nature of unicorns and magicians and heroes while telling stories about them, and mixes categories with abandon.

Schmendrick the magician, for instance, is inept, but he is the unicorn's only chance. Schmendrick tells the imprisoned unicorn that the magic on her is only magic and can be removed, but "the enchantment of error that you put on me I must wear forever in your eyes. We are not always what we seem, and hardly ever what we dream."

Prince Lir, the hero of the story, tries to win the Lady Amalthea by killing dragons and rescuing maidens in distress. The novel observes at one point that Lir "knew how to make [women] stop crying—generally you killed something." It also notes that adventures are good for the constitution: that Lir's "adventures had made him much handsomer and taken off a lot of weight." It is this combination of the fantastic juxtaposed with the commonplace that gives *The Last Unicorn* its unique flavor.

At another point, the entrance of a band of outlaws brings in comparisons to Robin Hood and his Merry Men—literally brings them in. And the outlaws themselves turn out to be trapped in roles. In fact, throughout the novel the characters get caught up in the roles they are required to play, thus asking readers to consider the storytelling process while they enjoy the story.

The magic is that it works. The reason it works is Beagle's sorcery with words and the wit and wisdom slipped into the narrative as delicately as butterfly wings. There are talking animals, too, and all sorts of fantastic creatures. And revelations about all of them, such as the fact that unicorns cannot have human emotions.

An animated film version of *The Last Unicorn* was produced in 1982, with a screenplay by Beagle. Beagle has written other screenplays, including one for an animated version of *The Lord of the Rings: Part One*, *The Dove*, and *The Greatest Thing that Almost Happened*. He has written an opera libretto, *The Midnight Angel*. His other novel is *The Innkeepers' Song*, published in 1993.

He has written nonfiction: *I See by My Outfit* (1965), *The California Feeling* (1969), *The Lady and Her Tiger* (1976, with Pat Derby), and *The Garden of Earthly Delights* (1982), and he has written for the *Ladies Home Journal* and the *Saturday Evening Post*.

But, as Beagle has admitted, *The Last Unicorn* is the book by which people know him: "It will probably haunt the rest of my career, as *The Crock of Gold* came to haunt James Stephens." It may haunt readers as well. The last unicorn, happy in her forest, with her magic pool, can live forever, bringing joy and peace to her little part of the world. But she risks everything on the mere chance that she can find her lost fellows and rescue them. Readers who venture into the pages of Beagle's novel must take their chances, like the unicorn, of losing their hearts forever.

LITTLE, BIG
JOHN CROWLEY

One familiar fantasy concerns the knight who goes off to rescue maidens and slay the dragons who hold them prisoner. But a colleague of mine has a cartoon in his office window that shows a reclining dragon, surrounded by shattered pieces of armor; the dragon is picking his teeth with a lance. The caption reads: "Sometimes the dragon wins." That's realism, and it's funny. The reason it is funny is that realism comes as a comic surprise in a romantic environment; for generations fantasy writers such as L. Sprague de Camp and Gordon R. Dickson have used such contrasts for humor.

Across the centuries realism and romanticism have battled for sway over the popular mind. Sometimes realism prevails; sometimes romanticism; but usually individuals alternate between them as the situation demands. Realism tells us that the universe pays no attention to the way people feel about it, and no amount of complaints about injustice will improve the human condition. Romanticism says that reality is only skin deep, and that underneath is a world that can be shaped by human desires, or at least that may reflect human moods.

We live in a skeptical, realistic age, but romanticism keeps trying to soften our hard-headed pragmatism. Literature imitates life: science fiction, the fantastic literature of a pragmatic age, is romanticism harnessed by realism; fantasy, the literature of humanistic rebellion against an uncaring universe, is romanticism unleashed. In a collection of his SF stories, George R. R. Martin commented that his all-time champion theme "has got to be reality's search and destroy mission against romance."

A considerable amount of fantasy is devoted to what Edgar L. Chapman in *The St. James Guide to Science Fiction Writers* has called "the magic lying beneath the surface of existence." Such fantasy stories suggest that the fantasy world is not restricted to the other side of the mirror but permeates the real world if we only could perceive it. The very young see the world that way, as a place of wonder. The dean of romantic poets, William Wordsworth, described the experience in the opening lines of "Intimations of Immortality From Recollections of Early Childhood":

> There was a time when meadow, grove, and stream
> The Earth, and every common sight,
> To me did seem

Appareled in celestial light,
The glory and the freshness of a dream.

Fantasies based on the concept that reality is an illusion, sometimes deeply disturbing, sometimes comforting, can shock us awake with vicious attacks from unleashed demons or can lull us into a state of reverie in which we give credence to their tales of hidden truths. The latter must work with the greatest delicacy—a wrong word, a too-close inspection, the forcible entry of skepticism may break the spell. Everything must be just beyond one's reach, a glimpse out of the corner of one's eye, a furtive movement that turns into the commonplace when one looks at it straight on.

Such a novel is John Crowley's *Little, Big*, which Thomas M. Disch called "the greatest fantasy novel ever" and Ursula K. Le Guin, "a book that all by itself calls for a redefinition of fantasy." It is a novel that convinces by implication rather than by argument, that develops through contrasts and inconsistencies, as its title suggests. At one point Dr. Bramble explains the existence of fairy folk and the nebulous realm they occupy: "The explanation is that the world inhabited by these beings is . . . another world entirely, and it is enclosed within this one, with a peculiar geography I can only describe as *infundibular*." He paused for effect. "I mean by this that the other world is composed of a series of concentric rings, which as one penetrates deeper into the other world, grow larger. The further in you go, the bigger it gets."

Other contrasts are at work in the Little and the Big, as David Pringle has pointed out in *Modern Fantasy: The Hundred Best Novels*: "the country and the city, the inside and the outside, the private and the public, the faerie and the human." The story of *Little, Big* deals with a city dweller named Smoky Barnable who leaves his dull job to marry Daily Alice Drinkwater. She lives in a rambling house built by her great-grandfather next to a wood that may be inhabited by fairies of various kinds. Alice's father writes children's books based on the stories told him by the fairies. Other members of the family are blessed or cursed by fairy gifts.

While Smoky and Alice consummate their marriage and raise a son, Auberon, and while Smoky continues his long effort to enter the world of Faerie, the world outside gets uglier. A fascist president is elected who attempts to destroy everyone who cherishes nature and the imagination—a personification, perhaps, of "reality's search and destroy mission against romance."

It is a time of personal sacrifice and discovery and renewal, all as indirect as a dreamscape. "The reader," Pringle says, "trembles on the brink of successive revelations, as the author plays with masterly skill on the emotional nerves of awe, rapture, mystery and enchantment."

Crowley, born in Maine in 1942, earned a B.A. from Indiana University and worked as a photographer and commercial artist for two years before turning to writing and since has worked in documentary films and television. His first SF novel, *The Deep*, was published in 1975 to considerable acclaim. It is a novel about a mysterious Being who has brought humans from their own dying planet to an artificial disk world and now engages them in interminable warfare.

Beasts (1976) describes a post-collapse world in which Crowley's persistent theme gets stated for the first time: the conflict between rational organizers who want to control nature as well as the people who want to live within it, and the romantics and lovers of nature who resist the government's dehumanizing effects. The "beasts" are hybrids, created from humans and animals.

Engine Summer (1979) is another post-holocaust world in which Rush That Speaks relives his youthful search for meaning and understanding. He also learns of the vanished twentieth-century science and technology that finally is revealed as excessive rationalism that has brought an end to its own world. And Rush discovers that he is a personality recorded within a memory cube.

Little, Big, which won the World Fantasy Award for best novel of 1981, was followed by new breakthroughs in fantastic concepts. *Aegypt* (1987) weaves together, as Edgar L. Chapman points out in *The St. James Guide to Science Fiction Writers*, "the Grail legend, the quests of Giordano Bruno, the adventures of the Elizabethan astrologer and occultist John Dee, a fanciful life of Shakespeare, and the quest of a modern Parsifal, Pierce Moffett." The Aegypt of the title refers not to Egypt but to the Renaissance myth of the magical world of Platonism and neoPlatonism symbolized by the figure of Hermes Trismegestus. In this novel Crowley perfected his technique of stories within stories, of myths restated and relived, of lives revisited and reimagined in later times, all to achieve a depth of focus that suggests the palimpsests that history and literature write on the present and the wisdom that allows perceptive and sensitive people to read between the lines.

Aegypt, Chapman concludes, "consolidates [Crowley's] claim to be not merely a major fantasy writer, but a writer who deserves to be considered a major novelist by any standards." Crowley followed *Aegypt* with another novel set in the same fantasy world and using the same characters, *Love and Sleep* (1994). He also published a collection of stories in 1989 titled *Novelties* (also known as *Great Works of Time*), which includes the much-praised novella "In Blue."

But *Little, Big* was the novel that first made Crowley's readers aware of the fact that he not only was a skillful writer but one who was going to establish new standards for the fantasy novel. Crowley himself has commented that the novel was important to his development because he discovered for the first time "the extent of my own powers as a writer." "*Little, Big* has permeated the field," John Clute wrote in *The Encyclopedia of Science Fic-*

tion, and "his fantasies have established him as a figure whose work markedly stretches the boundaries of genre literature."

Chapman concludes, "This humorous, whimsical, inventive, and richly allusive fantasy deserves many readings and is likely to become a classic of the genre. Here, as in the rest of his world, Crowley defines his vision as that of a sophisticated romantic, suspicious of technology, committed to the cause of his imagination, and possessing prodigious literary gifts of humor, characterization, and lyrical description."

Open the door of the fabulous Drinkwater residence and find "a compound illustration of the plates of [Alice's grandfather's] famous book—several different houses of different sizes and styles collapsed together." It is a metaphor for *Little, Big* itself, a novel, like the Fairy woods, that is bigger on the inside that it is on the outside.

THE LORD OF THE RINGS
J. R. R. TOLKIEN

Contemporary fantasy begins with *The Lord of the Rings*. David Pringle wrote in *Modern Fantasy: The Hundred Best Novels* that "the great American publishing boom in fantasy really got under way in the mid to late 1960s. . . . The books that first defined the category were the rival US paper back editions of . . . The Lord of the Rings . . . , which appeared in 1965-6." And John Clute in *The Encyclopedia of Fantasy* called it "the paradigm 20th century fantasy text" and its author "the 20th century's single most important author of fantasy."

What did Tolkien's novel accomplish?

Before the mid-1960s, fantasy was a minor publishing category. It had a longer, and in some ways more distinguished, literary history; in fact, for much of literary history, fantasy was indistinguishable from literature itself, and it was only with the rise of the novel in the late eighteenth century and the short story in the first half of the nineteenth century, with their associated developments of realism and naturalism, that fantasy became a separate category. Meanwhile, science fiction, called "*voyages extraordinaires*" and "scientific romance" in the nineteenth century, was seldom considered part of the mainstream. Nevertheless, science fiction seemed peculiarly appropriate to the late nineteenth and the first half of the twentieth century—that is, fantasy seemed an escape from the realities of a world that had surrendered much of its faith in the supernatural to belief in what could be measured and tested. At the same time, science and technology seemed to explain so much that had formerly appeared mysterious and provided even ordinary citizens with the power to shape their environments and their lives.

After 1926, when Hugo Gernsback founded the first science-fiction magazine, *Amazing Stories*, science-fiction magazines proliferated while fantasy magazines were represented mostly by *Weird Tales*, which specialized in the horror story. A common belief in publishing circles was that fantasy didn't sell: fantasy magazines struggled to survive and even fantasy novels did not have the basic audience of science fiction. After World War II, the publishing of science fiction boomed, even the publishing of books, which had largely been neglected since 1926.

In the past quarter century the position of fantasy in the publishing spectrum has improved, as fantasy achieved equality with science fiction in numbers of books published and perhaps superiority in its potential readership; the reason was largely the popular and critical success of Tolkien's epic. Other novels, such as Robert E. Howard's Conan books revived by L. Sprague de Camp, helped confirm the changing tide of reader appeal. The mood of the times may have contributed, as well; Pringle commented that "Hundreds of thousands of Tolkien's and Howard's books were sold to a largely young audience which apparently wished to turn its back on a scientific and technological world."

In terms of writing craft, Tolkien revolutionized fantasy by developing a "secondary world" so thoroughly that it became as complex as the real world, rather like Jorge Luis Borges's famous story "Tlon, Uqbar, Orbius Tertius," in which secret masters generate *A First Encyclopedia of Tlon* that actually creates that world and work on a new edition that will turn Earth into Tlon. Tolkien's unprecedented world building, according to Clute, "gave final legitimacy to the use of an internally coherent and autonomous land of Faerie as a venue for the play of human imagination. . . . JRRT gave fantasy a domain." And, even though he is clearly a writer of fantasy, Tolkien is included in most science-fiction encyclopedias.

In a 1939 lecture "On Fairy Tales," later twice expanded as an essay, Tolkien outlined his theories about the "secondary world," so completely imagined and governed by its own rules that the reader believes in it as much as he believes in his own world. A secondary world is one in which, as Tolkien put it, "a green sun will be credible." Tolkien's "Encyclopedia of Tlon" was *The Silmarillion*, which he began working on before he went off to service in World War I and continued expanding until his death. It was finally published, still unfinished, in 1977, by his son Christopher, who also has published a dozen other posthumous works under the general title of *The History of Middle-Earth*.

The Silmarillion was the history of the world as written by the elves, and Tolkien intended it as a conscious mythology for England, which lacked, he thought, a true creation myth. The later posthumous publications filled in other parts of the "backstory" that lies behind and enriches the narrative of *The Lord of the Rings*. In Tolkien's mythology, the world Arda was created before time began by a Prime Being who conceived the gods (and then disappears). The gods sing Arda, a flat world consisting of one vast continent, into existence. Later the gods, known as Valar, are joined by the demigods, known as Maiar. One of the Valar, Melkor, rebels and is defeated. His Maiar servant Sauron fights on, eventually tricking elves into creating for him the nine Rings of Power while he himself creates the One Ring that controls the others. It is this ring, lost by Sauron and recovered by Frodo's cousin Bilbo in *The Hobbit*, that Frodo and his companions seek to destroy in *The Lord of the Rings*.

Other aspects of Tolkien's "secondary world" describe the creation of two magical lamps that light Arda, their destruction, and the creation of magical trees the Valar use for light; the creation of dwarfs (Tolkien calls them "dwarves"); the kindling of the sun and the moon; the creation of humans, hobbits, and elves; the sinking of Atlante (Atlantis); and the shrinking of Arda into a globe. There is much more to the creation story than that—enough, indeed, to fill a dozen books as big as *The Lord of the Rings* itself.

It was a lifetime work for someone who was an academic and a scholar of Anglo-Saxon, not primarily a writer of fantasy. Born in South Africa in 1892, Tolkien was brought to England in 1895 and educated at King Edward VI's School, Birmingham; St. Philip's School, Birmingham; and Exeter College, Oxford. He served as an officer in the Lancashire Fusiliers from 1915 to 1918, married in the midst of the war, had three sons and one daughter, became reader in English and then professor of the English language at the University of Leeds, and then at Oxford University, where he ended his academic career Merton Professor of English language and literature. Tolkien also was an artist, and his illustrations for *The Lord of the Rings* (and the "visions," which he considered "a gift," may have owed a great deal to his artist's eye) added to the appeal of his epic. He died in 1973. He won many awards, including World SF Convention's Gandalf and Hugo awards, both posthumously.

Another facet of Tolkien's fantasies was their style. As Donald L. Lawler commented in *The St. James Guide to Science Fiction Writers*, "More than any work of its type, *The Silmarillion* grew out of language, both received and invented," "the most lyrical prose ever written in English," and "Tolkien's genius for naming grew directly out of his interest in developing imaginary languages spoken by beings all the more imaginary for dwelling in the world of fairies." And John Clute calls attention to Tolkien's sensitive mixture of archaic diction and modern, so that "the ordinary and the marvelous— or the 'simple' event and the revelation that this present-day occurrence is a quote of profounder happenings from an immense back-story—inhabit the same overarching reality." One of the influences on Tolkien's style was his linguistic background; another was his association at Oxford before World War II with Owen Barfield, C. S. Lewis, and Charles Williams. The name they gave themselves was "the Inklings," and their custom of reading their works aloud may have helped shape their language.

The Hobbit, or There and Back Again, the first of the hobbit stories, was published in 1937 and later revised twice. *The Lord of the Rings* was published in three volumes in 1954, because publishers of that time were concerned not only about the difficulties of selling fantasy but about the problems of marketing a thousand-page fantasy novel. Even then it did not achieve a substantial impact until 1965, when it was published in two paperback editions in the United States, the first by Ace Books when publishers noticed that the novel was not in copyright in the United States, the second, somewhat revised to allow new copyright, by Ballantine Books. After that, there was no stopping the novel or those books that capitalized on its marketing success and its secondary-world model.

Clute calls attention to the unfortunate aftermath of *The Lord of the Rings*. Not only have fantasies been published in unending trilogies, in imitation of what was originally a publishing artifact, "countless purveyors of genre fantasy have reduced the secondary world to the Identikit fantasyland. . . . But there are compensations. Over and above the value of his works themselves, the dialogue between JRRT and writers like Peter S. Beagle and Stephen R. Donaldson (to name only two) has been immensely fruitful."

For those who come to *The Lord of the Rings* for the first time, welcome to Tolkien's secondary world.

LORD VALENTINE'S CASTLE
ROBERT SILVERBERG

Like the rest of history, literature seems to move in cycles. "To every thing there is a season, and a time to every purpose under the heaven," Ecclesiastes tells us. Although fantasy is the oldest form of storytelling and never seems to go out of style, sometimes it has had to struggle for recognition. The romantic period in English literature lasted for almost a century, and since fantasy is romantic—that is, it asserts the dominance of human desire over nature and its processes—fantasy was in fashion. Even realism, which developed in the latter half of the nineteenth century in response to a growing reliance on science for explanations rather than on the supernatural, left room for fantasy as a reaction.

But naturalism, with its emphasis on Darwin's theories, supplanted realism. Everything *evolved*, or changed by natural processes, over time—sometimes geologic time—and nothing was *transformed*. People who were dedicated to changing the world, or their own place in it, began looking to science and technology. Fantasy survived for a time in the early twentieth-century adventure-pulp magazines such as *Argosy* and *All-Story*, but it, too, finally succumbed to the pragmatism of the times. When Hugo Gernsback created *Amazing Stories*, the first science-fiction magazine, in 1926, it seemed as if the fantastic imagination had chosen nature. Science fiction was in; fantasy was out.

Not all the way out, of course. Fantasy survived here and there, sometimes revived, as in *Fantastic Mysteries*, which in 1939 began reprinting the old Munsey-magazine pulp stories, and sometimes disguised as something else—a mystery novel, for instance, or a thriller, or even as a kind of fantasy-based science fiction, as in Street & Smith's *Unknown*.

By the time a young Robert Silverberg began publishing stories and novels in the mid-1950s, he turned naturally to science fiction. He wanted "to experience the future," he said in a 1996 interview published in *Locus*. "There was no reason to write fantasy then—there was no place to publish it. *Unknown* had been gone for about ten years, and the only magazines that published anything like fantasy were the almost invisible *Weird Tales* and the very trashy *Fantastic Adventures*."

Publishing wisdom of the times said that "fantasy doesn't sell," and the short life of several fantasy magazines, as well as the sales records of the few books that got published, seemed to bear that out. But in the 1960s everything changed again. What transformed publishing history was the unprecedented success of J. R. R. Tolkien's *The Lord of the Rings*, which appeared from two different U.S. publishers in 1965–1966. That astonishing event was reinforced by the paperback popularity of Robert E. Howard's Conan books, edited and later supplemented by L. Sprague de Camp. As David Pringle pointed out in his *Modern Fantasy: The Hundred Best Novels*, other books came along in the late 1960s, such as Ira Levin's *Rosemary's Baby* (1967) and Ursula K. Le Guin's *A Wizard of Earthsea* (1968) and Peter Beagle's *The Last Unicorn* (1968). All showed what fantasy was capable of, both artistically and commercially. Fantasy was back in; fantasy sold.

Today fantasy rivals science fiction in popularity and the numbers of books published. *Locus* reported that 224 original fantasy novels were published in 1996, as compared with 253 original science-fiction novels. Numbers, of course, are no measure of artistic success, nor is popularity. And yet the opportunity to be published and the financial return that allows an author to continue writing in his or her chosen field determine what will be available to be read. As Silverberg remarked, "I still require an audience. I'm a professional writer, a commercial writer. I want people to read what I write."

He also said, "Fantasy is the dominant commercial artform of our genre now, though you couldn't give fantasy books away in the '40s, '50s, and early '60s." Those were the years when Silverberg was making his mark, first as a fan, then a published author at the age of nineteen while still a student at Columbia University, and subsequently as the consummate writing professional, turning out publishable material first draft and upon editorial order, being named the most promising new writer of 1955. Only when the science-fiction market began to collapse in the late 1950s did he depart to become a prolific author in other fields, under a variety of pseudonyms and in a variety of areas, including some scientific popularizations.

He made a sizable fortune at it, so that when he returned to science fiction in the later 1960s he could afford to do so as the consummate artist, polishing and repolishing his prose until it met his own difficult standards. During the next dozen years he published one artistic success after another, winning two Hugo Awards and three Nebulas; later he would win several more. In 1972 he moved to California and a couple of years later announced his retirement, exhausted by the strain of his production and his agonizing writing discipline, and disillusioned by the publishing situation that saw most of his books out of print.

In 1980 he made a triumphal return with a novel that earned him the largest advance in the field up to that time and was a significant departure from his previous publications and from his writing methods. The result was the long, colorful science-fantasy *Lord Valentine's Castle*. As if a dam had been broken, a great pool of imagination was released and words poured out. In a 1996 SFWA *Bulletin*, he recalled how, in 1978, he set down on the back of an envelope the following words:

> 1979 NOVEL
> The scene is a giant planet-sized city—an urban Big Planet, population of billions, a grand gaudy romantic canvas. The city is divided into vast subcities, each with its own characteristic tone. The novel is joyous and huge—no sense of dystopia. The form is that of a pilgrimage across the entire sphere. (For what purpose?) A colossal odyssey through bizarre bazaars. Parks & wonders...
> Deliver a positive commodity. The book must be fun. Picaresque characters. Strange places—but all light, delightful, raffish. Cornie novel. Magical mystery tour.

And then:

> Young man journeying to claim an inheritance that has been usurped—his own identity has been stolen & he now wears another body.

The genre that Silverberg had turned to was science-fantasy—not quite science fiction because it involved strange powers and hierarchical, even mythical concerns such as the usurpation of authority, rightful succession, and personal development; not quite fantasy because it presumed a natural origin for all its background, including the nature of a giant planet colonized by humans some thousands of years earlier and the shapechangers who were once its dominant species. It was a kind of imaginative fiction that had once been more popular in the days of Planet stories or *Startling Stories* (in which Jack Vance's *Big Planet* had been serialized in 1952) or even *Fantastic Adventures*. Much of A. E. van Vogt's science fiction in *Astounding* was science-fantasy.

Sometimes science-fantasy seems more like science fiction, sometimes more like fantasy depending on the amount of explanation provided and the plausibility of the explanation. *Lord Valentine's Castle* leaned toward science fiction as did its sequels, *Majipoor Chronicles* (1982), *Valentine Pontifex* (1983), and *The Mountains of Majipoor* (1995). The next in the series, *Sorcerers of Majipoor* (1997), explores the magical side to which Silverberg has announced he now intends to devote most of his efforts. He thinks there may be another two or three novels yet to be told about Majipoor.

In his interview, he said, "I *am* very interested in writing fantasy, and not the occasional short story but novels or even, lord help me, series of novels. There are a couple of reasons for this. One is obviously commercial, and one is artistic. It's been my attempt for the last 30 years or so, to manage this trick of being commercial and artistic at the same time, and I've had occasional success with it, occasional catastrophe with it. But I've done pretty well at both of them."

"Pretty well" is an understatement. Born in 1935 in New York City, Silverberg fulfilled his ambition to write science fiction, and to become a full-time writer, at an early age, and he has not only written innumerable stories collected in more volumes than most authors have novels, but hundreds of novels. They have been honored by Silverberg's readers and by his fellow writers. He served as the second president of the Science Fiction Writers of America, edited its first *Science Fiction Hall of Fame* volume (and dozens of other anthologies), has been guest of honor (and frequent toastmaster) at the World Science Fiction Convention, and he has become, in his mature years, one of science fiction's master craftsmen and elder statesmen.

In an autobiographical essay for *Hell's Cartographers* (1975), he wrote: "I am a man who is living his own adolescent fantasies." Who better than Silverberg to turn to writing fantasies for others? Few are more colorful than the adventures of Valentine, cast adrift in a fantastic world to find his own way through incredible difficulties and over incredible distances back to Castle Mount, whose thirty-mile height, surrounded by fifty spectacular cities, is no more intimidating than Valentine's task of regaining himself—and his lost throne.

Signed First Editions of Science Fiction

Signed First Editions of Science Fiction got created at the World Science Fiction Convention in Atlanta in 1986. I had persuaded Eric Stones to attend so that he could meet some of the writers he was reprinting and some of the people who were writing introductions for him, and he had persuaded me to attend as well. Over dinner one evening he said that Easton was considering a new series of signed first editions of science fiction and asked what I thought. I thought it would be popular. How would we choose which books to include? he asked. I agreed to read manuscripts and bound proofs and recommend which books to include and then to write introductions for them. That process lasted until 1997, when Easton at first decided to instead expand its list of introducers, then, shortly thereafter, to choose the books in house, dispense with introductions, and use collector's notes.

FALLING FREE
LOIS MCMASTER BUJOLD

Coincidence is at work here. Or destiny.

I was in New York in April of 1988 at the Nebula Award weekend. I hadn't attended an award event for several years, and I had been invited to speak about science fiction at the Hayden Planetarium. As a former SFWA president, I was invited to present one of the Nebula awards, by chance for the novel. I was handed the list of nominees and the name of the winner in a sealed envelope. The winner was: *Falling Free* by Lois McMaster Bujold. The novel had been published as a four-part serial in *Analog* in late 1997 and early 1998, and would be published as a book that year by Baen Books. I hadn't yet read *Falling Free*, and I hadn't met the charming Ms. Bujold, so it was a totally new experience.

Only a year later, I got the manuscript for *Borders of Infinity* in the mail from Easton and wrote the first of nearly half-a-dozen introductions to Bujold books in Easton's Signed First Editions of Science Fiction. All of the Easton editions concern Bujold's handicapped hero, Miles Vorkosigan. All are placed in the distant future when humanity has colonized the stars through the use of wormhole. They provide transportation systems that make connections with remote spots of the galaxy through hyperspace shortcuts. Through the isolation of time and distance and collapses of civilization and technology, in the Miles Vorkosigan saga, human colonies have developed socially, politically, and technologically in sharply divergent ways.

In *Borders of Infinity*, a collection of three short novels about Miles that included the Nebula Award–winning "The Mountains of Mourning," I placed the novel in the science-fiction consensus future history that Donald Wollheim described in his 1971 book about science fiction, *The Universe Makers*. The Miles Vorkosigan books are located late in that future history, between "the barbarism of the Interregnum" and "the rise of a Permanent Galactic Civilization." *Falling Free* comes earlier, between "trips to the stars" and "the rise of the Galactic Empire." Earth and Earth-controlled corporations are still key players in the Great Game of galactic politics, and the politics and personal relationships are those with which we are familiar. We don't need much background to understand where we are and what is at stake.

But a little background might be helpful. We understand, without much instruction, that spaceflight and the instant transportation over light distances provided by wormholes has taken humanity to a number of other solar systems. We also discover that many of these have been settled and exploited by giant interstellar corporations whose purpose is that of all corporations, making profits. The corporations are not as soulless as those postulated by William Gibson's *Neuromancer* and its cyberpunk successors. Some of its employees are ordinary human beings with normal human concerns, and the corporations are as handicapped by their own bureaucracy as are its employees. Part of the fun of *Falling Free* is the pleasure of observing people manipulate the system in the way that employees have learned to do ever since complicated systems demanded complicated procedures.

Falling Free, however, is driven by more important concerns: genetic engineering practiced on humans in ways with which we have only recently become familiar, and the treatment of experimental human beings as capital equipment. The title of the novel has a double meaning. Almost all the action takes place inside a giant habitat—a space construction in orbit around the barren, inhospitable planet Rodeo—in an environment of zero gravity. It is literally falling around the planet at a speed that keeps it at a constant altitude, and the people who live inside the Habitat are in perpetual free fall. In this kind of environment, ordinary humans are handicapped by their evolutionary origins and development on planets. Their coordination doesn't work right, their bodies don't function properly, their muscles deteriorate, and their bones lose mass.

Then one geneticist realizes that humans could be created for whom space would be a natural environment. New developments and the invention of the uterine replicator make his concept workable. The result is the quaddies—humans designed with four arms instead of two (what use are legs in space?), internal organs that function best in zero gravity, and bones that don't deteriorate. Since these are the product of a corporate society, the corporation that invested in them expects to make a profit by using the quaddies for handling freight and manning weightless spaceships and stations.

But something happens, as it always does, to alter everybody's plans. In this case a new invention destroys the potential value of the quaddies. That brings into play the secondary meaning of the title: freedom. How do you explain freedom to children and near-children who have experienced only corporate care and constant supervision by manipulative adults? And how do you liberate the quaddies from a corporation for whom they are at best an embarrassment and at worst a continuing financial burden and even living proof of corruption? How do you enable the quaddies to fall free?

It won't be easy. Readers familiar with Bujold's Miles Vorkosigan saga can be sure of that. Obstacles will be raised by individuals, by the immobility of corporate operations, by physics, by inevitable accidents, by the attempts to do what has never before been done, and by the intransigence of human nature and the natural world.

In *Falling Free* Bujold deals with two of the major themes of science fiction: the expansion of humanity into space, which Jack Williamson has called "the central myth" of science fiction; and the continuing evolution of humanity. *Falling Free* makes a significant contribution to science fiction's dialogue about humanity's future, but it also speaks eloquently about the necessity for freedom if humanity is to thrive in this new, hostile environment of space. Bujold has drawn upon many predecessors—that, after all, is what a genre means—but most of all upon Isaac Asimov, and his Foundation novels, and Robert A. Heinlein, and his concerns about freedom and individual responsibility.

Bujold belongs to a newer group of science-fiction writers, women who create "hard" science fiction. Hard SF is a term used to describe stories in which the science is important, plausible, and often central. Not many women belong to this group: Kate Wilhelm, C. J. Cherryh, Vonda N. McIntyre, Pamela Sargent, Nancy Kress, perhaps a few others. They write other kinds of science fiction as well, including sociological, anthropological, and social science fiction, and even science-fantasy (so do most male "hard SF" writers), and when they write hard science fiction they do not overlook graceful prose, social concerns, and believable human characters.

So it is with Bujold. "I try to write," she says in *The St. James Guide to Science Fiction Writers*, "the kind of book I most like to read: character-centered adventure." And later, "I don't see the fact that I write genre or even subgenre as requiring me to hobble my novelistic ambition. Not either/or, but character and plot and theme, adventure and psychology and symbol, motion and meaning: everything, all at once, all the time." Most of her novels have involved the small, fragile Miles Vorkosigan, handicapped in every way except intelligence, common sense, and courage. It is no accident that one of Bujold's literary favorites is C. S. Forester: Miles is a kind of Horatio Hornblower, an ordinary man thrust into extraordinary circumstances (Miles comes with even more handicaps than Hornblower), and his space adventures are reminiscent of Hornblower's sea battles of the Napoleonic wars.

Bujold's career took off like Hornblower's. After publishing a couple of short stories in 1985 and 1986, the first Miles novel, *The Warrior's Apprentice*, was published in 1986, and also *Shards of Honor* and *Ethan of Athos*, followed by the Nebula Award novel *Falling Free* the next year and the Nebula Award short novel "The Mountains of Mourning," which also won a Hugo Award, in 1989. *The Vor Game* won a Hugo for 1990 novels; *Barrayar*, a Hugo for 1991 novels.

Bujold also has written what she has described as "a ghost story set in 15th century Italy," *The Spirit Ring* (1992), and has edited (with Martin H. Greenberg and Roland J. Green) *Women at War*, an anthology. Her most recent Miles Vorkosigan novel is *A Civil Campaign* (1999).

Bujold writes with authority about many things, including, in *Falling Free*, welding. The principal protagonist of the novel, Leo Graff, is an expert in welding who comes to the space habitat to teach quality-control procedures in free-fall welding to the quaddies and becomes involved in their struggle for survival and freedom. In a prefatory paragraph Bujold gives thanks to an expert on space physiology and medicine, to a welding engineer (named McMaster), and to an explosives technology consultant. A writer of hard SF does her research and notes her sources. And it helps that she is the daughter of a professor of welding engineering at Ohio State University, the late Robert C. McMaster.

ANCIENT SHORES
JACK MCDEVITT

Science fiction is the literature of change, and one of the ways to explore the impact of change on people is to change the cast—that is, to introduce humanity to new kinds of intelligent beings and see how the two species interact. For that reason science fiction has been dealing with alien encounters almost as long as science fiction has been in existence.

In addition, science fiction offers the opportunity to literalize the metaphor. In this case, the metaphor is "the other," which in traditional fiction stands for the problems of the individual in dealing with the reality of people outside, either as individuals or as groups. The most extreme example of "the other" is the person from another culture, a foreigner or a stranger because of race, gender, appearance, mental condition, or sexual orientation. Traditional fiction must work hard to make readers see and identify the strangeness in the other; science fiction can make alienness concrete and isolate what is most alien in it.

As in many other prototypical expressions of what later came to be science fictional concerns, aliens in fiction prior to the middle of the nineteenth century were projections of familiar human attributes or character flaws, or of supernatural fears or hopes. With the French astronomer Flammarion, however, speculations about extraterrestrial beings began to get more realistic in *Real and Imaginary Worlds* (1864), *Lumen* (1887), and *Urania* (1889). But aliens entered most dramatically in H. G. Wells's *The War of the Worlds* (1898), when they raised their repulsive shapes from their Martian cylinders.

That aliens might have "minds that are to our minds as ours are to those of the beasts that perish, minds vast and cool and unsympathetic" and that they might covet Earth and perhaps see humanity only as a food supply or as slaves was a concept that dominated science fiction for decades. It was countered in the 1930s and 1940s with stories such as Stanley Weinbaum's "A Martian Odyssey" (1934) and Raymond Z. Gallun's "Old Faithful" (also 1934), in which aliens were comprehensible, even sympathetic.

The notion of aliens as potential or actual threats competed with the concept of aliens as creatures of good will throughout the 1930s, 1940s, and 1950s, with such stories as Murray Leinster's "Proxima Centauri" and its carnivorous plant creatures (1936), John W. Campbell's "Who Goes There?" with its frozen shapeshifter (1937), and a variety of dangerous aliens created by A. E. van Vogt beginning with "Black Destroyer" (1939), many of them collected in *The Voyage of the Space Beagle* (1950). On the other side were Murray Leinster's pragmatic story "First Contact" (1945) and Eric Frank Russell's sentimental "Dear Devil" (1958).

Robert A. Heinlein exhibited the same kind of ambivalence about aliens in such contrasting novels as *The Puppet Masters* (1951) and *The Star Beast* (1954); he adopted a more even-handed approach in *Have Spacesuit—Will Travel* (1958), in which, as in Jack Williamson's *The Trial of Terra* (1962) and Gordon Dickson's "Dolphin's Way" (1964), superior aliens judge humanity. More recent film and television treatments also have alternated between menace in such scenarios as the *Alien* films, which took their inspiration from Wells and van Vogt, and the benevolence or innocence displayed in *2001: A Space Odyssey*, *E.T.*, and *Close Encounters of the Third Kind*, as well as *My Favorite Martian*, *Mork and Mindy*, and *Third Rock from the Sun*.

More recently SF authors, in the light of recent scientific speculations, have begun to take a new look at the possibility of other intelligent creatures in the universe and to suggest that they may more likely view humanity not only as a rival, as in Arthur C. Clarke's "The Sentinel" (1951), but as a threat. Greg Bear's *The Forge of God* (1987) and *Anvil of Stars* (1992) and George Zebrowski and Charles Pellegrino's *The Killing Star* (1995) suggest that the first contact with aliens may be a preemptive strike.

All these fictional speculations about encountering aliens do not take into account the likelihood that technological civilizations may not overlap. The fact that life has existed on Earth for several billion years and intelligent life for several million and civilized life for ten thousand, and that humanity has had technology capable of emitting radio signals for only a bit more than a hundred years and of picking up radio signals from the stars only about fifty—all these suggest that a key determinant of whether aliens will contact Earth, or vice versa, is the duration of technological civilizations. Astronomer Frank Drake included that factor in his alien contact equation. Technological civilizations may endure only a few hundred or a few thousand years, and even though billions of stars may have planets that bring forth life, and even though millions of these may develop intelligent life and even technological civilizations, the universe has existed so long that technological civilizations may not coincide.

Alien-contact possibilities can be improved by dealing not with aliens themselves but with their artifacts. Human history suggests that artifacts last longer than civilizations. Authors have taken advantage of this fact by basing their stories on encounters with what aliens have left behind. In Boris and Arkady Strugatsky's *Roadside Picnic* (1972), the artifacts were trash discarded by aliens, dangerous but valuable. Often, however, the artifact has been a transportation system; if aliens have visited the solar system, or even Earth, they would need convenient ways to travel to and from other stars.

Jack McDevitt's new novel *Ancient Shores* is in that tradition. The most famous example of the theme has been Frederik Pohl's *Gateway* (1977), which won the Hugo, Nebula, and Campbell Awards and spawned several sequels. A more recent example is George Zebrowski's *Stranger Suns* (1991), a consideration of the metaphysics of instantaneous transportation to the stars.

The appeal of such concepts is the elimination of interstellar distance with one grand "open sesame." The arduous construction of spaceships, the step-by-step exploration of the solar system, and the problems of surviving the interminable passage through interstellar space are eliminated; from their positions light-years and human life spans away, other worlds can be moved just next door.

A second attraction of alien transportation systems, like the lure of archaeology, is the exploration of the artifact itself. What will we find when we open this cave, when we break through this barrier? What indescribable treasures, what unimaginable experiences lie in front of us? A third feature is the adventure of uncertainty. What will happen if we push this button? Will we live or die, or end up in some terrible or wonderful place? Everything considered, the alien transportation system is an admirable device for telling a story.

McDevitt uses it well in *Ancient Shores*, a rousing story that deals with ordinary people encountering the alien in the midst of their everyday lives. What McDevitt brings to the idea, as well, in keeping with his career as a customs officer, are the consequences of bringing alien artifacts into this world. The introduction of alien technology into our contemporary circumstances will lead, he points out, to economic displacements that will have political consequences. McDevitt traces actions and reactions in ways that seem convincing in their commonplace reality.

The author of this new consideration of the alien-contact scenario started life in Philadelphia in 1935 as John Charles McDevitt. He earned a B.A. degree from Lasalle University in 1957 and a master of library science from Wesleyan University in 1967, wrapped around four years of service in the U.S. Navy. He was an English teacher for ten years and a customs officer for twenty. He began publishing SF stories in 1981 with "The Emerson Effect." "Cryptic" (1984) earned a Nebula nomination. His first novel, *The Hercules Text* (1986), picked up his persistent theme, alien contact, and his persistent concern, the effect of that contact on personal and international relations. *A Talent for War* (1988) dealt with war between aliens and humans, but also with the impact of revelation on people. *The Engines of God* (1995), a selection of Easton's Signed First Editions of Science Fiction, introduced the topic of alien artifacts, in this case a statue on Saturn, the abandoned ruins of an alien civilization, and a space station; it is another archaeological puzzle.

The Encyclopedia of Science Fiction sees McDevitt wrestling "valiantly with the task he has set himself: that of imposing an essentially contemplative structure upon conventions designed for violent action." He is doing it full time now, and readers can look forward to more valiant wrestling.

BLUE MARS
KIM STANLEY ROBINSON

Humanity has enjoyed a peculiar love affair with its nearest neighbors in space. The moon, of course, was the nearest celestial object, and it was easy to believe that it was a world much like Earth. On a clear night viewers might even be able to see on its surface what looked like continents and seas; some of the dark areas still bear the Latin word for sea, "mare," as in Mare Serenatis and Mare Cristum. The imagination of writers seeking un-Earthly locales for their adventures and satires landed first on the moon and fostered an entire genre of lunar voyages, so many that Professor Marjorie Hope Nicholson devoted a 1948 book to them.

When Galileo focused his telescope on the moon and the "stars" that moved, he discovered (what he later was forced to recant) not only that the Earth was not the center of the universe but that the moon was airless (and probably lifeless) and that the stars that moved were worlds like the Earth. That didn't stop writers from using the moon as a setting for their stories, but it did focus their attention on the nearest planets, Venus and Mars.

Other than the moon, they had always been the most fascinating objects in the sky, Venus the brightest star and Mars the red star. Venus, however, was enigmatic in its shroud of clouds (which later turned out to be literally a shroud around a world born dead because of heat and poisonous gases), but Mars, with its thin atmosphere, exposed its white polar caps and its red deserts to any peeping telescope.

The Italian astronomer Giovanni Schiaparelli focused his telescope on Mars in 1877 and reported seeing a network of "canali," or channels. English-speaking people interpreted the word as "canals," particularly American astronomer Percival Lowell, who spent a career staring at the Red Planet and reporting on it as a desert world keeping itself alive through canals that led melting water from the poles to oases nearer the equator. Earlier novels such as Percy Greg's *Across the Zodiac* (1880) and Gustavus Pope's *A Plunge into Space* (1894) had speculated about civilizations on Mars but such visionary works as Lowell's *Mars* (1896) provided a strong stimulus to authors looking for an off-world setting. The German author Kurd Lasswitz published *Auf Zwei Planeten* in 1897, the same year H. G. Wells speculated about a Martian civilization in "The Crystal Egg."

Wells's *The War of the Worlds* in 1898 established Mars in the public's imagination as a world that may have developed faster than Earth, and decayed more rapidly, and thus, perhaps, the possessor of a more advanced technological civilization than Earth and the envy of a dying planet for one still moist and green and mild. Wells used his advanced (and ruthless) Martians to chasten humanity's hubris, but Edgar Rice Burroughs, the second great creator of the Martian image, used Mars for a different purpose in his Mars novels, beginning in 1912 with "Under the Moons of Mars" (*A Princess of Mars*): the ancient world, with its dead sea bottoms, was a place where a gentleman and a former Confederate officer could still exercise his gallantry and indulge his love for adventure.

As more information about the actual conditions on Mars became available from scientific observations, the stories placed there became more realistic. Stanley Weinbaum, although he still presumed the existence of livable conditions on Mars, wrote in "A Martian Odyssey" (1934) about Martians who could exist for valid environmental reasons. But Ray Bradbury, in

A Martian Chronicle (1946–1950 stories collected in 1950), could still describe Martians (and humans) living on the surface of Mars, although, to be sure, for his own metaphorical purposes.

The colonization of Mars became a subject for the 1950s, with Robert A. Heinlein's juvenile *Red Planet Mars* (1949), Arthur C. Clarke's *The Sands of Mars* (1951), Cyril Judd's (Cyril Kornbluth and Judith Merril) *Outpost Mars* (1952), Lester del Rey's *Marooned on Mars* (1952) and *Police Your Planet* (1956, as by Erik van Lhin), D. G. Compton's *Farewell Earth's Bliss* (1966), James Blish's *Welcome to Mars* (1967), and many others, including Isaac Asimov's novelete about competition with the home planet in "The Martian Way" (1952). Film, as usual, was several decades behind the literature, contributing *Robinson Crusoe on Mars* (1964; which was similar to Rex Gordon's 1956 novel *No Man Friday,* but uncredited) to such earlier exploration of Mars films as *The Conquest of Space* (1955).

More pragmatic, in some cases grimly realistic, portrayals of the colonization of Mars emerged in the 1970s with such novels as Frederik Pohl's *Man Plus* (1976); he later expanded his 1967 *Dangerous Visions* story "The Day After the Day the Martians Came" into the satirical collection *The Day the Martians Came* (1988). Meanwhile, Ian Watson dealt with Mars colonization in *The Martian Inca* (1976) and so did John Varley "In the Hall of the Martian Kings" (1977).

The gaze of science-fiction writers became fixed firmly on Mars in the 1990s. Novels about the colonization of Mars have come so frequently, as I wrote in 1992 in the introduction to Kim Stanley Robinson's *Red Mars*, that "they seem like the expression of a racial subconscious, foretelling humanity's next manifest destiny." In part those novels were inspired by the reports radioed back by the Mariner flyby and its later orbiting observations beginning in 1966 and the stark observations of the two Viking landers in 1976. Mars was cold, barren, and apparently lifeless. Rather than being depressed by such news, SF writers were inspired to work such difficulties into their fiction.

Terry Bisson's *Voyage to the Red Planet* (1990) treated the subject satirically, but Jack Williamson's *Beachhead* (1992) and Ben Bova's *Mars* (also 1992) incorporated the difficulties of establishing a foothold on Mars with the same rigorous realism, and even suggested the same dangers from microorganisms. S. C. Sykes's *Red Genesis* even came with a scientific essay. Greg Bear's *Moving Mars* won a Nebula Award for 1993. But for some writers the challenge of the Viking lander reports developed into schemes for remaking the climate of Mars, for transforming it into something more closely resembling Earth's, for what scientists have called "terraforming." Proposals have been advanced by such authorities as Carl Sagan for the terraforming of Venus, but Mars, with its smaller size and greater distance from the warmth of the sun, has seemed less promising. But that lasted only until the science-fiction writers got started, led by speculative physicist Robert L. Forward and his *Martian Rainbow* (1991), which described the process in detail. Kim Stanley Robinson had presented the basic concept, for what later became his Mars trilogy, in his 1985 novella "Green Mars." The first volume of the trilogy, *Red Mars*, was published in 1992 and its sequel, *Green Mars*, in 1993. Now he winds up a massive consideration of the problem of Mars, and the people who will conquer its bleak terrain, with *Blue Mars*.

Robinson's Mars trilogy emphasizes that the conquest of Mars is not simply a technical problem. More than anything else it is a human problem. In *Blue Mars*, as in the early novels in the series, the terraforming process is background to the human process, and for that reason the terraforming seems more convincing.

Clearly Robinson has done his homework. The science and technology may not be at hand, but clearly they are within our reach. In *Red Mars*, *Green Mars*, and *Blue Mars*, we see it happen and we know, as surely as we knew that humanity would one day put its footprint on the moon, that it is possible. But clearly, also, the technology is not Robinson's primary interest. Here, as in his other writings, he is fascinated by human behavior in extreme circumstances, what kind of people undertake such challenges and how they meet them and are changed by them when they become immediate. The Mars trilogy offers not only the epic story of how a handful of humans, with marvelous machines, transform a lifeless world into another Eden, but the human drama. Other writers have presented the romantic derring-do of the adventurer, the agonies and heroism of the explorer; Robinson presents the other realities, the psychology, the economics, and the politics.

Robinson's earlier work, particularly the Orange County trilogy (*The Wild Shore*, 1984; *The Gold Coast*, 1988; and *Pacific Edge*, 1990), revealed his fascination with the psychological aspects of change and the political possibilities of utopia. One of the few SF writers with a Ph.D. in literature (he wrote his dissertation on the novels of Philip K. Dick), he began publishing stories in 1975 while still a college student. His other novels include *Icehenge* (1984), *The Memory of Whiteness* (1986), and *A Short, Sharp Shock* (1990). His short fiction has been published in *The Blind Geometer* (1986, with *Return from Rainbow Bridge*, 1989), *The Planet on the Table* (1986), *Escape from Kathmandu* (1988), *Remaking History* (1991), *Black Air* (1991), and *A Sensitive Dependence on Initial Conditions* (1991).

Martian Rainbow, *Beachhead*, and *Red Mars*, as well as *The Day After the Martians Landed,* have all been Easton Press Signed First Editions of Science Fiction (and Wells's *The War of the Worlds*, Pohl's *Man Plus*, and Heinlein's *Stranger in a Strange Land* have been selections of Easton's Masterpieces of Science Fiction series), which is testimony to Easton's belief in the immediacy of Mars. *Red Mars* won a Nebula Award and *Green Mars*, a Hugo Award. He also won a Nebula Award for "The Blind Geometer" and a John W. Campbell Award for *Pacific Shore*.

In the Mars trilogy Robinson prepared his colonists for Mars by exposing them to the rigors of the Antarctic. His next novel will be *Antarctica*. He prepared himself by spending five weeks recently on the frozen continent at the South Pole.

CLOUD'S RIDER
C. J. CHERRYH

C. J. Cherryh's *Cloud's Rider* continues the alien-world adventures of the boy named Danny, who became a man in *Rider at the Gate*, published by the Easton Press as a Signed First Edition of Science Fiction in 1995. *Cloud's Rider*, like its predecessor, has the feel of a Western: it deals with horses and riders, convoys, struggles against the elements, stockaded villages, and frontier rivalries. What makes it a science-fiction novel is that it happens on the alien world of Finisterre, where humans are trying to survive against great odds, and the alien creatures of that world are telepathic. Against all expectations, the Western and science fiction mixed well. But then, science fiction is a super-genre that can incorporate other genres: the adventure story as science fiction, the romantic story as science fiction, the horror story or the Gothic as science fiction, the detective story as science fiction—all these and more are commonplace. Seldom, if ever, however, have we had the Western story as science fiction. Cherryh proved that it could be done.

Cherryh seldom does anything in traditional fashion. She does not show us humans landing on Finisterre and discovering the peculiar nature of this world, joining up with their allies the Nighthorses, and beginning the construction of a new Earth. She does not show us the abandonment of the human colony, its loss of terrestrial technology, and its slow rebuilding of a frontier economy. Instead, like Homer, she begins "in medias res"—in the middle of things. All of the background, the past events that have led the characters to their present situation, is allowed to emerge as the occasion arises. Since Finisterre is a "lost colony," the occasion does not arise frequently. The human settlers have been abandoned for so long that they seldom talk, or even think, about how they got there.

Besides, as Cherryh pointed out in a *Locus* interview, "It's a Lost Colony scenario, and that has been done so many times I felt no need to go into exactly why and how they're lost. You could say probably it's a bad real estate deal! Somebody sold them a piece of goods and left them. . . . But human beings really have explored only a tiny element of this planet."

At one point early in *Cloud's Rider*, Cherryh allows a bit of background to emerge through Danny's thoughts about his predicament. Danny is trying to get the survivors of the ravaging of Tarmin, Carlo and Randy Goss and their willful, unconscious sister, Brionne, through a blizzard to safety in a high mountain village:

> . . . anything that faltered, anything that hesitated in the Wild, anything that took a wrong path and broke a leg—it died.
> When Men had come down to the world in their ships, horses had been the only thing that had come snuggling up to humans, wicked as they were, being the Beasts that God had set on the settlers—
> And some of them had to take the gift and be damned to save the rest, because the rest without horses, without riders, wouldn't have made it.

The symbiosis of humans and Nighthorses has been a dream come true, like the relationship between human and dog in Clifford Simak's story "Desertion," in which the consciousnesses of Fowler and Towser were projected into the Lopers native to Jupiter and were able to experience the terrible reality of the planet, with their Loper senses, as almost supernatural beauty; and to experience the true communion of telepathy. Man and dog have finally become equals, real best friends. To some, the relationship between human and horse may represent something even more satisfying.

The possibility of a more perfect union has occupied a privileged position in humanity's dreams, and sometimes in its nightmares—the possibility of communicating mind to mind rather than through the flawed mechanism of speech or gesture or depiction. Any horseman, fascinated by the way in which his mount seems to understand his intentions even before they are announced by a voiced signal or a twitch of the reins, must have considered telepathy as the ultimate connection.

All that has come true on Finisterre. It is a world in which evolution has favored telepathy; the occurrence of one telepathic species would have created an environment in which telepathic variants would have been naturally selected in other species. And on this world in which humans have been unceremoniously set down and forgotten, non-telepathic humans would need telepathic allies simply to survive.

The Nighthorses *liked* humans, *needed* humans, and immediately sought human partners and, it turned out, human riders. As Danny reflects, "Horses had become addicted to human minds. Horses had never been predators on humans—just curious, just vastly and immediately curious when ships came to the worlds and landed in the horses' range down near Shamesey."

But Cherryh rations out all such information, preferring in *Cloud's Rider* to start with the past as unspoken history. John W. Campbell, the long-time editor of *Astounding/Analog* who presided over science fiction's Golden Age, once urged his writers to "assume your gadgets and get on with your story." Cherryh assumes the background of the Lost Colony, the meeting and bonding between Nighthorses and humans, and their efforts to create a frontier society in the midst of perils worse than the American pioneers experienced in the settlement of the West, because on this world the wildlife is hungry, omnivorous, and telepathic.

Cherryh views a story as something like a holograph, in which every fragment contains the information of the whole. In her *Locus* interview she commented, "My books do not tend to follow their outlines without protest, though I make the outlines in good faith! Plot to me is like casting a stone into a pool of water. The ripples go out and obviously are going to intersect a lot of objects before they get through. So you can start at almost any place with an incident, and in a tightly controlled environment the ripples will touch practically everything in the world, eventually."

Cherryh begins her story after something unexpected has gone wrong. The something that has gone wrong is the unintended consequence—rather like Fowler and Towser in "Desertion" finding the experience of being Lopers so much better than their existences as human and dog that they don't want to go back. And then there is the further unintended consequence, described in Simak's novel *City*, which incorporates "Desertion," of their going back, the transformation of all humanity into Lopers, leaving Earth to be inherited by intelligent dogs.

If, Cherryh speculates, the telepathic bond is unique, and uniquely strong, what happens when it is broken? That was the starting point for *Rider at the Gate*, which began with a rogue Nighthorse sending into the ambient its pain and anger at what turned out to be its rider's accidental death. And what happens when the controlling partner, the human, is immature and irresponsible, and perhaps even mentally unstable? The rogue Nighthorse finds a response from a girl half-crazed with longing to be a rider and super-sensitive to telepathic sendings.

Rider at the Gate ended with the killing of the rogue Nighthorse in a climactic scene in which another rider, Guil, is wounded, Brionne lapses into a coma, and the rider of another Nighthorse is killed. All of this becomes clear as Danny and his Nighthorse, Cloud, as *Cloud's Rider* begins, struggle up a treacherous mountain road in a blizzard to get Danny's small human party to a place of warmth and safety and medical attention for Brionne. They are pursued by the telepathic image of "blood on the snow." Before their adventure is over they will discover that human exploration of the planet of Finisterre has only scratched the surface of the surprises it holds.

The author of what seems now like a trilogy in the making is versatile and prolific. Born Carolyn Janice Cherry (she added the "h" to her pen name at the request of her first publisher) in St. Louis in 1942, she earned a B.A. in Latin from the University of Oklahoma and an M.A. in classics from Johns Hopkins (where she was a Woodrow Wilson fellow). She taught Latin and ancient history in the Oklahoma City public schools from 1965 to 1976. Her first story, "The Mind Reader," was published in *Analog* in 1968, but she didn't discover her writing potential until her first novel, *Gates of Ivrel*, was published in 1976. A science-fiction novel, *Brothers of Earth*, was published the same year, and she left teaching for full-time writing, winning the John W. Campbell Award for best new writer for her work that year.

Since then, twenty years ago, Cherryh has published fifty-four books, edited another seven, and translated four, averaging more than three books a year. In fact, she has published more novels than short stories, although one of her short stories, "Cassandra," won a Hugo Award for 1978. Characteristically, however, two of her novels have won Hugo Awards, *Downbelow Station* in 1982 and *Cyteen* in 1989.

Cherryh publishes with equal versatility in both science fiction and fantasy. Her greatest recognition, however, has come from her science fiction, particularly the future history of human expansion and alien interaction that includes *Downbelow Station* and *Cyteen*. She brings to the task not only her background in classics and ancient history but a keen interest in contemporary science. "I use the form of English literature," she wrote about her work for the *St. James Guide to Science Fiction Writers*, "but bring into it a great many things which are pertinent to the sciences, or to the far corners of the world. This in my estimation is what science fiction ought to do to literature, create new symbologies and new understandings appropriate to the space age, not forgetting the traditions of our culture, but widening its viewpoints."

That, surely, is what *Cloud's Rider* does: spreading science fiction's generic wings to cover the stern and exploring the wish fulfillment and the costs of the symbiotic union between aliens and humans through telepathy.

COSM
GREGORY BENFORD

Gregory Benford is an astrophysicist who writes science fiction, or a science-fiction writer who practices astrophysics. Choose one. Or both.

The answer: it depends on the time of day or the season of the year, or simply your point of view. No doubt there are scientists who do not know that Benford writes some of the most provocative speculations in the science-fiction world; there may even be some SF readers who do not know that Benford is a professor of physics at the University of California, Irvine, and a contributor to the ongoing study of the universe; but to the world the most important aspect of Benford's split personality may be that his science informs his science fiction (and, perhaps, his science fiction inspires his science).

Benford is a staunch proponent of what is called "hard science fiction," or science fiction that operates within the limits of the known or that which can logically be extrapolated into the future, and which builds its narrative around its scientific content. He may be the most effective of today's SF authors in writing stories and novels in which the scientists and the scientific enterprise are portrayed realistically.

So it is with Benford's newest novel *Cosm*, which deals with the reality of atomic colliders and nuclear experiments, of cosmological theory, and of academic life and academic politics, as well as the private lives of professors and scientists. More than any other author, Benford has convinced his readers that scientists *have* private lives just like everybody else, and that those lives, though often similar to the lives and human problems of other people, also exhibit characteristics peculiar to their choice of careers. Scientists and professors, for instance, tend to intellectualize their emotional lives. That's good for an SF author: it allows him to explore the emotions of his characters in a way that is difficult for authors whose characters only feel and react. *Cosm* also deals with the scientists who make nuclei collide, and who make sense out of the chaotic aftermath and what it means to science and to the rest of us who depend upon scientists to explain to us the ever-more-curious operation of the universe in which we live.

For those of us who think physicists are physicists, Benford distinguishes between theorists and experimenters: "Theorists were Platonists, trusting detectors to peer coolly into reality. Experimenters were Cartesians, endlessly worrying over the reliability of their senses." And he reveals how particle theorists rank themselves: "The highest status attached to the field theorists who developed new models to bring more order to the particle zoo. Below them came the even more mathematical types, whose work often seemed abstruse and not intuitive. . . . Below came the phenomenologists, which merely meant those who tried to fit existing theory to the bewildering thicket of experimenters' data." And the relationships between theorists and experimenters is even more complicated:

> Experimenters usually avoided theorists and vice versa. "Theorists believe anything on graph paper," was a common put-down. If an experiment's data contradicted an existing theory, usually experimenters thought that probably something was wrong with the experiment. Theorists would think the error lay in the theory.

And:

> To physicists the universe was particles and waves, or more deeply, the interplay of fields. To a theorist it was deeper still, the unfolding of symmetries that God the Mathematician ordained would be obeyed, or broken, at various inscrutable energy levels. They shared a rather chilly vision of an abstract seethe, prickled by radiation, space-time warped and puckered by blunt mass. But she felt physics as a gut, hands-on experience, not an airy labyrinth of disembodied ideas.

Few writers are as well equipped as Benford to write the kind of story constructed on a foundation of science fact and speculation, and shaped by human desires and their predicaments. Born in 1941 in Alabama, one of twins, he earned his bachelor's degree from the University of Oklahoma and his master's and Ph.D. in physics from the University of California, San Diego. After working for two years at the Lawrence Radiation Laboratory in Livermore, he accepted a teaching and research position at the University of California, Irvine, where he has remained except for stints as visiting professor at Cambridge, Torino, the Florence Observatory, and MIT.

But Benford also had another life as a teenaged SF fan, even producing a well-regarded fanzine. He began publishing SF in 1965. His first novel, *Deeper Than Darkness*, came out in 1970. Since then he has published many short stories and sixteen novels, most particularly his award-winning *Timescape* (1980) and his more recent galactic-center six-book series. His 1997 Signed First Edition was a contribution to Isaac Asimov's Foundation series, *Foundation's Fear*. He has said, "I am a scientist by first choice and shall remain so," but he seems as productive as many full-time SF authors, and he was recently featured as both a scientist and as a SF author on the six-part PBS series *Stephen Hawking's Universe*.

Cosm, which stands for something like but just a little less grand than "cosmos," is the novel that goes deeper into the world of physics and university life than anything Benford has written yet. From the moment its heroine, the as-yet-untenured physics professor Alicia Butterworth, launches her experiment at the Brookhaven National Laboratory on Long Island, the reader is involved in the scientific chase as well as the politics and bureaucracy and interpersonal relationships that go along with it. "This shiny sphere," Alicia thinks, "was plain evidence for a universe that still held mystery and enormous implication, not buried down in infinitesimal particles no eye could ever see, but smack in your face, obvious." And in an act that can only be classified as hubris, Benford has placed his heroine at his own University of California, Irvine, with her evaluations of university life, students, colleagues, administrators, and procedures. One can imagine Benford's peers searching through the novel as a roman à clef, perhaps the most notable such exercise in SF since Anthony Boucher's 1941 *Rocket to the Morgue* portrayed the Los Angeles science-fiction community of that period. Is there something intoxicating in the southern California air?

More important, *Cosm* offers an insight into the world of particle physics, Big Bang theory, wormholes, and alternate universes, complete with diagrams. It could function as a textbook were it not for the engrossing story of scientific discovery and individual accomplishment around which it is wrapped. In the process, Benford allows the reader glimpses into what motivates scientists, from the acquisitiveness and ambition that leads Alicia to spirit from coast to coast the surprising object created in the Brookhaven

Collider, to the thrill of research. Two passages suggest the insights *Cosm* provides:

> Some of her first love of physics had come from that hope: that humanity could loft above the dark plain of incessant strife and passion, glimpse a serene beauty hovering beyond the veil of tribe and language. Such visions came to the great, soaring intellects, who passed them down to those struggling below.

And:

> In research there came enchanted moments when one seemed to be peering into the heart of reality. Often they came to the solitary gaze, in gliding quiet times of concentration. She had experienced moments like that and remembered them clearly.... He had died as a scientist, not out of accident, but out of the irreducible danger that went with the unknown.

In *Cosm* Benford has exchanged the standard metaphors and motifs of science fiction, the exploration of space, of alien worlds, even of alien universes, for the metaphors and motifs of science itself. Instead of the public lives of adventurers, he offers the private lives of scientists. Instead of conflicts with aliens, he offers the political battles of academia. Instead of the unknown, he offers Brookhaven and the University of California, Irvine—and for the SF reader, these may be almost as alien.

But not any longer.

DESTINY'S ROAD
LARRY NIVEN

Larry Niven made his reputation among science-fiction readers as the creator of cosmic artifacts such as Ringworld and of such hard SF concepts as "Neutron Star," "Inconstant Moon," "The Hole Man," and "Borderland of Sol," all of which won Hugo Awards. Some critics considered him the successor to Hal Clement as a writer who was able to make fascinating stories out of physics and astronomy, and William Laskowski Jr. wrote in the *St. James Guide to Science Fiction Writers*, "When the New Wave began to flourish in the mid-1960s, paradoxically a writer appeared whose work embodied many of the genre conventions which that movement was rejecting: science fiction as the depiction of technical problem-solving, faith in the infallible efficacy of science, and a belief in humanity's implicit ability to overcome any obstacle."

But Niven also has written comic satires in *The Flying Sorcerers* (with David Gerrold) and *Inferno* (with Jerry Pournelle), what might be called hard fantasies in *The Magic Goes Away* (1978) and *The Time of the Warlock* (1984), and best-selling catastrophe novels in collaboration with Jerry Pournelle, *The Mote in God's Eye* and *Lucifer's Hammer* and others. Now, with *Destiny's Road*, he demonstrates that he is capable of handling the small-scale, everyday reality of planetary colonization. Niven is a multitalented author it is risky to categorize.

Destiny's Road, for instance, is the story of Jemmy Bloocher, whose agricultural settlement, Spiral Town on the southern tip of a peninsula on the planet Destiny, is the terminus of a road that extends north toward the mainland. Twice a year caravans from the north bring manufactured goods and, most of all, life-sustaining "speckles," but nobody goes north except outcasts and "yutzes" who sign on for a season or two as temporary caravan labor, and nobody except caravan regulars are allowed north of the peninsula. That's what makes Destiny's road (and *Destiny's Road*) mysterious and fascinating, and what keeps pushing Jemmy north to discover the answer to its riddle and the riddle of the human settlement on this alien planet.

Destiny's Road is about Jemmy's experience as a young man, as a fugitive, as a young husband, as a "yutz" on a caravan, as a windfarm refugee, as a cook and innkeeper, and as a caravan regular once more—always pursued by the threat of death, always pursuing the elusive truth about Destiny and its road. Niven tells a compelling story but he never neglects his interests in hard SF. The novel is an extended metaphor for science: Jemmy's pilgrimage is a quest for knowledge, because knowledge sets humanity free from its dependence upon good fortune or the kindness of strangers.

The literature of science fiction has a special category for the colonization of alien planets. It is the Earthly settlement of distant islands or remote continents writ large against a background that not only is strange but as alien as the imagination of SF authors can make it. Sometimes it is a story of hardships, of battles against alien climates and native lifeforms; sometimes it is a triumph of human ingenuity over difficulties; sometimes it is a stepping stone to larger discoveries. Niven wrote such a novel himself, in collaboration with Pournelle and Steven Barnes, *The Legacy of Hereot* (1987). What Niven offers in *Destiny's Road* is the hard SF version—that is, if this is not the way it would be in every detail, at least it has the feel of the way things will be and a concern for the problems terrestrial colonizers are likely to encounter.

In a hard SF novel, the reader knows that every mystery will have a solution, that every detail has a place in the completion of the puzzle. Why are the two-hundred-year-old machines failing and why can't they be repaired? Why did the landers that created a road with their exhaust flames avoid the beaches? Why are "speckles" essential to the health of the settlers; and where do they come from and why are they rationed? Why are the caravans so secretive about their operations, and why is it death for a yutz to go north of the peninsula? Answers to all these questions, and more, the reader expects to discover.

But *Destiny's Road* is not a mystery in the ordinary sense of the word. The mysteries to be solved are inextricably involved with the problems of alien settlement. One problem, for instance, is the inevitable characteristic of alien planets: their lifeforms, their soil, their very chemistry are going to be alien to terrestrial biology. Where some novels of colonization skip over that important fact, Niven makes it the focus of his novel: the landers sterilize Destiny's soil with their exhausts before seeding it with Earth flora and fauna. Not only are the plants and creatures of Destiny indigestible, trace elements necessary to human survival may be missing. If this is true, why is it true, and what can be done about it, and why may temporary solutions become long-term problems? All these are questions for which a reader of hard SF expects answers, and Niven does not disappoint them.

Niven knows his science fiction as well as his science. The landers that brought the settlers to the surface and did most of the preparation for their survival are named the "Columbiad" and the "Cavorite." The Columbiad is the name Jules Verne gave his giant cannon that shoots a group of intrepid adventurers toward the moon in the 1865 *From the Earth to the Moon*, and "Cavorite" is the name H. G. Wells gave the anti-gravity metal that propels Caver and his assistant Bedford to the moon in the 1901 *The First Men in the Moon*. Niven also may have been aware of a 1954 novella by Isaac Asimov, "Sucker Bait," about the wiping out of a colony on an alien planet because its dust contains beryllium, a metallic element that damages enzymatic reactions.

The author of *Destiny's Road*, so different from anything he has written previously, was born in Los Angeles in 1938. He began a career in science fiction in 1964 with "The Coldest Place" after earning a B.A. at Washburn University majoring in mathematics and studying for a year at UCLA. He emulated Robert A. Heinlein's early practice of setting his first stories in a consistent future history. Niven called his "Tales of Known Space," carried it back a billion years, and peopled it with imaginative aliens such as the Thrint, the Pak, the Kzin, the Pierson's puppeteers, and many others. The stories culminated in 1970 with Niven's third novel, the Hugo and Nebula Award–winning *Ringworld*, which places its adventures on a vast living space constructed by long-ago engineers from the material of a sun's planets into the shape of a gigantic ring. Since then Niven has written two sequels, *The Ringworld Engineers* (1992) and The *Ringworld Throne* (1996).

Three novels after *Ringworld*, in 1974, Niven produced, with Jerry Pournelle, science fiction's first best-seller in *The Mote in God's Eye* and followed it with *Lucifer's Hammer* (1977), *Oath of Fealty* (1981), *Footfall* (1984), and other collaborations, a number of them with Barnes. On his own he created a Known Space series, *The Integral Trees* (1984) and *The Smoke Ring* (1987), and participated in a series of novels and story collections based on his Known Space future history, the Man-Kzin wars.

Niven has written more than thirty novels, alone or in collaboration, and published twenty collections. About his work, John Clute has remarked in *The Encyclopedia of Science Fiction*, "There can be no doubt that hard-[SF] writers dominant in the 1980s . . . owe much to the scope of [Niven's] inventiveness, the sense he conveys of technological ingenuity as being ultimately beneficial, and his cognitive exuberance," and called his *Tales of Known Space* "the most energetic future history ever written." His lasting achievement, Laskowski wrote, paraphrasing Wagner on Brahms, has been "to show what can be done with old forms in a new time."

DRAGONSEYE
ANNE MCCAFFREY

Few imaginary worlds have been as thoroughly chronicled as Anne McCaffrey's Pern, currently back for further exploration in *Dragonseye*. Since it was first contacted in the October 1967 issue of *Analog*, McCaffrey has followed the colonization of this alien planet through eighteen books, including *The Dragonlover's Guide to Pern*. So much focus on a single concept means two things: (1) readers find Pern, its people, and its problems, as involving as does its author; and (2) the narrative has all the characteristics of a science-fiction epic, and some of its requirements.

What is it about Pern that inspires such devotion? First of all, there are dragons. Well, they aren't actually dragons, but they look like dragons and breathe fire like dragons, and they are *lovable*! They like people, they can *communicate* with people telepathically, they can inspire love and loyalty in return, they can transport themselves, and their riders, telekinetically through space (and even through time), and they are essential to preserving life on Pern by destroying with their fiery breath the deadly mycorrhizoid Thread that falls periodically from the rogue planet called the Red Star.

The most moving scenes in the Pern novels are those of dragons hatching and each bonding with one special and sympathetic human for life (*Dragonseye* contains such a scene early in the book; watch for it). Who could ask for a better companion than a Pern dragon? Certainly none of the dragon riders, whose dragons come first, even before lovers, and *Dragonseye* not only offers examples of how this occurs, it reveals the early stages through which the bond between dragon and human is developed and strengthened.

All this may justify what *The Encyclopedia of Science Fiction* has to say about Pern's (and McCaffrey's) success: "The author appears to have achieved in these novels a mode and intensity of feeling that broke new ground in fitting SF to the imaginative needs of alienated teenage girls, thus helping to break the masculine mold of most previous SF." The dragons created some problems, however. They are the stuff of fantasy (which traditionally has been considered more appealing to teenage girls than science fiction), and they and the Gothic environment in which they were first encountered gave McCaffrey the fantasy writer reputation that she has had difficulty refuting. She writes, she has always maintained, science fiction, not fantasy, appearances to the contrary notwithstanding.

That fact should have been apparent from the beginning: the first Pern story "Weyr Search" appeared in the determinedly science-fiction magazine *Analog* edited by the rigorously science fictional John W. Campbell. It won the novella a Hugo Award, and its sequel, "Dragonrider," published in the December 1967 and January 1968 issues of *Analog*, won the Nebula Award. Campbell understood immediately what became apparent to others only with the publication of more recent novels, that there was a background to these novellas of Holds and Weyrs and flying dragons that would place everything into a real-world context. The two novellas were brought together as *Dragonflight* in 1968, and the dragon books were off and flying. It took twenty years, however, and seven more Pern novels before the science-fiction background began to be filled in with *Dragonsdawn* (1988).

Through these prequels, McCaffrey establishes the origin of human customs, the discovery of the fire-breathing lizards and their bioengineering into the beloved dragons of the later books, and the first fall of Thread with its threat of wiping out all land life on Pern. And in the process she even answers some of the questions that may yet lurk in the minds of determined science-fiction skeptics. In *Dragonseye*, for instance, she deals with the question of why, over the centuries, Pern has never contacted Earth, or Earth, Pern. It is important to the science-fiction reading of the Pern novels, of course, that the Pern colonists have no recourse to Earth technology, either to leave the planet for a world less threatened by horrible death falling from the sky or to find a technological solution to the problem of fighting Thread. There must be a reason for dragons and their riders.

But everything began with *Dragonflight* and its corollary novels *Dragonquest* (1971) and *The White Dragon* (1978), as well as the juvenile novels *Dragonsong* (1976), *Dragonsinger* (1977), and *Dragondrums* (1979), and *Mereta, Dragonlady of Pern* (1983) and *Nerilka's Story* (1986). They established the mythology of Pern and its dragons against the background of the fall of Thread every two hundred years. Mythologies, of course, are the ways in which people without histories and natural science explain the ways their universe and their culture behave. The prequels provide the historical facts on which the myths are based. *Dragonseye*, for instance, describes the deliberate creation of folk songs that will communicate the history of Pern after the last terrestrial computers fail, and why the eyerocks were constructed that sit on ridges of every Weyr on Pern.

Dragonsdawn described the first human landing on Pern and the colonization of Pern, and the discovery of the lizards who will be bioengineered into dragons. *The Renegades of Pern* (1989), *All the Weyrs of Pern* (1991), *The Chronicles of Pern: First Fall* (1993), *The Girl Who Heard Dragons* (1994), *The Dolphin's Bell* (1993), and *The Dolphins of Pern* (1994) continued the process and filled in a panoramic view of the planet and its development.

Now *Dragonseye* takes up the story two centuries after First Fall. What happens, it asks, after a great struggle for survival, when records (that are turning into legends as Earth-brought technology begins to fail and cannot be replaced) warn the Pernese that a new fall of Thread is imminent? The growing human colony, now scattered into Weyrs and Holds, are faced with the threat of ultimate attack from the heavens, and they do not know whether the records of the Red Planet's return and the fall of Thread are accurate. What if there are leaders who do not believe in the danger, or for whom disbelief is profitable? It is the story of Noah, only in this case everyone believes, more or less, except for one stubborn disbeliever, and what is to be done about him—and about his unprepared people? And behind it all is the difficulty of keeping up preparation for a threat that is fulfilled only every two centuries and for a period of crisis that will last a lifetime—for fifty years. How are people motivated to devote energy and wealth to a danger that will arrive long after they or their children or their children's children are dead? And how do people gird themselves for a war against a deadly foe that will last their lifetimes? Would the humans who fought the Hundred Years' War have kept on fighting if they had known how long it would last?

All this calls for dedication and determination seldom found in human history, and its development on Pern helps make the series an epic. McCaffrey records it all and records it with a focus on human relationships, including romance between likely and unlikely pairs, as well as the overarching ideal relationship between dragons and humans.

Although much of her work has been devoted to the Dragonriders of Pern series, McCaffrey has other books and even other series. Born in Cambridge, Massachusetts, in 1926 and now living in Ireland, she earned a B.A. degree from Radcliffe in Slavonic languages and literature. Her first story, "Freedom of the Race," was published in Hugo Gernsback's *Science Fiction Plus* in 1953, but she didn't pick up her career again until 1967 with the novel *Restoree* and the first Pern stories. She has written a series about parapsychological investigators, the Pegasus books, two Ireta books about a *Dinosaur Planet*, three Killashandra novels, the Planet Pirates books, the Rowan sequence, and the Petaybee sequence. She also wrote *Decision at Doona* (1969) and two sequels and *The Ship Who Sang* (1969)—McCaffrey's personal favorite—and several sequels. In fact, in the past thirty years, she has published something like forty-four SF novels, eleven collections of stories, seven other novels, and a nonfiction guide to Pern, plus editing three books, two of them science-fiction cookbooks.

McCaffrey has been called "one of the most beloved authors in the science fiction field." That is difficult to document but it is clear that her admirers have formed a McCaffrey-appreciation society based on her Pern novels, with members assigned to Weyrs and Holds according to their geographical locations; they imagine, among other activities, riding their own fire-breathing dragons.

It's not too late to join—if not a McCaffrey-appreciation group at least the even-broader readers of the Pern epic. The world of the Dragonriders is spread out before you, and, like any good history, you can enter at any point and read forward, or back.

DREAMFALL
JOAN D. VINGE

Joan D. Vinge's new novel *Dreamfall* raises the question of telepathy and the other parapsychological abilities that we have yet to demonstrate unequivocally in the real world.

Telepathy is one of those fantasies that have been folded into science fiction, like time machines and faster-than-light space travel, because it is a convenient concept and makes for interesting stories. And it might, it just *might*, be possible. There is no convincing evidence that telepathy exists, and no plausible scientific theory by which it might exist, but anecdotes multiply, stage magicians demonstrate, and a good many people believe in telepathy, as they believe in miracles and demons and UFOs.

Science-fiction writers, being natural skeptics, do not *believe* in telepathy, but they are willing to use it sometimes in their stories because it allows interactions in a different arena, and it makes an excellent metaphor for all buried talents. Moreover, to ease their consciences, writers can justify as scientific advance abilities not currently accepted by science, that is, as Arthur C. Clarke noted in his Third Law, "a sufficiently advanced technology is indistinguishable from magic." Perhaps on that basis U.S. military intelligence explored a number of psychic powers in response to a possible "psi-power" gap with the Soviet Union.

So far, at least, parapsychology has been unable to gain legitimacy in the scientific community. At Duke University, Professor J. B. Rhine gave parapsychology its first veneer of respectability in the 1930s, by constructing experiments using statistical methods. John W. Campbell, editor of *Astounding Science Fiction*, who obtained a degree in physics from Duke in 1932, was familiar with Rhine's work and used him as an authority when he urged writers, in the postwar years, to put away the used-up ideas of atomic bombs and atomic power and turn to the unexplored possibilities of psychic phenomenon.

Telepathy is just one of several psychic powers on which Rhine and other parapsychologists have experimented. Others include telekinesis (the movement of objects by the mind alone), teleportation (the movement of people by the mind), clairvoyance (perception from a remote location), precognition (perceiving the future), and other, more specialized powers, such as pyrokinesis (setting fires by mind alone) and mental control of others.

The first fictional treatments of telepathy were influenced by the movement of abilities from the magical to the everyday—they had the unsavory taint of the forbidden along with the attraction of fairy-tale powers, like the alchemists' transmutation of base metals into gold or the elixir of life. Although telepathy was used in novels in the latter part of the nineteenth century and the early twentieth, the first significant treatments were by J. D. Beresford in *The Hampdenshire Wonder* (1911) and Olaf Stapledon in *Last and First Men* (1930) and *Odd John* (1935), particularly *Odd John*, in which superhumans began to appear here and there and were persecuted because of their superior abilities.

In subsequent stories and novels, superiority and persecution seemed to be the common lot for superhumans, particularly those with parapsychological powers. A. E. van Vogt, who dealt obsessively with psychic abilities in most of his stories, carried superiority and persecution to its ultimate expression in *Slan* (1940), in which normal humans declare open season on a scattered group of superhumans, whose telepathy seems linked to tendrils in their hair.

Theodore Sturgeon used telepathy in *More Than Human* (1953) as part of a bundle of powers assembled by a group of outcasts who combine into a single gestalt being. Alfred Bester, in *The Demolished Man* (1953), imagined telepathy (he called telepaths "espers") circumscribed by laws and ethics, and, in *The Stars My Destination* (1956), teleportation (Bester called it "jaunting") transforming society. John Brunner in *The Whole Man* (1964) and Roger Zelazny in *The Dream Master* (1966) saw telepathy as a tool in psychotherapy. But most such fiction dealt with the basic response of normal human beings to these new powers. Wilmar H. Shiras, in a series of 1948–1950 stories gathered together as *Children of the Atom* (1953), suggested that the suspicion and hatred of society would force superior children to hide their abilities.

Mark Clifton may have taken John Campbell's suggestions about parapsychology most seriously. He wrote a series of stories with Alex Apostolides such as "What Thin Partitions" (1953) and "Sense from Thought Divide" (1955) and the novel *They'd Rather Be Right* (Hugo, 1995) with Frank Riley, in which the focus was society's response to psychic abilities. Katherine MacLean, who also was an *Astounding* writer, dealt with the psychic distress of telepathists in the series of stories collected as *Missing Man* (1975; "The Missing Man" won a Nebula Award in 1971). Robert Silverberg in *Dying Inside* (1972) treated telepathy as a metaphor, in the story of a man whose mind-reading ability had meant little but psychological torment, but who felt terrified about the possibility he was losing it.

All these and more are part of the background for Joan D. Vinge's *Dreamfall*. Vinge uses telepathy as a symbol of difference; it makes outcasts and inferiors of its alien catlike humans, the Hydrans, who possess it. They may be feared and suspected by the dominant human culture, which isn't generally telepathic, but Hydran weakness allows them to be ghettoized and despised, even on their home planet.

Dreamfall is the third in a series of novels that began in 1982 with *Psion*, which introduced Cat, half human, half Hydran, with catlike eyes, born literally into an underworld as a despised half-breed whose psionic abilities only make him more an outcast. Cat's efforts to lift himself out of the ghetto bring him into contact with the human community, teach him about love and trust, and about loss and mind-rape, and force him, eventually, to kill a criminal named Rubiy and, in the process, lose his telepathic abilities.

In the best science-fiction fashion, Vinge takes a new development and imagines its consequences. That includes its drawbacks; new developments always have drawbacks. Telepathy, she reveals, is not a blessing in a society where few others have it and it can be destroyed by killing someone else. That makes sense, psychologically and practically: the agonies of a dying mind might well overload the telepathic mind that is impacted by those thoughts and is responsible for that death.

The sequel, *Catspaw* (1988), continued Cat's experiences when he hires out as bodyguard to a member of one of Earth's great corporations, and his personal growth as he regains his telepathy through drug patches and learns more about interpersonal communication and personal development. In *Dreamfall* Vinge transports Cat to Refuge, the home world of the Hydrans. Cat ought to feel at home at last, but he is telepathically deaf, and he is as much an outcast in the Hydran ghetto as he is in the powerful corporation that employs him. To kill someone and lose one's psionic powers is as great a perversion to the Hydrans as to be half-human. The availability of the Hydran community leads Vinge to another insight: telepathy may become such a burden that some Hydrans take drugs to turn it off.

Once more, on a fully imagined alien world, Vinge reveals how a person damaged by society and the difficulties of growing up an outcast can assume responsibility for his own fate and learn how to be a whole person. Vinge contributes another great imaginary concept: the cloud-whales and "their cast-off musings," called "dreamfall," which form reefs of an "amino acid stew of recombinants," that has the potential for great financial gain, great good, or great danger, and psionic potential as well, which is why it is sacred to the Hydrans. But the corporation wants to harvest it . . .

Science fiction itself is a kind of dreamfall. The author of this particular "reef" was born in Baltimore in 1948 and earned a bachelor's degree in anthropology from San Diego State University in 1971. There she married Vernor Vinge, then an assistant professor of mathematics at the university and a science-fiction writer who has become even better known since their divorce in 1979. In 1980 Joan Vinge married editor and publisher Jim Frenkel.

In 1980, as well, Vinge's first great science-fiction success was published. *The Snow Queen* won a Hugo Award. She had earlier distinguished herself with short fiction, beginning in 1974 with "Tin Soldier." Her story "Eyes of Amber" won a Hugo Award for 1977. Her short fiction has been collected in *Fireship* (1978), *Eyes of Amber and Other Stories* (1979), *Phoenix in the Ashes* (1985), and *Tin Soldier* (1990, bound with Norman Spinrad's *Riding the Torch*).

Easton reprinted *The Snow Queen* as part of its Masterpieces of Science Fiction series and *The Summer Queen* (1991) in its Signed First Editions of Science Fiction. The middle book in the trilogy is *World's End* (1984). Vinge's first novel was *The Outcasts of Heaven Belt* (1978). She went through a period in the mid-1980s when she wrote a number of film novelizations: *Star Wars: Return of the Jedi: The Storybook* (1983), *Tarzan, King of the Apes* (1983), *The Dune Storybook* (1984), *Return to Oz* (1985), *Mad Max III: Beyond Thunderdome* (1985), *Ladyhawke* (1985), *Santa Claus: The Movie* (1985), *Santa Claus, the Movie Storybook* (1985), and *Willow* (1988).

Telepathy and the other parapsychological abilities have the power, like fairy tales, to fulfill our dreams. There is a fairy-tale attraction to much science fiction, and yet the psychic powers are not simply wish fulfillment. Dreamfall, for instance, is not simply a fascinating concept; it reminds us of the potential that lies in repressed memories and the unconscious mind. Psionics, like all dreams, represents something important in our lives, in this case our sense of individual worth and the difficulties we encounter in identifying and then expressing it, and the need to develop our particular talents, through hard work and discipline, so that we can display them, unashamed, to others. Because those talents are what we are.

Dreamfall tells a fascinating story of adventure, imagination, and self-discovery, but it also helps understand that we cannot reveal who we are without exposing ourselves.

EVOLUTION'S SHORE
IAN MCDONALD

The title of Ian McDonald's new novel, *Evolution's Shore*, suggests the emergence of sea-bred creatures onto the land. But the novel's subtitle is: "A

Novel of Africa, Ambition, the Alien, and Football." That is broad enough, but it doesn't begin to do justice to the novel, which encompasses the entire world (plus parts of the solar system). It takes place largely in Kenya, where evolution that produced the first hominids is once more at work, but this time through alien intervention.

Roz Kaveney in *The Encyclopedia of Science Fiction* wrote about the comparison of McDonald's first novel, *Desolation Road* (1988), with *The Martian Chronicles* crossed with *One Hundred Years of Solitude*, "a joke limited in accuracy only by its failure to add Cordwainer Smith to Ray Bradbury and Gabriel Garcia Marquez." And Kaveney went on to comment that McDonald was "not so much being influenced or writing pastiche as appropriating deftly from other writers the precise gestures needed to make ideological or emotional points about the human implications of terraforming or cyborgization." McDonald's earlier Signed First Edition of Science Fiction was *Terminal Cafe* (1994), which some reviewers compared with Robert Silverberg's *Born with the Dead* (1974). That is not a criticism but an observation. Since science fiction is a continuing dialogue about the impact of change on humanity, every SF author is the heir of all the authors who have gone before. The basic changes that humanity can experience may not have been exhausted, but new concepts are limited; most SF builds on what has gone before or argues against the earlier consensus. For readers to benefit fully from a new SF story or novel, then, it is useful to be aware of elements appropriated from prior SF and to move from there to a consideration of what the author has done with his inheritance.

McDonald, born in 1960 and a resident of troubled Belfast, Northern Ireland, seems to be a keen student of science fiction; he sprinkles references to science fiction throughout his latest novel, such as the space vehicles named for Isaac Asimov, Arthur C. Clarke, and Robert A. Heinlein, and references, among others, to *The Encyclopedia of Science Fiction*. *Evolution's Shore* incorporates two major SF themes united by a single agency: continuing evolution and alien intervention. They are executed in an apocalyptic mode, which David Ketterer in *New Worlds for Old* (1974) wrote "finds its purest outlet in science fiction." In the process of playing out these themes, McDonald incorporates various subthemes such as biological catastrophe (what one of McDonald's characters calls "environmental armageddon") and Big Dumb Objects (BDOs).

Biological catastrophe, with or without alien influence, has been treated by a number of SF writers, particularly after the publication of Rachel Carson's *Silent Spring* (1962), when human pollution became the primary culprit, and John Brunner's *The Sheep Look Up* (1972) became its most savage indictment. Before that, and even afterward, environmental armageddon was principally a natural phenomenon, such as that chronicled in John Christopher's *No Blade of Grass* (1956) in which civilization crumbles when grass (which includes wheat) is destroyed by disease, or one of the earliest of the environmental stories, Murray Leinster's "The Mad Planet" (1920), in which carbon dioxide pours out of fissures in the Earth and destroys all terrestrial life except insects and fungi and a handful of mutated humans. That takes millennia to achieve, as does the Earth of Brian W. Aldiss's *Hothouse* (1962) in which, as in "The Mad Planet," humanity has devolved in the face of overwhelming environment. Earth's environment also has been changed by aliens, as in Thomas M. Disch's first novel *The Genocides* (1965), in which aliens seed Earth with giant plants and when humans become a nuisance, fumigate them.

The Big Dumb Object may have been named, oddly enough, by the author of McDonald's *Encyclopedia* entry, Roz Kaveney, in 1981. The term refers to the huge artifacts encountered by humanity as it explores the remote corners of the Earth, the solar system, and the universe. Usually constructed by aliens who have long vanished, the exploration of the artifact and its purposes and its powers becomes the plot of the narrative, while its size dwarfs the humans who venture onto it or into it as well as their concerns. The biggest of these have been Larry Niven's *Ringworld* (1970) and Bob Shaw's *Orbitsville* (1975), both influenced by Freeman Dyson's speculations about alien spheres entirely enclosing their suns. John Varley, in his Gaea trilogy, found his BDO within the solar system, but it was a sentient artifact. Greg Bear incorporated a BDO in *Eon* (1985) and *Eternity* (1988), a space habitat that was bigger on the inside than the outside. A major BDO was the alien spaceship in Arthur C. Clarke's *Rendezvous with Rama* (1973) and sequels, which came floating into the solar system and at the end of the novel, its essential mysteries unsolved, went floating out again. McDonald surely pays tribute to Rama at the conclusion of *Evolution's Shore*.

Perhaps the greatest single influence on science fiction was Darwin's *Origin of Species* (1859), which stressed the way in which environment and its changes selected appropriate traits for survival. From Darwin science fiction adopted its basic tenet, human adaptability to environment, but added another: the ability of intelligent creatures to recognize their adaptations and transcend them. Most people, and a number of SF writers, assume that evolution no longer applies to humanity, but other writers are not so sure, and they have chronicled the ways in which the human species may produce superior beings—or, in the case of devolution, inferior. H. G. Wells showed in *The Time Machine* (1895) how people, because of social influences, could devolve into Eloi and Morlocks. Once the concept of radiation influencing genetic change became general knowledge, authors such as John Taine in *The Iron Star* (1930) and *Seeds of Life* (1931) showed it accelerating evolution, and after the man-made radiation released in the post-atomic age, stories about super beings and super children began to appear more frequently. Olaf Stapledon in *Last and First Men* (1930) dealt with the evolution of the human species over a period of two billion years. A. E. van Vogt was continually searching for what would turn people into super beings of great power and wisdom, and Eric Frank Russell in "Metamorphosite" (1946) showed it happening.

The concept of aliens influencing evolution may have come not long after the *Origin of Species* controversy died down, as philosophers seeking some kind of meeting ground between religion and science suggested that God worked through evolution. H. G. Wells, in 1937, wrote a quiet novel about people possibly being *Star Begotten*, ending with the notion that this process might lead to superior humans. Arthur C. Clarke's *Childhood's End* (1952) portrayed aliens enforcing peace on a troubled Earth so that the children of humanity could fulfill its destiny and evolve to join the Overmind. But the definitive treatment of the idea of alien influence on evolution was Clarke's novelization of the Kubrick-Clarke film *2001: A Space Odyssey* (1968), in which an alien black monolith is shown shaping apelike creatures' evolution into *Homo sapiens* and then into a super child.

What McDonald has brought to the concepts is not only a weaving of themes into a seamless whole, and a compelling narrative that displays the epic events, but the knack of making it all seem believable and contemporary. The characters are treated like real people with needs for sex and food and sleep and power and survival and getting ahead (the "ambition" of the subtitle), and even though they may be dwarfed by the BDOs they encounter, they do not surrender their selves to the Big Idea but cling, humanly, to the constants of their lives.

McDonald excels at the science-fiction crafts as well. The test of an SF author's skills and responsibility is the way in which he or she accepts the challenge of the essential passage. The first is the demonstration to the reader of the reality of the change that has come over the world. In the case of BOOs, where plausibility is critical, the description must make the case for strangeness and believability at the same time. McDonald succeeds not only in making convincing the BDO that has been transformed out of Saturn's moon Hyperion, he doesn't shirk the alien infestations of Earth. Sprouting from capsules landing on Earth in different parts of the world (like H. G. Wells's Martians in the 1898 *The War of the Worlds*), the "Chagas" (sometimes called "Bucky jungles" after the molecules shaped like Buckminster Fuller's geodesic domes) spread inexorably over various parts of the world, transforming everything, including humans, in their path. McDonald makes the Chagas and their alienness seem as real as the Africa in which much of the action takes place.

Evolution's Shore, however, is more like a novel inspired by science-fiction concepts than it is a science-fiction novel, and readers can expect to meet real suffering, joyful, passionate, petty, often mistaken people trapped by their pasts but occasionally able to free themselves from them, to transcend the limitations of being human. Because ultimately that is what the novel is about, transcendence, which Alexei and Cory Panshin, in their 1989 book *The World Beyond the Hill*, called SF's basic quest. In *Evolution's Shore*, as in *2001: A Space Odyssey*, humanity needs some help in achieving transcendence, but McDonald makes convincing the way, in the welter that is the human world of emotions and conflicts and misunderstandings, humanity can bring itself to understand what is happening and to accept what is being offered to it: change, not only in the world they live in and their prospects for the future but in the nature of humanity itself.

A FISHERMAN OF THE INLAND SEA
URSULA K. LE GUIN

Ursula K. Le Guin may be the mostly highly praised author of modern science fiction. Other writers have won more awards, but Le Guin's honors have been numerous within the field and without. *The Encyclopedia of Science Fiction* commented, "Her reputation has extended far beyond the readership of genre SF, while within the genre she has been honored with 5 Hugos and 4 Nebulas." She also won a National Book Award and is one of the few SF writers who has been well received, and well reviewed, by mainstream critics writing in mainstream media. She shares with Ray Bradbury the honor of representing SF to non-SF readers in many high-school and college textbooks; both display the mainstream virtues of sensitivity to language and character, but Le Guin's SF virtues—plausible and consistent world creation—are sometimes overlooked.

So it is an event when Le Guin publishes a new collection of SF short stories. Moreover, it may be significant. In recent years, a few critics within the field have suggested that Le Guin has deserted SF in favor of the mainstream, an accusation that Le Guin has vigorously denied. An even more effective denial is *A Fisherman of the Inland Sea*. It is, if nothing else, clearly a collection of SF stories. Moreover, Le Guin has provided an introduction in which she explains, and defends, the process of reading and writing science fiction. Of course, since this collection is by Le Guin, it is something else. These are Le Guin stories.

What is a Le Guin story?

Le Guin is a mixture of anthropology and the humanistic. The anthropology comes from her parents, Alfred L. Kroeber, a famous anthropologist who taught at the University of California at Berkeley, and Theodora Kroeber, who wrote, among other things, an important anthropology study titled *Ishi in Two Worlds*. Le Guin's humanistic leanings were evidenced in her undergraduate degree at Radcliffe and her master's degree at Columbia in medieval and renaissance Romance literatures, mostly French.

Le Guin turned to SF after writing poetry and some unpublished European novels. Her first story, "April in Paris," was published in 1962 in *Fantastic*. Her first novel, *Rocannon's World*, was published in 1966, and was followed immediately by *Planet of Exile* the same year and *City of Illusions* in 1967. Though apprentice works, they established the background for her best-known (and perhaps her best) novels, *The Left Hand of Darkness* (1969) and *The Dispossessed: An Ambiguous Utopia* (1974). Each won both Hugo and Nebula Awards.

That background, which also provides the background for the last three stories in *A Fisherman of the Inland Sea*, establishes the origin of human life on Earth and on all the other inhabited planets. They were seeded by humans of the planet Rain, and their different shapes and customs allow Le Guin to explore alternative ways of social behavior as well as people's reactions to it and to "the other," the alien. The notion of "forerunners" and stranded or abandoned human settlements had been used before, but largely for political comparisons; Le Guin's was anthropological and humanistic and peculiarly her own.

The Hainish stories and novels share other developments: the Ekumen, for instance, a loose association of planets for economic, artistic, scientific, and intellectual purposes; spaceflight at nearly the speed of light, which means time dilation or the passage of time much more slowly under acceleration than on the planets; and the ansible, a device for instantaneous radio communication. All these came together in 1969 with the publication of *The Left Hand of Darkness*, which offered an anthropological study of a Hainish experiment in sexual difference treated with humanistic concern about character, language, myth, and culture. An envoy seeking to persuade an ice-age planet to join the Ekumen must cope with a people who are neuter most of the month but come into a period of sexual readiness when they can be either female or male and be either mother or father to offspring. The people of Gethen have no differentiation by sexual role, a fact that informs almost everything in their social and political relationships. The novel was an early contribution to feminist issues in SF.

Another Hainish novel, sometimes preferred by critics, *The Dispossessed*, describes an experiment in anarchy and the invention of the ansible. A short story set before *The Dispossessed*, "The Day Before the Revolution" (1974), concerning the last days of the founder of the anarchic society, won the Nebula Award, and *The Word for World Is Forest* (1972), which describes an exploited native race, won the Hugo.

Le Guin had already ventured into fantasy in 1968 with *A Wizard of Earthsea*, ostensibly a juvenile but read as often by adults; it presented a richly detailed world in which the practice of magic is as rigorous as a science. It was followed by *The Tombs of Atuan*, in 1971, and *The Farthest Shore* in 1972, the last of which won the National Book Award. She returned to the world of magic in 1990 with *Tehanu: The Last Book of Earthsea*. Another fantasy novel, *The Beginning Place*, was published in 1980.

Le Guin also has published three earlier collections of short stories: *The Wind's Twelve Quarters* (1975), *The Compass Rose* (1982), and *Buffalo Gals and Other Animal Presences* (1987). Another direction Le Guin's interests took her was into criticism with a series of articles and lectures that were brought together as *The Language of the Night: Essays on Fantasy and Science Fiction* (1979), edited by Susan Wood, and *Dancing at the End of the World: Thoughts on Words, Women, Places* (1989). In 1989 the Science Fiction Research Association presented her their Pilgrim Award for her contributions to SF criticism and scholarship.

After *The Dispossessed* Le Guin focused most of her efforts on work that seemed of more interest to general readers than to her SF audience: *Orsinian Tales* (1976), for instance, and *Malafrena* (1979), and even *Always Coming Home* (1985), an experimental collage of verse, reports, tales, drawings, recipes, and a cassette of folk music. Although *Always Coming Home* drew upon Le Guin's anthropological background, it also was influenced by what Peter Nicholls in *The Encyclopedia of Science Fiction* called her "strongly utopian impulse.... Because utopian fiction tends not to be plot-driven ... it demands a more contemplative kind of attention than that dictated by most sf." Le Guin herself has traced traditional linear fiction to the male hunting-for-game pattern and the female "basket" alternative, to the women's "gatherer" role.

That Le Guin can excel as a hunter as well as a gatherer is evidenced not only by her Hainish novels and stories but by her 1971 *The Lathe of Heaven*, a novel about a young man who can bring alternate realities into being through his dreams. It received an effective dramatization on PBS.

Le Guin also has edited four anthologies and published four volumes of poetry: *Wild Angels* (1975), *Hard Words and Other Poems* (1981), *In the Red Zone* (1983), and *New Poems* (1988). Her 1993 textbook anthology with Brian Attebery, *The Norton Book of Science Fiction*, was a significant breakthrough for science fiction into one of the academic publishing houses that had up to that time neglected the field; its focus on contemporary and literary SF also led to discussion and (probably not unwelcome) disagreements about focus and inclusions and omissions.

A Fisherman of the Inland Sea, which takes its title from the final story in the collection, displays Le Guin's varied and considerable talents. "The Rock that Changed Things" is a parable like her Hugo Award–winning story, "The Ones Who Walk Away from Ornelas." "The Ascent of the North Face" is an anthropological spoof like "The Author of the Acacia Seeds," and "The Kerastion" is an anthropological slice-of-life. "The First Contact with the Gorgonids" is a feminist jape at first-contact stories; "Newton's Sleep" is a serious SF look at the psychological problems of survival guilt in orbit. But the heart of the collection, if placement and space have relevance, are the three final stories, "The Shobies' Story," "Dancing to Ganam," and "Another Story or A Fisherman of the Inland Sea."

If *The Dispossessed* pivots around the invention of the ansible, which makes possible the Ekumen, the last three stories of *A Fisherman of the Inland Sea* pivot around the invention of churten theory, the process for instantaneous transmission of matter. Other writers have dealt with matter transmitters and what they make possible, including catastrophe. Le Guin deals with their psychological reality.

The problem with "transilience," as Le Guin terms it, is simultaneity. It is not simply that simultaneity contradicts Einstein's speed-of-light limitation; it embodies paradoxes that render untenable any conceivable theory about the structure of the universe. Le Guin uses churten theory as a device, as a metaphor for the problems we have in reaching a consensus about reality, as a way of exploring the human predicament. "All fiction is metaphor," she wrote in an introduction to *The Left Hand of Darkness*. "Science fiction is metaphor. . . . The future, in fiction, is a metaphor." And "science fiction is not predictive; it is descriptive." Thus Hideo writes in "Another Story . . . ," "Story is our only boat for sailing on the river of time, but in the great rapids and the winding shallows, no boat is safe." And Shan says in "Dancing to Danam," "It's very difficult to live without the notion that there is, somewhere, if one could just find it, a fact." "Only fiction," Forest replies. "Fact is one of our finest fictions."

At the same time, the reader can observe Le Guin paying attention to the SF realities, the statements that reflect the differences made possible by science-fiction thought experiments. "The *Shoby*," Le Guin writes in "The Shobies' Story," in one of those sentences that some readers may allow to pass unnoticed, "had been built on Hain about four hundred years ago, and was about thirty-two years old." "What sets (science fiction) apart from older forms of fiction," she wrote in her introduction to *The Left Hand of Darkness*, "seems to be its use of new metaphors, drawn from certain great dominants of our contemporary life—science, all the sciences, and technology, and the relativistic and the historical outlook, among them. Space travel is one of these metaphors; so is an alternative society, an alternative biology; the future is another. The future, in fiction, is a metaphor."

Le Guin pays attention to the difficult job of describing simultaneity in a language built on cause-and-effect, when she describes Gveter's problems in even thinking about what had happened: "Unduring a nonperiod of no long, he perceived nothing was had happening happened that had not happened."

Le Guin also uses the perspective of a galactic culture to call attention to contemporary chauvinism. "Shan knew that heroes were phenomena of primitive cultures; but Terra's culture was primitive," she notes in "Dancing to Danam." And in the same story: "Shan had not realized how white-skinned

Dalzul was, but the deformity or atavism was minor." Le Guin also pays tribute to the passage of time by getting sayings slightly wrong, like "How many cooks spoil a soup?" And the universality of story by the desert fox who reenacts the Orpheus story or the fisherman who undergoes the Rip Van Winkle experience.

At the same time, Le Guin retains her commitment to principle, particularly in her attention to sexual roles and alternative cultures. "Anthropologists solemnly agree that we must not attribute 'cultural constants' to the human population of any planet," she writes in "The Shobies' Story," and cultural variation is what she offers, from the mixed crew of the *Shoby* to the religion of Ganam and the marriage customs of O, which must find four compatible people for both heterosexual and homosexual relationships in a network complicated by assignment to Morning or Evening moieties. It is not that she is "prescribing" this kind of arrangement, as she denies that she was prescribing the androgynous relationships of Gethen, but the fact that the people of the planet O are so serious about their marriage arrangements, and the fact that those arrangements work at least as often as marriages of here and now, suggests that all such cultural patterns are arbitrary.

Finally, however, *A Fisherman of the Inland Sea* is about narrative. The collection is filled with stories, and with "story." Just as the Nearly As Fast As Light drive's time-dilation experience is echoed in the fable of "the fisherman of the inland sea," churten theory offers an opportunity to tell stories about story, metafiction. It is what writers do. "A novelist's business is lying," Le Guin wrote in her introduction to *The Left Hand of Darkness*. "In reading a novel, any novel, we have to know perfectly well that the whole thing is nonsense, and then, while reading, believe every word of it. Finally, when we're done with it, we may find—if it's a good novel—that we're a bit different from what we were before we read it, that we have been changed a little, as if by having met a new face, crossed a street we never crossed before."

And that applies to stories, too.

ILLEGAL ALIEN
ROBERT J. SAWYER

Robert J. Sawyer's *Illegal Alien* returns to one of the basic themes of science fiction: encounter with aliens. Only science fiction is equipped to speculate about intelligent creatures totally different from humans, or feels a need to do so. Science fiction is the literature of change, and nothing is likely to change humanity more than meeting intelligent extraterrestrials.

Earlier writers wrote about angels or demons or human-like creatures on other worlds. In the second century AD, for example, Lucian of Samosata wrote about strange creatures on the moon; in the seventeenth century Cyrano de Bergerac's flying Frenchman landed in the Garden of Eden when he reached the moon; and in the eighteenth century Voltaire brought giants from Sirius and Saturn to the Earth. But aliens were popularized in the mid-1860s by another French author—not Jules Verne, who never wrote about aliens, but the astronomer Camille Flammarion.

Flammarion's nonfictional *Real and Imaginary Worlds*, published in 1864, described sentient plants. He wrote about aliens again in *Urania* (1889). But it was H. G. Wells who caught the world's imagination in 1898 with the rapacious Martians of *The War of the Worlds*, and the threat of alien invasion dominated the literature until Stanley G. Weinbaum introduced more plausible aliens in "A Martian Odyssey" (1934). The same year Raymond Z. Gallun's "Old Faithful" suggested that aliens could be friends. Three years later Olaf Stapledon's *Star Maker* speculated about an entire galaxy of alien life forms, each with its own history and reason for existence, and SF consideration of aliens broke free from its preoccupation with invading monsters.

As SF writers have pondered astronomers' reports on the solar system and other possible planetary systems, Earth has seemed peculiarly favored by a modest, stable, long-lived sun and a planet large enough to retain its atmosphere and its oceans and located at about the right distance from the sun to allow water to remain liquid most of the time in most latitudes. Aliens might well find it an enviable piece of real estate. But other possibilities began to seem more reasonable.

Where Wells (picking up on Percival Lowell's views of "canals" on Mars) had seen Mars as a dying planet that might have nurtured intelligent life, later authors realized that Mars was an unlikely birthplace for anything larger (or smarter) than bacteria. And Mars was more hospitable to life than any of the other planets. Writers also noted that if aliens elsewhere in the galaxy had developed under different conditions, they would have viewed those as more favorable than conditions on Earth. After Murray Leinster's "First Contact" (1945), the SF dialogue about what to do about aliens and what would happen when they were encountered shifted to a consideration of how humans and aliens could get along.

Nothing in SF gets entirely discarded, however, and the threat of alien invasion remained a viable concept, as Robert A. Heinlein's 1951 *The Puppet Masters* and 1959 *Starship Troopers* and Larry Niven and Jerry Pournelle's 1985 *Footfall* illustrate. Later treatments, however, have become more ambivalent: Orson Scott Card's *Ender's Game* (1985) concluded in remorse and its sequels showed Ender seeking expiation. Perhaps an interchange of goods and ideas and technology would be more valuable than real estate; perhaps humans and aliens could learn more from each other than they could take from each other. Hal Clement wrote a series of novels in which believable aliens dealt with environmental problems, sometimes with the help or observation of humans, as in *Mission of Gravity* (1954). Or perhaps, considering the overwhelming interstellar distances, radio communication might be the only plausible contact, as was suggested in James Gunn's *The Listeners* (1972).

The possibility of friendly relationships has been undercut in recent times by grimmer considerations. If there is intelligence life elsewhere in the universe, where is it? Why hasn't it contacted Earth? Are interstellar civilizations a threat to one another because they are capable of mutual destruction, and is a sudden onslaught a more likely possibility than invasion? Charles Pellegrino outlined some convincing scenarios involving projectiles hurled at relativistic speeds in *The Valhalla Project* and *The Killing Star* (with George Zebrowski), and Greg Bear offered an equally deadly prospect in *The Forge of God* and *Anvil of Stars*.

By calling his new novel *Illegal Alien*, Sawyer suggests that he approaches the concept of aliens with a sophistication possible only at the end of more than a century of SF dialogue. Sawyer offers a narrative of a plausible first contact with aliens that turns into something extraordinary when a human is murdered and one of the aliens is the chief suspect. The consequences for future relationships are fraught with unsuspected perils. What will aliens make of human laws and courtroom protocols? And how will they, and their home world, react if one of their own is convicted of murder?

Sawyer, who was born in Ottawa, Ontario, Canada, in 1960, calls himself the only native-born full-time SF writer in English-Canada. He earned a bachelor's degree in radio and television arts in 1982 from the Ryerson Polytechnical Institute of Toronto and has been a full-time writer since 1983. His career started with corporate news releases and articles for business journals, and an occasional SF story.

His work indicates that he has absorbed the dialogue SF has engaged in over the past century. Like *Illegal Alien*, his fiction occupies a position at the top of a mountain of prior speculation. Sawyer's work is sophisticated in SF terms because it displays an awareness of everything that has gone before while building engaging new scenarios with believable characters.

Sawyer's first SF story, "If I'm Here, Imagine Where They Sent My Luggage" was published in *The Village Voice* in 1981. His first novel, *Golden Fleece*, was published in *Amazing Stories* in 1988 and in book form in 1990, and he has specialized in SF ever since. A trilogy named the Quintaglio Ascension sequence, made up of *Far-Seer* (1992), *Fossil Hunter* (1993), and *Foreigner* (1994), concerns intelligent dinosaurs who had been transplanted to an alien world millennia before. *End of an Era* (1994) involves time travel into the Cretaceous era to check on Earth's dinosaurs. But it was with *The Terminal Experiment* (1995), in which a scientist discovers proof for the existence of the human soul, that Sawyer made a major breakthrough.

It was serialized in *Analog*, won a Nebula Award, and was a finalist for the Hugo. *Starplex* (1996) also was serialized in *Analog* and was a Nebula and Hugo finalist. *Frameshift*, described as "an SF thriller set against the backdrop of the Human Genome Project," was published in June 1997.

As someone who once aspired to be a paleontologist specializing in dinosaurs, Sawyer has a reputation as a writer of hard SF who develops believable characters. In a comment published in *The St. James Guide to Science Fiction Writers*, he wrote, "I think SF's most important role is not technological prediction, nor sounding warning bells about dangerous trends, but rather to allow us to examine what it means to be human by using a suite of literary tools unavailable to writers in other genres. . . . The tricky job is getting characters' reactions to both the mind-boggling and the mundane to ring true."

"My work," he continued, "often crosses the boundaries between science fiction and mystery." This is true, as well, of *Illegal Alien*, which offers, in what Sawyer calls "*Independence Day* meets John Grisham," a courtroom drama as gripping as anything encountered by Perry Mason. Courtrooms are less common in science fiction than aliens; two notable examples are Isaac Asimov's "Galley Slave" and J. T. McIntosh's "Made in U.S.A.," both, incidentally, dealing with artificial life. Sawyer's novel may be the first SF story to put an alien on trial.

Illegal Alien is the latest SF contribution to the discussion of the totally other. The different defines itself against the familiar, and *Illegal Alien* confronts mind-boggling aliens with mundane courtroom procedures—and with the customary surprising outcome.

LIFEHOUSE
SPIDER ROBINSON

Spider Robinson is a favorite with science-fiction fans. They have honored him with awards (even naming him one of the best new writers in 1973) and affection. He has returned it, and in his new novel, *Lifehouse*, he writes about them.

Science fiction used to be called a ghetto. It defined itself in the pulp magazines that originated in 1896 and began specializing in particular kinds of fiction in the category pulps beginning in 1915 with *Detective Story Monthly*. In 1926 science fiction got its own magazine, *Amazing Stories*. Critics thought that the pulp magazines were beneath literary consideration and took seriously only those SF stories and novels produced by mainstream authors, and even then only those that were not identified as science fiction. When I wrote my master's thesis about SF, back in 1950, one of my professors told me that science fiction was *at best* subliterary, and in 1959 Kurt

Vonnegut Jr. began to get reviews in the literary journals only when he insisted that the designation "science fiction" be removed from his second novel, *The Sirens of Titan*.

SF readers and authors didn't take kindly to being ignored, much less being scorned. Their magazines were different from other pulp magazines, springing out of the soil of the popular science magazines rather than the dime novels and the boys' magazines and the other pulps, and the writers wrote out of a sense of enthusiasm, even of mission, that readers responded to with dedication. If anything, SF readers and authors felt superior to the rest of literature, which they called "mundane," because it didn't consider the impact of change on the world, and they created their own little world of mutual admiration and support. It was called fandom and it was created out of the SF magazines themselves, within a few years of their first appearance.

The magazines had letter columns, and in those columns readers groped into contact with each other. Where they were close enough, as in Philadelphia and New York, they formed clubs. Where they were separated they kept in touch by exchanging letters and fan magazines. In the early 1930s Hugo Gernsback, the founder of *Amazing Stories*, who had lost that magazine and created others, announced in *Wonder Stories* the formation of the Science Fiction League. Clubs became regularized and publicized, and almost the first thing fandom did was to create conventions, with the first world convention being held in New York City in 1939.

Today it is difficult to consider science fiction a ghetto. It pervades contemporary society, through books, television, movies, music, art . . . It is not a minority literature anymore (what Damon Knight called "the mass medium for the few"); everybody is aware of it and most people read it or view it. Its world conventions attract thousands, rather than the two hundred who attended the first convention, and local and regional conventions take place every weekend of the year. SF even appears regularly on the best-seller lists, and SF films are the top-grossing films of all time.

Nevertheless, SF fandom has survived scorn and it has even survived prosperity; the attitudes, the traditions, and the culture have survived as well. Fandom has even been celebrated in the fiction itself. One of the earliest instances of SF entering fiction was in Anthony Boucher's 1942 *Rocket to the Morgue*, a detective story in which Los Angeles SF authors are thinly disguised. Mack Reynolds placed a murder mystery at a science-fiction convention in *The Case of the Little Green Men* (1951), Barry Malzberg dealt with a fading SF writer in *Herovit's World* (1973), Sharon McCrumb included fandom in her farcical mysteries *Bimbos of the Death Sun* (1987) and *Zombies of the Gene Pool* (1992), and Larry Niven and Jerry Pournelle brought SF authors into *Footfall* to brainstorm solutions to an alien invasion and, with Michael Flynn, looked to fandom for rescue in *Fallen Angels*

(1991). Other authors have participated in what *The Encyclopedia of Science Fiction* has called "recursive SF."

Now Spider Robinson has joined in the fun. In a remarkably symmetrical narrative, Robinson offers a story in which a con man comes up with an ingenious scenario that would work only on two bright, sympathetic fans, only to discover that his scheme has run head-on into reality and that everyone is in danger of being eliminated as a means of preserving one of the biggest secrets of all time. How the SF fans manage to find a solution to this predicament uses all their ingenuity and all their accumulated SF wisdom as well as the expertise of two experienced grifters.

It helps, though it is not essential, to be aware of the nature of fandom. Regional conventions like Vancon really do have budgets of $100,000 and more. Probably more fans are networked by e-mail than any other nontechnical group, and fans are accustomed to responding to requests for information, or help, from other fans. Fandom has developed a language, mostly composed of initial slang or portmanteau words. In one paragraph in *Lifehouse*, one of the characters uses three such words: "Truphan," "gafiated," and "corflu." Some of the meanings can be pieced out through context; "Truphan," for instance, is a sincere, dedicated, and experienced true fan; "gafiated" is initial slang for "get away from it all," to leave fandom for good (or at least for some time); and "corflu" is short for "correction fluid," which was used on the mimeograph stencils that once were the basic tools for creating fanzines (another portmanteau word that means "fan magazine").

The reader doesn't have to be a fan to enjoy all this—only to recognize that fandom shares a body of literature from which it draws an attitude toward the world and in terms of which it communicates with other fans, a language that reflects the reading experience as well as fandom itself, and a quickness of mind honed by the experience of reading the literature of change. SF demands attention and a broad body of knowledge about the world and possible changes in it. The characters pick up on matters quickly. There is no asking for explanations, and there are no lectures. The reader who is aware of this will pick up on things, as well, and realize that a great deal of badinage goes on among fans and that such hyperbole conceals not only affection and respect but information. The reader who understands all this, and allows himself or herself to float with the story, will enjoy an engrossing and sometimes comic narrative and pick up a great deal of knowledge about fandom in the process. Fandom is not everybody's cup of tea, but for some it is the stuff of existence itself (or, as they would say, "fiawol"— fandom is a way of life). Maybe some readers will be led to join it.

Robinson, born in New York City in 1948, became a fan favorite with his first story, "The Guy with the Eyes," in *Astounding* in 1973 and became a full-time writer the same year. It inaugurated a series of "club" stories told in Callahan's *Crosstime Saloon*, a volume in which the first of these were collected in 1977. Robinson moved to Canada in 1973, first to Nova Scotia and later to Vancouver. In 1974 he shared with Lisa Tuttle the Campbell Award for best new writer. He wrote book review columns for *Galaxy*, *Destinies*, and *Analog*, and won a 1977 Locus award for best critic. The same year he won a Hugo for "By Any Other Name," which became the first four chapters of his first novel, *Telempath* (1976). In 1978 he and his wife, Jeanne, won a Hugo and a Nebula for "Stardance," which was expanded into the novel *Stardance*. In 1983 he won a Hugo for "Melancholy Elephants."

Robinson's later work includes *Mindkiller: A Novel of the Near Future* (1982); *Night of Power* (1985); *Time Pressure* (1987), a continuation of *Mindkiller*; *Starseed* (1991) with Jeanne Robinson, a sequel to *Stardance*; *Kill the Editor* (1991, expanded as *Lady Slings the Booze*, 1992) and *The Callahan Touch* (1993), both part of the Callahan saga; and *Starmind* (1995), with Jeanne Robinson, the third part of the *Stardance* trilogy. His stories have been collected in *Antimony* (1980); *Melancholy Elephants* (1984); *Callahan and Company: The Compleat Chronicles of the Crosstime Saloon* (1987), which is composed of *Callahan's Crosstime Saloon* (1977), *Time Travelers Strictly Cash* (1981), and *Callahan's Secret* (1986); *Callahan's Lady* (1989); and *Copyright Violation* (1990).

Robinson's feeling for community pervades much of his fiction, the *Stardance* trilogy in which the community expands to include benevolent aliens who liberate human potential, and the Crosstime Saloon community, where humans and aliens conquer their own inherent difficulties by a sense of togetherness. In *Lifehouse* Robinson celebrates the science-fiction community that he joined in 1973.

THE MEMORY CATHEDRAL
JACK DANN

Jack Dann's big, colorful novel *The Memory Cathedral* reminds us that science fiction often deals with the future, but not always. Sometimes the story can happen in the present with an event in the here and now that will change human existence, such as a revolutionary scientific discovery or a revelation or a technology that will remake society, or something emerging from the natural world, from the very small to the very large, from deep beneath our feet to light-years beyond our grasp, that will change our relationship to the universe.

Sometimes SF can even happen in the past like the prehistory novels of Stanley Waterloo, H. G. Wells, Jack London, William Golding, and, more recently, Jean Auel, that deal with how *Homo sapiens* became modern humanity through evolution, insight, invention, or repelling competitors such as the Neanderthals. But what about historical times? Alternate history is a possibility, such as Ward Moore's *Bring the Jubilee* (1953) or Philip K. Dick's *The Man in the High Castle* (1962), in which the past upon which the novel's present is based has turned on events that happened differently, and the point is how slim a grasp we have on the reality we take for granted, or how the future will be determined by events that we can identify only by looking back upon them.

Finally, though less likely, SF can be based on history much as we know it but with the addition of a new element or insight, such as Mark Twain's *A Connecticut Yankee in King Arthur's Court* (1889) or L. Sprague de Camp's *Lest Darkness Fall* (1941). Most such SF operates by introducing a contemporary person with contemporary knowledge and sensibilities into the historical era. But some, like a traditional historical novel, deal with science-fictional issues from within the era itself, such as James Blish's biographical novel about Roger Bacon, *Doctor Mirabilis* (1971).

Such a novel is Jack Dann's *The Memory Cathedral*. It combines a rich evocation of the Renaissance with a portrait of the man for whom the term "Renaissance man" may have been invented, someone who might be called the first science-fiction man, that is, a person who bases his life upon the belief that the world is being changed by science and invention and that the pace of change will create an existence that contemporaries might find disorienting or disturbing. His name is Leonardo da Vinci, and he was a man of incredible and varied talents: artist, town planner, military tactician, and inventor, at least of concepts that the technology of his day could not turn into artifacts. One of the notebooks in which his inventions were sketched was bought at auction recently by Bill Gates, billionaire entrepreneur of Microsoft, for nearly $100 million. That alone makes Leonardo seem like science fiction.

To be sure, justifying *The Memory Cathedral* as science fiction takes some doing. Blish's novel about Roger Bacon, the thirteenth-century English monk who was thrown into prison for fifteen years because of his belief in the potential of experimental science, was published as a historical novel, bringing to life the times and experiences of the man who dreamed greatly and yet on his deathbed was reputed to have said, "I repent of having given myself so much trouble to destroy ignorance." The interest in Blish's novel, however, was in its speculations, in its science-fictional aspects, in the lost potential in Bacon's life for a different world. That is, it suggests an alternate history that did not happen. Philip Jose Farmer wrote a short story in which that alternate history happened; he called it "Sail On! Sail On!" and it described Columbus's first voyage in a world in which Roger Bacon was not persecuted but embraced by the Church and his principles incorporated in a brotherhood (of "Rogerians") who produced technology explained theologically.

The Memory Cathedral is like *Doctor Mirabilis* in that it involves the reader in its milieu, the raucous, colorful, roistering era of Renaissance Italy, experimenting with art, music, politics, nation-building, philosophy, and science, knowing that there were better ways to do almost anything and willing to try almost anything new. Moreover, Dann offers an alternate history reading as well, not only the possibilities of a different history having emerged if Leonardo's inventive genius had been the basis for technological development rather than unrealizable dreams but speculation that Leonardo's inventions may not have been beyond the technological capabilities of his times, that he may have tried out his flying apparatus, that he may even have been recruited into the services of a middle-eastern monarch who could have perfected his devices and actually used them in war.

In an article written for *The New York Review of Science Fiction*, Dann says, "I could not help but feel that this was like writing science fiction.... I would try to suspend the reader's disbelief by using H. G. Wells's technique of introducing only one fantastic element into a realistic setting and extrapolating from there; but to make it fly, so to speak, I would have to make every detail real and let my one fantastical element affect this fictive world in a natural way."

If Dann was going to gain a plausible reading from those who know something of Leonardo's life, he had to incorporate an explanation of why we have no more record of these actual inventions and accomplishments than the sketches that come down to us and some letters that may have been tall tales. The prologue performs that task, showing us the aged Leonardo (he was sixty-seven when he died in 1519) feeding the drawings of his actual inventions into the fire, lest someone else misuse them as he was forced to do. The reader, with his or her knowledge of what has come to pass, may be led to speculate about how the present might have been different if Leonardo's inventions, real or imaginary, had been developed at the time. De Camp's *Lest Darkness Fall* (1941) has a related interest: a modern man finds himself back in sixth-century post-imperial Rome and faces the imposing task of preventing the Dark Ages by the inventions he knows are possible; Martin Padway may suggest to the reader a Leonardo inserted into history a millennium earlier.

The prologue also serves the function of introducing us to the concept of "the memory cathedral" itself, a mnemonic device invented by Simonides of Ceos. Simonides, a fifth-century BC Greek lyric poet, advocated building a mental image of a great building in which every event, person, and fact worth remembering would be associated with a room, statue, painting, or other part of the structure. It is through Leonardo's imaginary cathedral that he (and Dann) lead us as we explore Leonardo's life and times.

The Memory Cathedral works like all good historical novels by creating in its readers an appetite for the times in which it is set. And what times they were: Johann Gutenberg was perfecting the craft of printing, which soon spread to England and France; Thomas More and Martin Luther and Copernicus were born; the Turks were conquering parts of Europe, including Bosnia, before being thrown back at Vienna; the Hundred Years' War between England and France ended, and civil war (the War of the Roses) sprang up again in England; universities were being founded and nations were being created; navigators and explorers were discovering the West Coast of Africa and the mouth of the Congo, Columbus discovered the New World, and Vasco da Gama and Ferdinand Magellan were born. And the artists: Botticelli, Bosch, Fillipo Lippi, Holbein, Durer, Michelangelo, Raphael, Pellugrino, della Robbia, del Sarto, Corregio ... the list seems endless.

In an afterword, Dann tells how much of the novel is history, how much is invented, and the research that took him through one crowded byway after another, catching a glimpse of something fascinating that led him away from his central task but ultimately returned him to it reinvigorated and richer for the experience. Perhaps it is enough to say here that we know a great deal about fifteenth century Italy, but there are gaps into which a skillful historical novelist can slip almost anything, even the working model of a glider or a hot-air balloon. Dann notes that Leonardo wrote letters to the Devatdar of Syria, ostensibly when Leonardo was in the Middle East, but also writes that "historians don't take these letters seriously and shrug them off as tall tales and fables." But Dann also points out that the standard biography of Leonardo allows for a four-year gap in Leonardo's life, between 1482 and 1486, when he cannot be proved to have been in Florence or Milan. And, Dann might add, Leonardo cannot be disproved to have been in the Middle East.

A few notes on the historical figures who figure prominently in the novel may be useful; our knowledge of actual history lends significance to alternate history:

Lorenzo the Magnificent (1449–1492), a Medici under whom Florence became the center of the Renaissance and humanism, was the patron of Botticelli and Michelangelo.

Girolamo Savonarola (1452–1498), who is mentioned in *The Memory Cathedral* but does not appear in it, was a Dominican who preached against moral corruption, became the virtual leader of Florence after the exile of the Medici in 1494, was excommunicated for his attacks on Pope Alexander VI, and during a period of rioting Florence city officials tortured and hanged him.

Andrea del Verocchio (1435–1488), born Andrea di Michele di Francesco de Cioni, was a Florentine sculptor and painter, many of whose paintings have been lost; he was a leading figure in the early Renaissance.

Leonardo da Vinci (1452–1519) is best known for the *Last Supper* and the *Mona Lisa*, painted long after the events of *The Memory Cathedral*. He is recorded as moving to the court of Ludovico Sforza in Milan about 1482 where he is believed to have composed most of his notebooks. He did theoretical work on mathematics and studied anatomy in the hospitals of Florence. He worked as a military engineer for Cesare Borgia and studied swamp reclamation; as architect and engineer for Louis XII, he continued his scientific investigations into geology, botany, hydraulics, and mechanics and spent his last four years continuing his studies in a castle in France.

Sandro Botticelli (1444–1510), born Alesandro di Mariano Filipepi, became a favorite of the Medici and specialized in mythological paintings such as *Spring*, *Birth of Venus*, and *Mars and Venus*; late in life he turned to religious scenes such as the *Nativity* and *Last Communion of St. Jerome*.

Amerigo Vespucci (1454–1512) sailed to South America in 1499, discovered the mouth of the Amazon, evolved a system for computing exact longitude, and accepted South America as a continent, earning the naming of the Americas after himself rather than Columbus.

Niccolo Machiavelli (1469–1527) became defense secretary for the Florentine republic and substituted a citizens' militia for the mercenary forces common to the period. He worked on diplomatic missions where he learned about power politics. When the Medici regained power in 1512, he was imprisoned and tortured, after which he retired to his country estate and wrote on politics, most famously *The Prince*, with its "Machiavellian" advice on statescraft, but he also wrote *Discourses* and a history of Florence and poems and plays such as *Mandragola*.

The author of this long, rich novel was born in Johnson City, New York, in 1945. He earned a B.A. in social science and political science from the University of New York in Binghamton in 1968 and launched a writing and editing career in 1970, not straying far from the New York–Pennsylvania area until 1993, when he moved to Australia but has been commuting several times a year.

Dann's work was characterized by Gregory Feeley in *Twentieth-Century Science-Fiction Writers* as featuring "a solitary, obsessive young man whose disaffection with the stratified society he belongs to leads to a dramatic encounter with a larger strangeness that resonates in the telling with a powerful and sometimes disturbing psychic resonance." His short fiction has often been nominated for awards, some of it collected in *Timetipping* (1980). He published three novels, *Starhiker* (1977), *Junction* (1981), and *The Man Who Melted* (1984), but much of his work before *The Memory Cathedral* was in such innovative anthologies as *Wandering Stars* (1974), featuring SF about Jews, and *More Wandering Stars* (1981), *Faster Than Light* (1976), *Future Power* (1976), and *In the Field of Fire* (1987), about Vietnam. Many of the anthologies were edited in collaboration, most of them with Gardner Dozois.

The Encyclopedia of Science Fiction concludes its entry on Dann by suggesting that with *The Man Who Melted* he may have lost his need to write SF, but that speculation may have been only a misapprehension created by the six years of research and writing that went into *The Memory Cathedral*. Up to the time of its publication, Dann's work, even at the novel length, had been like Renaissance miniatures; now with his new novel he is painting on a giant canvas with bold, bright strokes. Like the Renaissance artists among whom he lived, in his imagination, for six years, he is reaching out in new directions.

MOONRISE
BEN BOVA

The moon has always been an object of fascination: so near, so world-like, and yet so out of reach. The moon is an unusually large satellite for a planet the size of Earth, so large, indeed, that the moon and Earth are nearly a double planetary system, and some scientists have speculated that the oversized moon, with its oversized tides, may have helped life develop on Earth.

The size and proximity of the moon also has influenced human fantasies, and all sorts of myths and folklore and superstitions have developed around it. One of those fantasies has been about travel to the moon. The earliest science-fiction-like narratives—"A True Story" by Lucian of Samosata in the second century AD, for instance—were about imaginary trips to the moon, and the literature of the fantastic was dominated throughout the Middle Ages and the Renaissance by voyages to Earth's satellite. When the Industrial Revolution and the Age of Enlightenment made real science fiction possible, trips to the moon became not only more frequent but more credible. Edgar Allan Poe wrote one (as did one of his University of Virginia professors), Jules Verne wrote the most famous in his *From the Earth to the Moon*, and even H. G. Wells, who was not noted for getting his characters off the Earth, wrote *The First Men in the Moon*.

The evolution of science fiction toward the realizable is evidenced in Ben Bova's new novel *Moonrise*. Even after the creation of the American science-fiction magazine, *Amazing Stories*, in 1926, stories retained a major element of the romantic until the Golden Age, when John W. Campbell, editor of *Astounding Science Fiction*, urged writers to create stories in which the science was credible and the technology worked, stories, he said, that might be published in a magazine in the twenty-fifth century. Isaac Asimov responded in 1939 with the first story he would publish in *Astounding*, "Trends," which described a future in which the first flight to the moon was opposed by an evangelical religious group and its charismatic leader. And Robert A. Heinlein in his third story in *Astounding*, "Requiem," described the triumphant final trip to the moon by the entrepreneur who had made it all possible; a decade later, Heinlein published a novella about the earlier life of D. D. Harriman, "The Man Who Sold the Moon."

Bova was the heir to Campbell's editorship in 1971, when he took over, after Campbell's death, the magazine that was then (as it still is) named *Analog*. In another sense, with his most recent novel, he has become Heinlein's heir as well. Where Heinlein described, in credible detail, the way in which a human colony might be established on the moon, Bova has described in even greater detail life on the moon and the way in which humanity might struggle to realize the potential of a moon base so that it can be used as a stepping stone to the stars. Where Heinlein dwelt upon the ways in which the human imagination might be stimulated and the practical problems of financing and boardroom intrigue might be resolved, Bova has focused on the human problems of love and hate and jealousy and revenge, as well as the need to make a profit. Both, however, might have agreed about the philosophy offered to one of the protagonists, "If it is to be, it's up to me." Although there may be in Heinlein's fiction a greater sense of the inevitability of historic movements, he, like Bova, always saw the need for competent people, aware of how things get done in their own social system, to make matters come out right.

Genres are like science: they build on what has gone before. As Brian Attebery has pointed out, unlike mainstream works, which rest on the authority of the author alone, a genre is like a giant volume in which the more one reads the more one understands, and every author contributes to what has gone before. Science is like that; even the great Sir Isaac Newton wrote, "If I have seen further than other men, it is because I stood on the shoulders of giants."

Science-fiction authors also are the heirs to events in the real world. As scientific and technological possibilities come closer to realization, SF becomes more realistic. Stories and novels dealing with atomic power and atomic bombs were clean, romantic dreams, or nightmares, until it seemed that they might be achieved, and then Heinlein wrote "Blowups Happen" and "Solution Unsatisfactory" and Lester del Rey wrote "Nerves." That was before 1945. The stories and novels that followed World War II were even grimier and grimmer.

Now it seems that although U.S. astronauts have landed on the moon and explored a bit of it, and even brought back some samples of lunar rocks and dust, the public has lost its enthusiasm for extraplanetary adventures, and governments no longer seem likely to fund anyone's lunatic dreams. Like Heinlein (in "Requiem" and the 1950 movie he wrote, *Destination Moon*), Bova speculates that developments in space will have to be financed by corporations in search of profit, and so he must imagine the ways a lunar colony might carve out a way of life on the moon and in which a lunar operation can be profitable—as a source of raw materials for orbital factories, for instance, or even, maybe, intercontinental rocket craft made out of diamond.

The partnership of human ambition with entrepreneurial profits comes naturally to Bova. Born in Philadelphia in 1932, he earned a B.S. from Temple (and an M.A. from SUNY, Albany, twenty-nine years later—and recently a Ph.D.), Bova worked for two years as technical editor for Project Vanguard, for a year as a screenwriter for the MIT Physical Science Study Committee, and then for a decade as science writer for Avco Everett Research Laboratory before taking over *Analog*. He earned the Hugo Award for best editor six out of the seven years he served, before moving on to become, for four years, fiction editor and then executive editor of *Omni*. He has served as president of the Science Fiction Writers of America.

Bova's first published SF was a children's novel, *The Star Conquerors*, in 1959. Since then he has written nearly fifty novels, nine collections of short stories, and more than two dozen nonfiction books and edited more than a dozen anthologies. Like Heinlein, he understands the political component of public action, and perhaps even more than Heinlein he understands the possibility of public reaction. Part of the problem to be solved in *Moonrise* is the fear of releasing new biological agents into the environment. Such fears are not unreasonable, but then every scientific advance, every journey to new worlds, has involved risks, most of them unforeseen. If those who counsel caution, or even pullback from the frontiers of knowledge, had been in charge during most of the history of the human species, people would still be living in caves. And, since every change means struggle, sacrifice, even the introduction of new evils, if people had known ahead of time all the problems each new step forward would entail, Columbus would never have brought back syphilis (and slaves) from the New World, Watt would never have been allowed to perfect the steam engine and create social upheaval, Bell would never have been permitted to introduce the telephone, nor Edison, the phonograph, the motion picture camera, and electric lights.

Part of the problem faced by the moon colonizers in *Moonrise* is the growth to political power of a religious conservatism opposed not only to scientific progress but to spaceflight. In this the novel picks up the warning of Asimov's first *Astounding* story and Heinlein as well. In the "Future History" into which Heinlein placed many of his early stories, Heinlein predicted the rise of religious fanaticism shortly after the turn of the century. In one of his classic novels, *The Moon Is a Harsh Mistress* (1966), he also dealt with the need for a moon colony to fight for its political freedom.

The future of the human species is much on Bova's mind. He not only has published many science popularizations, the majority of them for children, his science fiction also has been aimed at the next steps in humanity's evolutionary progress toward the stars. Among other future-history stories and novels, his Kinsman Saga (*Millennium*, 1976; *Kinsman*, 1979) traces the events at the turn of the century that lead to the colonization of space, and his

Mars (1992) describes in realistic detail the first manned interplanetary flight.

Not everything will happen on the time scale that SF authors propose. Asimov placed the first trip to the moon in 1973, four years after the real thing occurred, but by private enterprise and some years before the rise to political power of religious conservatives. In his Future History chart (published in the May 1941 *Astounding* and reprinted in *The Past Through Tomorrow*), Heinlein dated "The Man Who Sold the Moon" past the middle of the twentieth century, and "Requiem" and Harriman's death (after the founding of Luna City) before the year 2000. He also dated the rise of religious fanaticism (and a religious dictatorship in the United States) after the turn of the century, and the reestablishment of civil liberty and the creation of "The First Human Civilization" toward the end of the twenty-first century.

Bova wisely specifies no dates in *Moonrise*, but a moon colony has been established and nanotechnology has been invented (although opposition keeps it from being used on Earth except in a few isolated places). Interestingly, Asimov's protagonist is named John Harmon, and Heinlein's, D. D. Harriman. What can one make of that? Bova's heroes are named Stavenger, but the original head of the aerospace company that founds the moon base is named Masterson.

Will it happen? Will humanity inherit the stars? If that's what humanity must do, it depends on you.

Index

77 Sunset Strip, 56
1984, 45, 46, 47–48, 48–49, 51, 52
1984: The End of the World News, 52
2001: A Space Odyssey, 31, 39, 45, 87, 93, 167, 191
2010, 86

A. Merrit Magazine, 63
Abbott, Edwin A., 92
ABC, 9
The Abyss, 73
Ace Books, 1, 82, 97, 138, 158
Across the Zodiac, 170
Ad Astra "Per Aspera", 28
Adams, Douglas, 83–86
Aegypt, 154
After London, 43
After Such Knowledge, 142
Agnew, David, 84
Alas, Babylon, 43, 77
Aldiss, Brian W., 51, 52, 58, 110–113, 190
Alice in Wonderland, 120
All Flesh Is Grass, 91
All the Weyrs of Pern, 183
"All You Zombies", 119
All-Story, 63, 158
All-Story Magazine, 60
Alternate Worlds: The Illustrated History of Science Fiction, 26, 229
Altshuler, Harry, 5, 9, 12, 13
Always Coming Home, 194

Amazing Stories, 26, 36, 55, 63, 97, 128, 136, 156, 158, 198, 199, 207
Amazon, 206
American Weekly, 61
"Among the Beautiful Bright Children", 26
Analog, 26, 27, 28, 29, 140, 163, 174, 175, 182, 183, 198, 201, 208, 209
Ancient Shores, 168, 169
The Ancient Engineers, 134
"And He Built a Crooked House", 119
"... And Searching Mind", 17, 136
"And the Light Is Risen", 43
"... And Then There Were None", 18
Anderson, Poul, 18, 129–132
The Andromeda Strain, 16
"The Angry Man", 12
Anthony, Piers, 7
Anvil of Stars, 168, 198
Apostolides, Alex, 186
Ardrey, Robert, 79
"Arena", 67
Argosy, 36, 61, 63, 133, 158
Armageddon, 107
The Artificial Kid, 74, 76
"The Ascent of the North Face", 194
Ashes and Stars, 89
Ashley, Mike, 118
Asimov, Isaac, 1, 6, 18, 27, 33–35, 36, 39, 40, 54, 74, 80, 86, 90, 93, 97, 134, 141, 165, 171, 181, 189, 199, 207, 209, 210

Astounding, 6, 8, 13, 17, 22, 34, 35, 36, 40, 54–55, 56, 67, 90, 116, 117, 118, 119, 131, 132, 134, 137, 140, 141, 142, 143–144, 145, 160, 174, 185, 186, 201, 207, 209, 210
Astounding Days, 87
At the Earth's Core, 99
"The Atoms of Chladni", 27
Attebery, Brian, 124, 208
Audran, Marîd, 81
Auel, Jean, 202
Auf Zwei Planeten, 170
"The Author of the Acacia Seeds", 194

Babbage, Charles, 75
Babel-17, 93
"Baby Is Three", 18, 19
Bacon, Roger, 67, 142, 203
Baen Books, 163
"The Ballad of Lost C'Mell", 18
Ballantine Books, 138, 158
Ballard, J. G., 43, 58, 77
Balmer, Edwin, 77
Bantam Books, 5, 8–10, 12, 20, 87, 97
Barefoot in the Head, 112
Barfield, Owen, 157
Barnes, Steven, 107, 180, 181
Barrayar, 166
Battle of Helm's Deep, 107
Baxter, John, 37
Beachhead, 171, 172
Beagle, Peter, 14, 107, 126, 139, 144, 149, 150, 151, 158, 159
"Beanstalk", 141
Bear, Greg, 68, 69–70, 96, 168, 171, 190, 198
Beasts, 154
"The Beautiful Brew", 14
"Beep", 141
The Beginning Place, 193
The Belgariad, 122
Bellamy, Edward, 45
Bellamy, Ralph, 9
"Belsen Express", 144
Belson, Jane, 84
Beneath a Red Star: Studies in International Science Fiction, 90
Benford, Gregory, 78, 90, 176–177, 178–179

Beresford, J. D., 77, 186
Berle, Milton, 9
Bernal, J. D., 69
Bester, Alfred, 6, 74, 186
Bethke, Bruce, 74
Beyond, 13–14, 140
Beyond Heaven's River, 70
Beyond This Horizon, 18
"The Bicentennial Man", 27
"The Big Front Yard", 18, 91
Big Planet, 160
The Big Time, 144
"The Big Wheel", 4
Billion Year Spree, 113
Bimbos of the Death Sun, 200
The Bird of Time, 81
Bisson, Terry, 171
Black Air, 172
"Black Destroyer", 40, 41, 167
Black Easter, 113, 140–141, 142
The Black Sun, 136
The Black Wheel, 61
Blade Runner, 74–75, 82–83
Blair, Eric Arthur, 45
Blake, Ken, 115
Blatty, Peter, 14
The Blind Geometer, 172
"The Blind Geometer", 172
Blish, James, 6, 18, 19, 41, 53, 97, 113, 139, 140–142, 171, 203
Bloch, Bob, 1, 7
Blond Barbarians and Noble Savages, 134
Blood Music, 69, 70
"Blowups Happen", 208
Blue Book, 36
Blue Mars, 171–172
"The Blue Pagoda", 61
The Blue Star, 135
Bok, Hannes, 61
The Bone Forest, 115
Bonestell, Chesley, 4
A Book of Nonsense, 148
The Book of Ptath, 134
The Book of the New Sun, 95, 96, 143
"Borderland of Sol", 179
Borders of Infinity, 164
Borges, Jorge Luis, 156
Born with the Dead, 189
Boucher, Anthony, 1, 7, 15, 64, 178, 200

Bova, Ben, 171, 207–209, 210
The Boy Who Hooked the Sun: A Tale from the Book of Wonders of Urth and Sky, 96
Boys' Life, 36
Bradbury, Ray, 37, 77, 170, 189, 192
Bradley, Marion Zimmer, 126, 128–129, 139
Brain Wave, 131
Brave New World, 52
Breaking Point, 7, 25
Breuer, Miles J., 136
A Brief History of Time, 70
The Brightfount Diaries, 112
Brin, David, 76–78, 95
Bring the Jubilee, 66, 202
The Broken Sword, 131, 132
Brothers of Earth, 175
Brown, Fredric, 64–67
Brunner, John, 3, 52, 186, 189
Brute Orbits, 89, 90
Bryant, Ed, 2, 3
Budrys, Algis, 13, 18
Buffalo Gals and Other Animal Presences, 194
Bujold, Lois McMaster, 163–166
Burgess, Anthony, 50, 51–54
Burn, Witch, Burn!, 61
The Burning, 20, 23, 26
Burroughs, Edgar Rice, 60, 99, 108, 117, 170
Burroughs, William, 54
"By Any Other Name", 201

Cabel, James Branch, 120, 150
Caidin, Martin, 80
"Call Me Joe", 18
Callahan's Crosstime Saloon, 201, 202
Cameron, James, 10
Campbell, John, 1, 6, 7, 8, 13, 14, 17, 18, 22, 29, 34, 36, 40, 42, 54–55, 56, 67, 88, 90, 113, 116, 117, 131, 132, 133, 134, 137, 140, 141, 143, 145, 167, 174, 183, 185, 186, 207–208
A Canticle for Leibowitz, 37, 42, 45, 53, 77
Card, Orson Scott, 71, 72–73, 197
Carlsen, Holger, 130
Carrie, 101
Carroll, Lewis, 103, 116

Carson, Rachel, 189
A Case of Conscience, 53, 142
The Case of the Little Green Men, 64, 200
The Castle of Iron, 129, 135
The Castle of Otranto, 146, 150
The Castle of the Otter, 96
Castle of Wizardry, 122
Catastrophe!, 26
"Catch That Zeppelin", 144
Catspaw, 187
"The Cave of Night", 4, 20, 21, 229
Cave of Stars, 89
CBS, 26
Chalmers, Reed, 135
Chamberlin, Bert, ix, 32
Chambers, Everett, 9
Chandler, Raymond, 25, 81, 101
Chapman, Edgar L., 152, 154, 155
Charles Scribner's Sons, 24
Charly, 93
Cheap Truth, 74
Cherryh, C. J., 165, 173–176
"Child of the Sun", 26
Childhood's End, 86, 191
Children of Dune, 39
Children of the Atom, 186
"The Children's Hour", 56
A Choice of Gods, 91
Christopher, John, 16, 43, 45, 189
"The Chronicler", 41
Chronicles of Amber, 106
The Chronicles of Thomas Covenant the Unbeliever, 123
The Citadel of the Autarch, 95
Cities in Flight, 141
City, 86, 91, 175
A Civil Campaign, 166
Clareson, Thomas D., 118
Clarke, Arthur C., 31, 39, 45, 69, 79, 86–87, 143, 168, 171, 185, 189, 190, 191
"Clash by Night", 56–57
The Claw of the Conciliator, 95
Clement, Hal, 179, 197
"Cloak of Aesir", 145
A Clockwork Orange, 50, 51–53
Close Encounters of the Third Kind, 167
Cloud's Rider, 173–176

Clute, John, 44, 108–109, 116, 123–124, 125, 137, 147, 148, 154, 155, 156, 157, 158, 182
Cogswell, Theodore, 18
"The Coldest Place", 181
Collier, John, 18–19
Collier's, 4
Colossus, 80
The Coming of the Quantum Cats, 69
The Compass Rose, 194
The Complete Enchanter, 140
Compton, D. G., 171
Conan, 14, 144, 146
"Conditionally Human", 45
Conjure Wife, 13, 120, 134, 140, 144
A Connecticut Yankee in King Arthur's Court, 127, 129–130, 133, 203
Contact, 27, 28, 68
The Conquest of Space, 4
The Conquest of the Moon Pool, 60
Corman, Roger, 112
Cosm, 177–179
Cosmic Engineers, 91
Cosmos, 27
The Courts of Chaos, 106
The Craft of Fiction, 120
The Craft of the Lead Pencil, 148
Creations: The Quest for Origins in Story and Science, 90
Creatures of Light and Darkness, 105
Creep, Shadow!, 61
Crichton, Michael, 16
Crisis!, 26
Crispin, Edmund, 15
The Crock of Gold, 151
Crowley, John, 152, 153–155
Crown Publishers, 90
"Crucifixus Etiam", 45
"Cryptic", 169
"The Crystal Egg", 170
Crystal Express, 74
Cummings, Ray, 99
cyberpunk, 76
Cyteen, 176

da Vinci, Leonardo, 203, 205
Damnation Alley, 105
Dancing at the End of the World: Thoughts on Words, Women, Places, 194
Dangerous Visions, 171
Daniels, Les, 133
Dann, Jack, 202–206
"The Darfsteller", 45
Dark Valley Destiny, 134
Darker Than You Think, 13, 134, 136, 137, 138, 139
Darkness and Dawn, 43
A Darkness at Sethanon, 108
Darkover series, 128
Darwin, Charles, 46, 68, 158, 190
Daughter of Regals and Other Tales, 125
Daughter of the Empire, 110
Daw Books, 7
The Day After, 77
The Day After Judgment, 113, 140, 142
The Day After the Martians Landed, 172
"The Day Before the Revolution", 193
The Day of the Triffids, 43, 77
"The Day the Magic Came Back", 27
The Day the Martians Came, 171
de Bergerac, Cyrano, 196
de Camp, Catherine Crook, 135
de Camp, L. Sprague, 13, 36, 54, 117, 121, 129, 130, 132, 133–135, 140, 150, 152, 156, 159, 203, 204
The Dead Ringer, 67
The Dead Zone, 101, 102
"Dear Devil", 167
Decision at Doona, 184
The Deep, 153
The Deeper Meaning of Liff, 85
Deeper Than Darkness, 178
del Rey, Lester, 7, 18, 54, 171, 208
Del Rey Books, 24
Delany, Samuel R., 3, 74, 93
Dell Books, 1, 7, 10, 14, 23
Deluge, 37
The Demolished Man, 186
Demon Lord of Karanda, 122
Demon Moon, 143
"Desertion", 174, 175
Desolation Road, 189
Destination Moon, 37, 118, 208
Destinies, 201
Destiny's Road, 179–181
Detective Story Monthly, 199
The Devil Doll, 61
"The Devil Makes the Laws", 13, 118, 134

The Devil's Game, 132
"The Diamond Lens", 27
The Diamond Throne, 122
Dick, Philip K., 66, 82–83, 172, 203
Dickson, Gordon, 131, 152, 167
The Difference Engine, 75
Dinosaur Planet, 184
Dirk Gently's Holistic Detective Agency, 84
Dirk Wylie Literary Agency, 97
Dirty Tricks, 81
Disch, Thomas M., 153, 189
Discover, 68
A Dish of Orts, 108
"The Disintegration Machine", 98
Disney Pictures, 10
The Dispossessed, 193, 194, 195
The Dispossessed: An Ambiguous Utopia, 193
Do Androids Dream of Electric Sheep?, 82
Dockweiler, Joseph, 97
Doctor Mirabilis, 142, 204
Doctor Who, 84
The Doings of Raffles Haw, 98
The Dolphins of Pern, 183
"Dolphin's Way", 167
Domes of Fire, 122
Donaldson, Stephen R., 123–126, 158
"Donor", 8
Doomsday Book, 87–88
The Door into Summer, 39
"The Doors of His Face, the Lamps of His Mouth", 105
Doorways in the Sand, 105
Double Star, 37, 39
Doubleday, 82, 138
Downbelow Station, 176
Doyle, Arthur Conan, 98–99
Dozois, Gardner, 74, 81, 206
Dr. Strangelove, 77
Dracula, 146, 150
Dragondrums, 183
Dragonflight, 183
Dragonquest, 183
"Dragonrider", 183
Dragonsdawn, 183
Dragonseye, 182–184
Dragonsong, 183
Drake, Frank, 23, 68, 168

The Dream Master, 186
Dream Park, 107
The Dreamers, 26, 29, 68, 229
Dreamfall, 185, 187, 188
Dreamsnake, 86
Dune, 39, 44, 93
Dungeons and Dragons, 107
Dunsany, Lord, 117, 120, 150
Dwellers in the Mirage, 61
Dying Inside, 186
Dyson, Freeman, 68, 190

"E for Effort", 18
E.T., 167
Earth Abides, 43, 77
Earthman, Come Home, 141
Earthman's Burden, 131
Eddings, David, 120, 121–123
Eddison, E. R., 120, 149, 150
Edwards, Carroll, 5
Effinger, George Alec, 69, 75, 79–82
Einstein, Albert, 68, 195
Eisler, Steven, 115
"The Elephant Circuit", 119
An Elephant for Aristotle, 134
Ellison, Harlan, 18, 26, 80
Elms, Alan C., 137
"The Emerson Effect", 169
Empires of Foliage and Flower: A Tale from the Book of Wonders of Urth and Sky, 96
The Encyclopedia of Fantasy, 14, 108, 109, 123, 125, 131, 132, 137, 155
The Encyclopedia of Science Fiction, 62, 74, 96, 107, 113, 116, 117, 147, 154, 169, 182, 189, 192, 194, 200, 206
"Encyclopedia of Tlon", 156
Ender's Game, 71, 72, 197
"The End-of-the-World Ball", 27
Engine Summer, 154
The Engines of Creation, 69
The Engines of God, 169
England, George Allan, 43
Eon, 70, 190
Epic Fantasy in the Modern World: A Few Observations, 125
"Escape", 109
Escape from Kathmandu, 172
Eternity, 70, 190

Ethan of Athos, 166
"Ether Breather", 40
Evolution's Shore, 188–191
The Exile Kiss, 81
The Exorcist, 14
The Exploration of Space, 86
Eye among the Blind, 115
"Eyes of Amber", 188
Eyes of Amber and Other Stories, 188

F&SF, 43
The Face in the Abyss, 61
The Faerie Queene, 130, 135
"The Fairy Chessmen", 56
Fallen Angels, 200
Falling Free, 163–166
Famous Fantastic Mysteries, 63–64, 117, 159
Famous Fantastic Novels, 135
Fantastic, 193
Fantastic Adventures, 159, 160
Fantastic Novels, 63
Fantastic Stories of the Imagination, 8
Fantastic Universe, 4, 12
Fantastic Worlds, 149
Fantasy Press, 138
The Fantasy Worlds of Peter Beagle, 150
Farewell Earth's Bliss, 171
Farmer, Philip Jose, 67, 203
Far-Seer, 198
The Farthest Shore, 193
Faster Than Light, 90, 206
"Fault", 26
"Fear", 13, 134
Feeley, Gregory, 206
Feist, Raymond E., 107–110
"Fiat Homo", 43
"Fiat Lux", 43
"Fiat Volutas Tua", 43
The Fifth Head of Cerebrus, 96
The Fifth Sally, 94
A Fine and Private Place, 150
A Fire in the Sun, 81
"Fire Watch", 87, 88
"The Firefly Tree", 136
Fireship, 188
Firestarter, 101
"First Contact", 72, 167, 197
A First Encyclopedia of Tlon, 156

The First Men in the Moon, 95, 181
A Fisherman of the Inland Sea, 192, 193, 194–195
"A Fisherman of the Inland Sea", 194
Flammarion, Camille, 77, 167, 196–197
Flatland, 92
Flaubert, 4
Flint, Homer Eon, 99
Flowers for Algernon, 86, 93
"Flowers for Algernon", 19, 93
The Flying Sorcerers, 179
Flynn, Michael, 200
Footfall, 181, 197, 200
Foreigner, 198
Forester, C. S., 166
The Forge of God, 70, 168, 198
Forster, E. M., 18
Fort, Charles, 68, 119
Forward, Robert L., 171
Fossil Hunter, 198
"Foundation", 34
Foundation and Earth, 35
The Foundation Trilogy, 32–35
Foundation's Edge, 35, 86
The Fountains of Paradise, 69, 87
"The Fox Woman", 61
The Fox Woman and Other Stories, 61
The Fox Woman and the Blue Pagoda, 61
Frameshift, 198
Frank, Pat, 37, 43, 77
Frankenstein, 37, 43, 146, 150
Frankenstein Unbound, 112
Frazer, James, 135
Frenkel, Jim, 188
Freud, Sigmund, 52
Friday, 86
From the Earth to the Moon, 5, 181, 207
From Unknown Worlds: An Anthology of Modern Fantasy for Grownups, 133
Fuller, Buckminster, 191
Fury, 54–58
Future Imperfect, 12, 23
"The Futurist", 26

Gagarin, Yuri A., 20
Galaxy, 4, 6–7, 13–14, 22, 23, 24, 25, 77, 91, 97, 141, 201
Galileo, 170
"Galley Slave", 199

Gallun, Raymond Z., 167, 197
Gandalf Grand Master, 144
Gap sequence, 125
The Garden of Earthly Delights, 151
Garrett, Randall, 120
Gates of Ivrel, 175
Gateway, 97, 168
Gather, Darkness!, 144, 145
The Genocides, 189
Genus Homo, 134
George, Christopher, 9, 21
Gernsback, Hugo, 36, 97, 156, 158, 184, 200
Gerrold, David, 80, 179
Gibson, William, 74–75, 76, 80, 164
Giesy, J. U., 99
Gift from the Stars, 28
"The Giftie", 27–28
Gilbert and Sullivan, 34
Gilgamesh, 117
"The Gingerbread Man", 27
The Girl Who Heard Dragons, 183
The Glassblowers, 148
Glory Road, 118
Gnome Press, 1, 2, 3, 92, 119
The Goblin Reservation, 91
The God Machine, 80
Gold, Evelyn, 7
Gold, Horace, 4, 6, 7, 13–14, 77, 117, 140–141
The Gold Coast, 172
Golden Blood, 138
Golden Fleece, 198
Golding, William, 202
Goldman, Stephen, 31
Goldstein, Emmanuel, 47
Goodwin, Walter T., 62
Gordon, Carolyn, 4
Gormenghast, 146, 147
Goslings, 77
Graff, Leo, 166
Grail legend, 154
Grand Master Award, 36, 97, 229
Grant, Richard, 147
"The Graveyard Rats", 55
Gravy Planet, 97
"The Great Kleinplatz Experiment", 98
Green, Rowland J., 166
The Green Magician, 135

"The Green Magician", 129
Green Mars, 171, 172
Greenberg, Martin H., 166
Greenberg, Marty, 2, 92
Greenland, Colin, 74
Greg, Percy, 170
Grisham, John, 199
"Grotto of the Dancing Deer", 91
"Guardian Angel", 86, 87
Guardians of the West, 122
"Guilt", 26
Gulliver's Travels, 60, 92
The Guns of Avalon, 106
"The Guy with the Eyes", 201
Gygax, Gary, 107

H. G. Wells: Critic of Progress, 137
The Hacker Crackdown: Law and Order on the Electronic Frontier, 76
Haggard, H. Rider, 99
Hall, Austin, 99
Halsey, Dorris, 10
The Hampdenshire Wonder, 186
The Hand of Oberon, 106
The Hand of Zei, 134
The Hand-Reared Boy, 112
Hard Words and Other Poems, 194
Harmon, John, 210
Harold Shea novels, 13, 133, 135
The Harp and the Blade, 133
Harrison, Harry, 7, 25, 112, 113
Harrison, M. John, 147
Hart's Hope, 73
Hartwell, David, 3, 136
Hawking, Stephen W., 70
Hawthorne, Nathaniel, 115
Hayakawa, S. I., 41
"He Who Shapes", 105
Heart of the Comet, 78
"Hedonics, Inc.", 12
"The Hedonist", 12, 20
Hegira, 70
Heinlein, Robert A., vii, 1, 13, 18, 36–39, 40, 44, 54, 80, 86, 90, 93, 116, 117, 118–119, 134, 137, 138, 140, 145, 165, 167, 171, 172, 181, 189, 197, 207–210
Hell's Cartographers, 161
Helliconia Spring, 112
Hemingway, Ernest, 32

Hendrix, Howard V., 89, 90
Henley, W. E., 94
Herbert, Frank, 39, 44, 93
The Hercules Text, 169
Herovit's World, 200
The Hidden City, 122
High Hunt, 122
Hines, Gregory, 85
The History of Middle-Earth, 156
Hitchhiker, 84, 85
The Hitchhiker's Guide to the Galaxy, 83–86
"Hoax", 4
Hoban, Russell, 43
"Hobbies", 91
The Hobbit, 156, 158
Hoka!, 131
Holdstock, Robert, 113, 115–116, 140
"The Hole Man", 179
The Hollowing, 115
"Home Is the Hangman", 105
Homer, 100, 147, 173
Hot Sleep, 73
Hothouse, 112, 189
Howard, Robert E., 14, 107, 120–121, 133, 134, 144, 146, 150, 156, 159
Hrolf Kraki's Saga, 132
Hubbard, L. Ron, 13, 41, 117, 134
Hugo Award, 19, 23, 37, 42, 69, 70, 71, 72, 73, 78, 80, 81, 82, 87, 88, 91, 93, 97, 105, 112–113, 131, 141, 144, 157, 160, 166, 168, 172, 176, 179, 181, 183, 184, 186, 188, 192, 193, 194, 198, 201, 209
The Hugo Winners, 93
Human Error, 69
Human Machines, 90
Human Voices, 25
The Humanoids, 17, 19, 136
Hundred Best Novels, 132
Huxley, Aldous, 52
Huxley, Thomas Henry, 94, 95
Hyden, Holgar, 29, 68
Hyland, Morn, 126
Hyman, Stanley Edgar, 53

I, Robot, 80
I Am Legend, 138
"I Have No Mouth, and I Must Scream", 80

Icehenge, 172
Idylls of the King, 127
If, 4, 22, 23, 97, 141
If This Goes On . . ., 18
"Ill Met in Lankhmar", 144
The Illearth War, 125
Illegal Alien, 196, 198, 199
The Immortal, 9, 105, 229
"The Immortal", 8, 9, 21
The Immortals, 7–10, 11, 12, 20, 21, 23, 229
Imposter, 83
Imprisoned in a Tesseract, 142
"In Hiding", 18, 19
In Search of Wonder, 141
In the Field of Fire, 206
In the Red Zone, 194
In the Valley of the Statues, 115
"Inconstant Moon", 179
Independence Day, 199
"The Indigestible Triton", 134
Inferno, 179
The Infinity Concerto, 70
The Innkeepers' Song, 151
Inside Science Fiction, 229
The Integral Trees, 181
International Fantasy Award, 91, 135
The Invisible Man, 37, 95, 101
Involution Ocean, 73
The Iron Dragon's Daughter, 143
The Iron Star, 190
Irrational Numbers, 81
Irwin, Robert, 147
Isaac Asimov: The Foundations of Science Fiction, 229
Isaac Asimov's SF Magazine, 74
Ishi in Two Worlds, 192
The Island of Dr. Moreau, 94–95
The Island of Lost Souls, 37
Islands in the Net, 73–76
Isle of the Dead, 105
"The Isolinguals", 134
The Issue at Hand, 141
"It", 13, 134

J. Lloyd Eaton Award, 113
James, Edwin, 6, 7
Jarrell, Randall, 15
Jeffries, Richard, 43

Jem: The Making of a Utopia, 98
Jeter, K. W., 83
John W. Campbell Memorial Award, 73, 87
Jonas, Gerald, 1, 3
Jones, D. F., 80
Jones, Langdon, 146
Jordan, Robert, 29
The Joy Makers, 8, 10–12, 20, 21, 23
Joyce, James, 141, 147
Judd, Cyril, 171
"Judgment Night", 56
Junction, 206
Just Imagine, 37

Kalevala, 135
Kampus, 23, 25, 29, 30, 229
Kaveney, Roz, 189, 190
Kell, Joseph, 51
"The Kerastion", 194
Ketterer, David, 142, 189
Keyes, Daniel, 19, 86, 93–94
The Killing Star, 89, 168, 198
King, Stephen, 99–102
King Kong, 37
The King of Elfland's Daughter, 120
King of the Murgos, 122
King Solomon's Mine, 99
The King's Buccaneer, 108
Kinsman, 209
Kirk, Richard, 115
Kirkland, Kyle, 29
Knight, Damon, 6, 28, 97, 103, 105, 141, 200
Knight of Shadows, 106
Kornbluth, Cyril, 52, 97, 171
Korzybski, Alfred, 41
Krech, David, 29
Kress, Nancy, 165
Kroeber, Alfred L., 192
Kroeber, Theodora, 192
Kubrick, Stanley, 45, 52, 54, 87, 191
Kuttner, Henry, 18, 54, 55–57, 58, 117

Ladies Home Journal, 151
The Lady and Her Tiger, 151
Ladyhawke, 188
Lake, David, 59
The Land of Mist, 98

The Land That Time Forgot, 99
Lands Beyond, 134–135
Language of the Night: Essays on Fantasy and Science Fiction, 194
Larson, Ron, ix, 32
Lasswitz, Kurd, 170
Last and First Men, 58, 186, 190
The Last Battle, 60
"The Last Canticle", 43
The Last Dangerous Visions, 26
The Last Man, 43, 77
The Last Unicorn, 14, 107, 126, 139, 144, 150, 151, 159
The Lathe of Heaven, 194
Lavondyss: Journey to an Unknown Region, 115
Le Guin, Ursula K., 14, 53, 69, 72, 107, 144, 150, 153, 159, 192–196
Le Morte d'Arthur, 127
The Left Hand of Darkness, 72, 193, 195, 196
The Legacy of Hereot, 180
The Legion of Space, 136
The Legion of Time, 136
Leiber, Fritz, 6, 13, 77, 107, 117, 120, 121, 134, 140, 142, 143–145, 150
Leinster, Murray, 72, 167, 189, 197
"The Lens of Time", 27
Lessing, Doris, 58
Lest Darkness Fall, 13, 129–130, 134, 203, 204
Levin, Ira, 14, 107, 150, 159
Lewis, C. S., 58–60, 76, 149, 157
Ley, Willy, 4, 134–135
Life, the Universe, and Everything, 84
Life in the West, 112
Lifehouse, 199–202
"Lifeline", 36, 40, 118
Lincoln's Dreams, 87
Lindsey, David, 120
The Lion, the Witch, and the Wardrobe, 60
The Listeners, 20, 24, 25–26, 27, 28, 68, 197, 229
"The Listeners", 23, 24, 25
Literary Swordsmen and Sorcerers, 134
Little, Big, 153–155
Llewellyn, Alun, 43
"Lobby", 91
Locus, 78, 88, 136, 159, 173, 175

London, Jack, 43, 77, 202
Lone Star Universe, 73
The Long Dark Tea-Time of the Soul, 84
The Long Loud Silence, 43
Looking Backward, 2000–1887, 45
Lord Foul's Bane, 123–125
Lord of Light, 105
The Lord of the Rings, 14, 61, 107, 108–109, 120, 123, 125, 140, 144, 146, 150, 151, 155, 156–158, 159
The Lord of the Sea, 46
Lord Valentine's Castle, 160, 161
"The Los Amigos Fiasco", 98
Lost Continents, 134
The Lost World, 37, 98–99
Love and Sleep, 154
Lovecraft, H. P., 18, 55, 62, 100, 114, 120, 134, 150
Lovell, Bernard, Sir, 23
Lowell, Percival, 170, 197
Lowndes, Robert A. W., 97
Lucian of Samosata, 196, 207
Lucifer's Hammer, 77, 179, 181
Lynley, Carol, 9

MacDonald, Anson, 145
MacDonald, George, 108, 150
"The Machine Stops", 18
MacLean, Katherine, 186
Macrolife, 69, 89
Mad Max III: Beyond Thunderdome, 188
"The Mad Planet", 189
"Made in U.S.A.", 199
The Magazine of Fantasy and Science Fiction, 26, 142
Magic, Inc., 118
The Magic Goes Away, 179
Magician, 108, 109
Magician: Apprentice, 108
Magician: Master, 108
The Magicians, 14
"The Magicians", 14
Magician's Gambit, 122
Majipoor Chronicles, 161
The Malacia Tapestry, 111–113
Malafrena, 194
Malzberg, Barry, 200
"Man in Orbit", 4, 21, 229
The Man in the High Castle, 66, 82, 202

"Man of Parts", 26
Man Plus, 171, 172
A Man Rides Through, 125
The Man Who Melted, 206
"The Man Who Sold the Moon", 207, 210
"The Man Who Traveled in Elephants", 119
Mandragola, 206
"The Maracot Deep", 98
"The Marching Morons", 18
Marion Zimmer Bradley Magazine, 128
Marooned on Mars, 171
Marquez, Gabriel Garcia, 189
Mars, 170, 171, 209
Marshall, E. G., 4
A Martian Chronicle, 170
The Martian Chronicles, 189
The Martian Inca, 171
"A Martian Odyssey", 167, 170, 197
Martian Rainbow, 171, 172
"The Martian Way", 171
Martin, George R. R., 152
Marvel Comics, 81
Marvel Tales, 94
Marvin, Lee, 4, 21
"The Masque of the Red Death", 69
The Mathematics of Magic, 135
"The Mathematics of Magic", 129
Matheson, Richard, 7, 138
Maverick, 56
McCaffrey, Anne, 182–185
McClary, Thomas Calvert, 43
McConnell, Frank, 68
McDevitt, Jack, 166, 168, 169
McDonald, Ian, 188–191
McIntosh, J. T., 199
McIntyre, Vonda N., 10, 86, 165
McNelly, Willis E., 42
The Meaning of Liff, 85
"The Medic", 21
Melancholy Elephants, 202
The Memory Cathedral, 202–207
The Memory of Whiteness, 172
The Mermen's Children, 132
Merril, Judith, 43, 77, 97, 171
Merritt, A., 60–64, 99, 117, 136, 150
Merwin, Sam, Jr., 5, 10, 64–65
The Metal Emperor, 63
"The Metal Man", 63, 136

The Metal Monster, 61, 63
"Metamorphosite", 190
Methusela's Children, 18
Metropolis, 37
"The Midas Plague", 18
The Midnight Angel, 151
A Midsummer Night's Dream, 115, 132
A Midsummer Tempest, 132
"Mikal's Songbird", 73
Millennium, 209
The Millennium Blues, 26, 27
Miller, P. Schuyler, 134
Miller, Walter, Jr., 37, 42, 43, 44, 53, 77
"The Million-Year Picnic", 77
Mills, Bob, 5, 8
"Mimsy Were the Borogoves", 56
"The Mind Reader", 175
Mindkiller: A Novel of the Near Future, 202
The Minds of Billy Milligan, 94
Mines, Samuel, 12
Minority Report, 83
The Mirror of Her Dreams, 125
Mirrorshades: The Cyberpunk Anthology, 74
"The Misogynist", 6
Missing Man, 186
"The Missing Man", 186
Mission of Gravity, 197
Mistress of the Empire, 110
The Mists of Avalon, 128, 139
Mitchell, Burroughs, 14
Mixed Feelings, 81
Modern Fantasy: The Hundred Best Novels, 107, 136, 153, 155, 159
Moffett, Pierce, 154
Mohan, Kim, 26
The Monadic Universe, 89
The Monster Show, 99
Moon, Elizabeth, 126, 139
The Moon Is a Harsh Mistress, 3, 37, 39, 71, 80, 93
"The Moon Moth", 18
The Moon Pool, 60–64
"The Moon Pool", 60, 63
Moonrise, 207, 209, 210
Moorcock, Michael, 132
Moore, C. L., 18, 54, 55, 56, 117
Moore, Ward, 66, 202

More Issues at Hand, 141
More Than Human, 86, 186
More Wandering Stars, 206
Mork and Mindy, 167
Morrison, Philip, 23, 68
Moskowitz, Sam, 61
Mostly Harmless, 84
The Mote in God's Eye, 180, 181
The Mountains of Majipoor, 161
Moving Mars, 171
Mr. Pye, 148
Murdercon, 64
My Favorite Martian, 167
Myers Myers, John, 133
Mythago Wood, 115–116, 140

"The Naked Sky", 12
"Name Your Pleasure", 12
Nativity, 206
Nerilka's Story, 183
"Nerves", 18, 19, 208
Neuromancer, 74, 80, 164
"Neutron Star", 179
The New Age, 141
"New Blood", 8, 21
The New Encyclopedia of Science Fiction, 62
New Worlds, 112, 115, 148
New Worlds for Old, 189
New York, 7, 12, 23, 56, 128, 141, 163, 200, 206
Newton, Isaac, Sir, 208
"Newton's Sleep", 194
Nicholls, Peter, 117, 194
Nichols, Ian, 108, 109, 110
Nicholson, Marjorie Hope, 169
The Night Life of the Gods, 14, 133
Night of Power, 202
Nightmare Blue, 81
Nightside the Long Sun, 96
"Nine Lives", 69
Nine Princes in Amber, 105–107, 114, 126, 139
Nineteen Eighty-Four, 45, 145
Niven, Larry, 68, 77, 96, 107, 179, 180, 181–182, 190, 197, 200
No Blade of Grass, 16, 43–45, 189
No Man Friday, 171
"No Woman Born", 56

"None but Lucifer", 13
"The North Wind", 26
The Norton Book of Science Fiction, 194
"Not So Great an Enemy", 8
Nova Two, 25
Novelties, 154
Now Wait for Last Year, 82
Null-A Three, 41

Oath of Fealty, 181
O'Brien, Fitz-James, 27, 47, 49
Odd John, 186
O'Donnell, Lawrence, 18, 55, 57
Of Worlds Beyond, 40
"Old Faithful", 167, 197
"The Old Folks", 25, 26
Omega, 77
The Omega Point, 89
Omni, 209
On the Beach, 16, 43, 77
The Once and Future King, 127
One Hundred Years of Solitude, 189
"The Ones Who Walked Away from Omelas", 194
"Open Warfare", 6
Operation Ares, 96
Operation Chaos, 132
Orbit, 96
Orbitsville, 68, 190
Origin of Species, 190–191
Orlando Furioso, 130, 135
Orsinian Tales, 194
Orwell, George, 45–51, 52, 145
Our Lady of Darkness, 144
"Out of Night", 145
Out of the Silent Planet, 58–60
The Outcasts of Heaven Belt, 188
Outpost Mars, 171

Pacific Edge, 172
Padgett, Lewis, 55, 57
Pall Mall Budget, 94
Palmer, Ray, 7
Panshin, Alexei, 82
Panshin, Cory, 191
Paradise Lost, 87
"Paradox", 5, 10, 65
"Passion Play", 105
The Past through Tomorrow, 210

Paul, Steve, 100
"Pauper's Plot", 115
Pawn of Prophecy, 121–122, 123
The Pawns of Null-A, 41
Paycheck, 83
Peake, Mervyn, 140, 145, 146–148
Pellegrino, Charles, 89, 168, 198
Penal Colony, 90
"The People of the Pit", 60
Perelandra, 58, 59
Phoenix in the Ashes, 188
The Pirate Planet, 84
A Planet Called Treason, 73
Planet of the Apes, 81
The Planet on the Table, 172
The Planet Savers, 128
"The Planners", 68
Plant Engineering, 96
A Plunge into Space, 170
Pocket Books, 10
Podkayne of Mars, 37
Poe, Edgar Allan, 77, 94, 100, 207
Pohl, Frederik, 1, 6–7, 8, 9, 10, 12, 18, 22, 24, 52, 69, 82, 97–98, 137, 168, 171, 172
The Poison Belt, 98
Police Your Planet, 171
The Postman, 76–78
Pournelle, Jerry, 77, 179, 180, 181, 197, 200
"Powder Keg", 4
The Practice Effect, 78
Pratt, Fletcher, 13, 129, 132, 133, 135, 140
Prentice Alvin, 73
Preuss, Paul, 69
Prince of Chaos, 106
Prince of the Blood, 108
A Princess of Mars, 60, 170
Pringle, David, 107, 120, 131, 132, 136, 150, 153, 155, 156, 159
"Private Eye", 56
"Proxima Centauri", 167
Psychlone, 70
The Puppet Masters, 39, 118, 167, 197
The Purple Cloud, 43, 77

Queen of Angels, 70
Queen of Sorcery, 122
Queen of Zamba, 134

Quest for Fire, 53
The Quincunx of Time, 141
Quinn, James, 4
Rabkin, Erik, 44, 149
Reading Science Fiction, 229
Real and Imaginary Worlds, 167, 197
Rebirth, 43
Red Genesis, 171
Red Mars, 171, 172
Red Planet Mars, 171
Red Prophet, 73
Reed College, 122
The Reign of Wizardry, 134, 138
"The Reluctant Witch", 7, 13, 14
Rendezvous with Rama, 87, 190
A Requiem for Astounding, 145
Resnick, Mike, 72
The Restaurant at the End of the Universe, 84
Restoree, 184
Return from Rainbow Bridge, 172
Return to Oz, 188
A Reverie of Bone and Other Poems, 148
Reynolds, Mack, 64, 200
A Rhapsody in Amber, 106
Rhine, J. B., 68, 185–186
Rhymes without Reason, 148
Riddley Walker, 43
Rider at the Gate, 173, 175
Riding the Torch, 188
Riley, Frank, 186
Ring around the Sun, 91
Ringworld, 68, 181, 190
Rite of Passage, 82
The River of Time, 78
The Road to Science Fiction, 39, 229
Roadside Picnic, 168
The Roaring Trumpet, 135
"The Roaring Trumpet", 129
Roberts, Dick, 8, 12, 20
Robinson, Jeanne, 202
Robinson, Kim Stanley, 169–173
Robinson, Spider, 199–202
Robinson Crusoe on Mars, 171
Rocannon's World, 193
"The Rock That Changed Things", 194
Rocket to the Morgue, 64, 178, 200
Rocketship Galielo, 37
Rogers, Alva, 145

"Rogue Moon", 18, 19
Rogue Queen, 134
Rosemary's Baby, 14, 107, 150, 159
Rosenberg, Aaron, 126
Rottensteiner, Franz, 149
Rucker, Rudy, 74
A Rude Awakening, 112
Russell, Eric Frank, 13, 18, 54, 117, 119, 167, 190

Sagan, Carl, 23, 27–28, 68, 171
"Sail On! Sail On!", 67, 203
"The Saliva Tree", 113
The Salmon of Doubt, 85
Sanders, Joe, 74, 76
The Sands of Mars, 171
"Sane Asylum", 6, 10
The Sapphire Rose, 122
Sargent, Joseph, 9
Sargent, Pamela, 89, 165
Saturn Science Fiction and Fantasy, 119
Sawyer, Robert J., 196–199
A Scanner Darkly, 83
The Scarlet Plague, 43
"The Scarlet Plague", 77
Schismatrix, 74
Schmitz, James H., 18
Scholes, Robert, 44
"Schrödinger's Kitten", 69, 81
Science Fiction, Fantasy, and Weird Fiction Magazines, 118
Science Fiction: History, Science, Vision, 44
Science Fiction Age, 27
Science Fiction Book Club, 24, 87
Science Fiction Hall of Fame, 18, 19, 67, 141
Science Fiction Plus, 184
Science Fiction Research Association, 2, 113, 137, 194, 229
Science Fiction World Convention, 1
Science Fiction Writers of America, 36, 70, 90, 97, 118, 131, 137, 161, 209
Scott, Ridley, 83
Screamers, 83
The Screwtape Letters, 60
Second Contact, 72
Second Foundation, 35
The Seedling Stars, 141

Seeds of Life, 190
The Seeress of Kell, 122
Seetee Ship, 136
Seetee Shock, 136
"Sense from Thought Divide", 186
A Sensitive Dependence on Initial Conditions, 172
The Serpent Mage, 70
Servant of the Empire, 110
Seven Footprints to Satan, 61
Seventh Son, 73
Severian, 95–96
SF Chronicle, 88
SF Horizons, 113
SFWA Bulletin, 34, 89, 160
Shadow of a Dark Queen, 108
The Shadow of the Torturer, 95, 143
Shadow on the Hearth, 43, 77
"Shambleau", 55
Shapes and Sounds, 148
Shards of Honor, 166
Shaw, Bob, 68, 190
She, 99
Sheckley, Robert, 6
Sheepfarmer's Daughter, 126, 139
Sheffield, Charles, 69
Shelley, Mary, 43, 77, 94, 146, 150
Sherred, T. L., 18
Shiel, M. P., 43, 46, 77
Shiner, Lewis, 74
The Shining Ones, 122
The Ship of Ishtar, 61, 62
"Ship of Shadows", 144
The Ship Who Sang, 184
Shiras, Wilmar, 18, 19, 186
Shirley, John, 74
Shklovskii, I. S., 68
"The Shobies' Story", 194, 195, 196
Shoby, 195, 196
"The *Shoby*", 195
A Short, Sharp Shock, 172
"Shottle Bop", 134
Shute, Nevil, 16, 43, 77
Siege of Minas Tirith, 107
Sign of Chaos, 106
The Sign of Four, 98
Sign of the Unicorn, 106
Silent Spring, 189
The Silmarillion, 156

Silverberg, Robert, 158, 159, 160–161, 186, 189
Silverthorn, 108, 109
Simak, Clifford, 1, 6, 7, 18, 86, 90–91, 174, 175
"The Simple Art of Murder", 81
"Sine of the Magus", 14
Sinister Barrier, 117, 119
"Sinister Barrier", 13
The Sirens of Titan, 31, 199
Sixth Column, 145
Skal, David J., 99
"Skylark", 138
Skylife: Space Habitats in Story and Science, 90
Slan, 18, 40, 186
Slaves of Sleep, 134
Slepyan, Norbert, 24
Slobbovia, 107
Smith, Clark Ashton, 120, 150
Smith, Cordwainer, 18, 95, 189
Smith, Doc, 138
Smith, Thorne, 14, 117, 133
The Smoke Ring, 181
The Snake Mother, 61
The Snow Queen, 188
So Long and Thanks for All the Fish, 84
Solar Lottery, 82
Soldier of Arete, 96
A Soldier Erect, 112
Soldier of the Mist, 96
"Solution Unsatisfactory", 208
Some Dreams Are Nightmares, 15
Songmaster, 73
Sorcerer, 107
Sorcerers of Majipoor, 161
Sorceress of Darshiva, 122
Space Cadet, 37
Space Is a Lonely Place, 5
The Space Merchants, 52, 97
Space Science Fiction, 7
Speaker for the Dead, 71, 72
Specht, Robert, 9–10
"The Spectre General", 18
Speculations on Speculation: Theories of Science Fiction, 229
Spinrad, Norman, 188
The Spirit Ring, 166

The St. James Guide to Science Fiction Writers, 88, 108, 112, 122, 126, 147, 152, 154, 157, 166, 176, 179, 199
Stableford, Brian, 117
Stand on Zanzibar, 52
Stapledon, Olaf, 58, 90, 186, 190, 197
"The Star", 43, 77
The Star Beast, 167
Star Begotten, 191
Star Bridge, 1–3, 137
The Star Conquerors, 209
Star Maker, 58, 197
Star Prince Charlie, 131
Star Science Fiction No. 4, 8
Stardance, 202
"Stardance", 202
Starhiker, 206
Starmind, 202
Starplex, 198
The Stars My Destination, 3, 186
The Stars Will Speak, 89
Starship Troopers, 37, 93, 118, 197
Startide Rising, 78
Startling Stories, 8, 12, 56, 64, 160
Station in Space, 5, 8, 12, 20
Stations of the Tide, 143
Sterling, Bruce, 73–76
Stewart, George R., 43, 77
Stilson, Charles B., 99
Stoker, Bram, 146, 150
The Stolen Dormouse, 134
Stones, Eric, 31, 163
Strange Dreams, 125
The Strange Invaders, 43
Strange Stories, 55
Stranger in a Strange Land, 37–38, 39, 44, 118, 172
Stranger Suns, 89, 168
Strength of Stones, 70
Strugatsky, Arkady, 168
Strugatsky, Boris, 168
Stuart, Don A., 145
A Study in Scarlet, 98
"Sucker Bait", 181
Sullivan, Barry, 9
Sullivan, Walter, 23–24
The Summer Queen, 188
Sundiver, 78
Sunspacer, 89

"Surface Tension", 19, 141
Surprising Stories, 64
Survey of Modern Fantasy Literature, 123
Survey of Science Fiction and Fantasy Literature, 125
Suvin, Darko, 104
Swanwick, Michael, 143
The Sword and the Stone, 127
The Sword of Aldones, 128
The Sword of the Lictor, 95
Swords and Sorcery, 134
Synergy, 27, 90

Taine, John, 190
A Talent for War, 169
"Tales of Known Space", 181
Tangents, 70
Tarzan, King of the Apes, 188
Tarzan of the Apes, 60
Teaching Science Fiction: Education for Tomorrow, 137
Tehanu: The Last Book of Earthsea, 193
Telempath, 201
Terminal Cafe, 189
The Terminal Experiment, 198
That Hideous Strength: A Modern Fairy-Tale for Grownups, 58
"There Will Come Soft Rains", 77
"They", 13, 118, 119, 134
They Walked Like Men, 91
They'd Rather Be Right, 186
Third Rock from the Sun, 167
This Fortress World, 2, 3
This Immortal, 105
Three Hearts and Three Lions, 129–132
Three Lines of Old French, 61
Thrilling Mysteries, 55
Thrilling Wonder Stories, 5, 10, 12, 36, 56
"Through the Dragon Glass", 60
Thru the Dragon Glass, 61
"Thunder and Roses", 77
Time and Again, 91
"The Time Machine", 18
The Time of the Warlock, 179
Time Pressure, 202
Time Travelers Strictly Cash, 202
Timescape, 178
Timetipping, 206
"Tin Soldier", 188

Titans' Daughter, 141
Titus Groan, 146, 148
"Tlon, Uqbar, Orbius Tertius", 156
To Say Nothing of the Dog, 87, 88
"To Serve Man", 28
The Tombs of Atuan, 193
"Tomorrow and Tomorrow", 56
Tomorrow Today, 90
Tom's A-Cold, 43
"Tools", 91
Total Recall, 83
The Touch, 94
Transatlantic Tunnel, 37
Transcendental, 229
"Trends", 40, 207
"Trial by Fire", 22
The Trial of Terra, 167
"Trip, Trap", 96
Tron, 74, 107
"The Trouble with Water", 13
"A True Story", 207
Trumps of Doom, 106
Tucker, Wilson, 43
Tuttle, Lisa, 201
Twain, Mark, 127, 129–130, 133, 203
Twentieth-Century Science-Fiction Writers, 59, 74, 78, 206
The Twilight Zone, 93
"Two Sought Adventure", 13, 134, 143
"Two-Handed Engine", 56
"The Twonky", 56
Tymn, Marshall, 118
"Typewriter in the Sky", 13, 134

Unaccompanied Sonata and Other Stories, 73
Uncovering Lives: The Uneasy Alliance of Biography and Psychology, 137
Under the Moons of Mars, 99
"Under the Moons of Mars", 60, 170
Ungar, George, 29, 68
"Universe", 18
The Universe Makers, 164
Unknown, 13–14, 40, 67, 113, 117–118, 119, 129, 131, 132, 133–134, 135, 137, 138, 140, 143–144, 159
The Unpleasant Profession of Jonathan Hoag, 119, 140

"The Unpleasant Profession of Jonathan Hoag", 118, 119, 134
The Unpublished Gunn, 6
The Uplift War, 78
The Urth of the New Sun, 95

Valentine Pontifex, 161
The Valhalla Project, 198
van Lhin, Erik, 171
van Vogt, A. E., 40–42, 54, 82, 86, 90, 134, 142, 160, 167, 186, 190
Vance, Jack, 18, 160
Varley, John, 171, 190
Vault of the Ages, 131
Venture, 5
Venture Science Fiction, 8
Verne, Jules, 5, 31, 37, 66, 78, 94, 181, 196, 207
Videodrome
Vinge, Joan D., 185–188
Vinge, Vernor, 188
"The Voices", 25
von Braun, Wernher, 4
Vonnegut, Kurt, Jr., 31, 85, 199
The Vor Game, 166
The Voyage of the Space Beagle, 41, 86, 167
A Voyage to Arcturus, 120
Voyage to the Red Planet, 171

The Wall of Serpents, 135
"The Wall of Serpents", 129
The Wanderer, 77, 144
Wandering Stars, 206
The Wanting Seed, 52
War of the Rings, 107
The War of the Worlds, 31, 71, 95, 167, 170, 172, 191, 197
Ward, David, 31
Warlocks and Warriors, 134
The Warrior's Apprentice, 166
Water Babies, 117
Waterloo, Stanley, 202
Watson, Ian, 171
"The Waveries", 67
Way Station, 91
The Way the Future Was, 97
We Are Not Alone, 23, 24
The Weapon Makers, 86

The Web between the Worlds, 69
Weinbaum, Stanley, 167, 170, 197
Weird Tales, 55, 117, 119, 121, 138, 156, 159
Welcome to Mars, 171
The Well of the Unicorn, 135
Wells, H. G., 18, 31, 39, 43, 58, 66, 71, 77, 88, 92, 94–95, 101, 112, 167, 170, 172, 181, 190, 191, 197, 202, 204, 207
Wendroff, Gail, 14, 23
The Werewolf Principle, 91
"Weyr Search", 183
What Entropy Means to Me, 81
What Mad Universe, 64–68
"What Thin Partitions", 186
"What You Need", 56
Whelpley, J. D., 27
When Gravity Fails, 79–81
When Harlie Was One, 80
"When the Bough Breaks", 56
When the Sleeper Wakes, 95
"When the World Screamed", 98
When Worlds Collide, 77
Where Late the Sweet Birds Sang, 43, 69
"Wherever You May Be", 7, 13
The White Company, 98
The White Dragon, 183
White Gold Wielder, 125
White, T. H., 127
"Who Goes There?", 18, 167
The Whole Man, 186
Why Call Them Back from Heaven?, 91
Wilcox, Robert H., 62
Wild Angels, 194
Wild Palms, 74
The Wild Shore, 172
Wilhelm, Kate, 43, 68–69, 165
Williams, Charles, 157
Williams, David, ix, 32
Williamson, Blanche, 2
Williamson, Jack, 1, 2, 3, 7, 13, 17, 18, 59, 63, 90, 117, 134, 136–139, 143, 165, 167, 171
Willis, Connie, 87–89
Wilson, John Anthony Burgess, 52
The Wind from a Burning Woman, 70

The Wind's Twelve Quarters, 194
"Witch Hunt", 22
"The Witches of Karres", 18
"Witches Must Burn", 22
The Witching Hour, 14, 23
"With Folded Hands . . .", 17, 18, 136
A Wizard of Earthsea, 144, 150, 159
The Wizard of Oz, 32
Wolfe, Gary K., 112
Wolfe, Gene, 95–96, 143
Wollheim, Donald, 24, 97, 141, 164
The Wolves of Memory, 81
Wonder's Child, 137–138
Wood, Susan, 194
The Word for World Is Forest, 193
The World beyond the Hill, 191
The World of Null-A, 40, 41
The World Set Free, 77
World SF Convention's Gandalf and Hugo awards, 157
The World, the Flesh, and the Devil, 69
World's Best Science Fiction, 24
World's End, 188
Worlds of Fantasy, 88
Worlds of Tomorrow, 97
The Worm Ouroboros, 120
The Worm-Runners Digest, 29
The Worthing Chronicle, 73
The Wounded Land, 125
Wurts, Janny, 110
Wyndham, John, 43, 77
Wyrms, 73

X Minus One, 4, 21

Year's Best SF, 136
The Years of the City, 97
"Yesterday Was Monday", 134
"Young Goodman Brown", 115

Zebrowski, George, 27, 69, 89–90, 119, 168, 198
Zelazny, Roger, 104, 105–106, 114, 120, 126, 139, 186
Zombies of the Gene Pool, 200

About the Author

James Gunn, emeritus professor of English at the University of Kansas, has led a double life as a scholar and teacher of science fiction and fiction writing, and as an author or editor of forty-two books in the field; sixteen novels such as *The Immortals*, *The Listeners*, *The Dreamers*, and *Kampus*; and his current novel, *Transcendental*. His scholarly books include *Alternate Worlds: The Illustrated History of Science Fiction*, *Isaac Asimov: The Foundations of Science Fiction*, and *Inside Science Fiction*, and he has edited such books as the six-volume *The Road to Science Fiction*, *Speculations on Speculation: Theories of Science Fiction*, and *Reading Science Fiction*.

He has served as president of the Science Fiction Research Association and the Science Fiction and Fantasy Writers of America and won the lifetime achievement awards of both organizations, the Pilgrim Award, and the Damon Knight Grand Master Award. His short story "The Cave of Night" was adapted for television's *Desilu Playhouse* as "Man in Orbit," and *The Immortals* was adapted into an ABC-TV Movie of the Week and a television series entitled *The Immortal*.

Lightning Source UK Ltd.
Milton Keynes UK
UKOW05n1645240714

235706UK00001B/15/P

9 780810 891227